# 1a

## HOLT McDOUGAL

# ¡Avancemos!

**HOLT McDOUGAL**
a division of Houghton Mifflin Harcourt

## Cover Photography

**Front cover**
View toward La Fortaleza, San Juan, Puerto Rico, Steve Dunwell/The Image Bank/
Getty Images
Inset: Windsurfing in Puerto Rico, © Mark Bacon/Latin Focus.com

**Back cover**
Level 1a: View toward La Fortaleza, San Juan, Puerto Rico, Steve Dunwell/The Image Bank/
       Getty Images
Level 1b: View of Buenos Aires through the Puente de la Mujer, Joseph Rodriguez/Gallery
       Stock Limited
Level 1:   Monumento a la Independencia on the Paseo de la Reforma at night, Mexico City,
       Mexico, Panoramic Images/Getty Images
Level 2:   Cibeles Fountain and Palacio de Comunicaciones at night, Madrid, Spain, Doug
       Armand/Getty Images
Level 3:   Plaza de la Constitución at night, Santiago, Chile, David Noton Photography
Level 4:   Santa Catarina Arch, Antigua, Guatemala, Jeremy Woodhouse/Masterfile

ISBN-10: 0-554-02534-5
ISBN-13: 978-0-554-02534-6

1 2 3 4 5 6 WMW 13 12 11 10 09

Internet: www.holtmcdougal.com

**1a**

HOLT McDOUGAL

# ¡Avancemos!

# Celebraciones

**Cultura INTERACTIVA** Explora las celebraciones del mundo hispano

El Día de los Muertos,
Santiago Sacatepéquez, Guatemala

# Online at CLASSZONE.COM

**Cultura INTERACTIVA** *pp. C2–C3, C4–C5, C6–C7, C8–C9, C10–C11, C12–C13, C14–C15, C16–C17, C18–C19, C20–C21, C22–C23, C24–C25*

New Year's Eve, Madrid, Spain

¡AvanzaRap!
**DVD**
Sing and Learn

## Cultura
- **Un mural en Nueva York** *p. 9*

PARA Y PIENSA

**Did you get it?**
**Student Self-Check**
*pp. 5, 9, 11, 15, 17, 19, 21, 24*

A performer wearing the colors of the Puerto Rican Flag

Dominican dancers in colorful costumes

Una playa de Miami Beach, Miami Beach, Florida

Paseo del Río, San Antonio, Texas

*¡AvanzaRap!*
DVD
**Sing and Learn**

# México
## ¡Vamos a la escuela!

**Cultura**
- **Explora México** *p. 90*
- **Uniformes escolares** *p. 102*
- **Los murales en México** *p. 109*
- **Una escuela internacional en México** *p. 114*

*¿Recuerdas?*
- after-school activities *p. 103*
- days of the week *p. 105*

**Did you get it?**
Student Self-Check
*pp. 97, 99, 103, 105, 109, 112*

## Online at CLASSZONE.COM

**Cultura INTERACTIVA**
*pp. 90–91*
*148–149*

**Animated Grammar**
*pp. 100, 106, 117*
*128, 134, 145*

**@HomeTutor VideoPlus**
*pp. 98, 104, 110*
*126, 132, 138*

 **Video/DVD**
Vocabulario
*pp. 94–96, 122–124*
Telehistoria
*pp. 98, 104, 110*
*126, 132, 138*

La fuente de San Miguel en el Zócalo,
Puebla, México

El patio de una escuela secundaria,
México

Lección
## 2

*Tema:* **En la escuela** . . . . . . . . . . 120

### VOCABULARIO

Describing classes, Describing location,
Expressing feelings . . . . . . . . . 122

Práctica . . . . . . . . . . . . . . . 125

Telehistoria escena 1 . . . . . . . . . 126

### GRAMÁTICA

The verb **estar** . . . . . . . . . . . 128

Práctica . . . . . . . . . . . . . . . 129

Telehistoria escena 2 . . . . . . . . . 132

The verb **ir** . . . . . . . . . . . . 134

Práctica . . . . . . . . . . . . . . . 135

### TODO JUNTO

Telehistoria completa . . . . . . . . . 138

Juegos y diversiones: ¿Cierto o falso? . . . . 141

Lectura cultural: Mi clase favorita . . . . . 142

Proyectos culturales: Arte de México
y la República Dominicana . . . . . . . 144

En resumen . . . . . . . . . . . . . 145

Repaso de la lección . . . . . . . . . 146

**Cultura**
- **El Museo de Antropología** *p. 130*
- **El autorretrato** *p. 137*
- **Mi clase favorita** *p. 142*
- **Arte de México y la República Dominicana** *p. 144*
- **Horarios y clases** *p. 148*

*¿Recuerdas?*
- class subjects *p. 127*
- adjective agreement *p. 128*
- telling time *p. 139*

 **Did you get it?**
**Student Self-Check**
*pp. 125, 127, 131, 133, 137, 140*

---

**UNIT 2**
**WRAP-UP**

Comparación cultural  Lectura y escritura:
Horarios y clases . . . . . . . 148

Repaso inclusivo ♺ Unidades 1–2 . . . . . 150

Entre dos ¿? . . . . . . . . . 280

¡AvanzaRap!
DVD
Sing and Learn

México
Contenido   **ix**

# Puerto Rico
## Comer en familia

La Plaza de Colón en el Viejo San Juan,
San Juan, Puerto Rico

Una familia come en casa,
San Juan, Puerto Rico

**Cultura**
- **Las elecciones en
  Puerto Rico** *p. 193*
- **Los retratos** *p. 199*
- **La quinceañera**
  *p. 204*
- **Instrumentos de
  Puerto Rico y Perú**
  *p. 206*
- **¿Qué comemos?**
  *p. 210*

 *¿Recuerdas?*
- the verb **tener** *p. 189*
- numbers from
  11 to 100 *p. 189*
- after-school activities
  *p. 191*
- describing others
  *p. 192*

 **Did you get it?**
**Student Self-Check**
*pp. 187, 189, 193, 195,
199, 202*

¡AvanzaRap!
DVD
Sing and Learn

# UNIDAD 4

# España
## En el centro

Una tienda de ropa, Madrid, España

El Teatro de la Comedia en la calle
Príncipe, Madrid, España

### Cultura

- **Los mercados** *p. 255*
- *Las meninas* *p. 261*
- **El fin de semana en
España y Chile** *p. 266*
- **Pinturas de España y
Chile** *p. 268*
- **¿Adónde vamos el
sábado?** *p. 272*

 *¿Recuerdas?*

- present tense of
**-er** verbs *p. 249*
- the verb **ir** *p. 251*
- direct object
pronouns *p. 259*
- **tener** expressions
*p. 261*

 **Did you get it?**
**Student Self-Check**
*pp. 249, 251, 255, 257,
261, 264*

¡*AvanzaRap!*
DVD
Sing and Learn

# Recursos

# ¡Avancemos!

# About the Authors

### Estella Gahala

Estella Gahala received degrees in Spanish from Wichita State University, French from Middlebury College, and a Ph.D. in Educational Administration and Curriculum from Northwestern University. A career teacher of Spanish and French, she has worked with a wide variety of students at the secondary level. She has also served as foreign language department chair and district director of curriculum and instruction. Her workshops and publications focus on research and practice in a wide range of topics, including culture and language learning, learning strategies, assessment, and the impact of current brain research on curriculum and instruction. She has coauthored twelve basal textbooks. Honors include the Chevalier dans l'Ordre des Palmes Académiques and listings in *Who's Who of American Women, Who's Who in America,* and *Who's Who in the World.*

### Patricia Hamilton Carlin

Patricia Hamilton Carlin completed her M.A. in Spanish at the University of California, Davis, where she also taught as a lecturer. Previously she earned a Master of Secondary Education with specialization in foreign languages from the University of Arkansas and taught Spanish and French at the K–12 level. Patricia currently teaches Spanish and foreign language/ESL methodology at the University of Central Arkansas, where she coordinates the second language teacher education program. In addition, Patricia is a frequent presenter at local, regional, and national foreign language conferences. In 2005, she was awarded the Southern Conference on Language Teaching's Outstanding Teaching Award: Post-Secondary. Her professional service has included the presidency of the Arkansas Foreign Language Teachers Association and the presidency of Arkansas's DeSoto Chapter of the AATSP.

### Audrey L. Heining-Boynton

Audrey L. Heining-Boynton received her Ph.D. in Curriculum and Instruction from Michigan State University. She is a professor of Education and Romance Languages at The University of North Carolina at Chapel Hill, where she teaches educational methodology classes and Spanish. She has also taught Spanish, French, and ESL at the K–12 level. Dr. Heining-Boynton served as the president of ACTFL and the National Network for Early Language Learning. She has been involved with AATSP, Phi Delta Kappa, and state foreign language associations. In addition, she has presented both nationally and internationally and has published over forty books, articles, and curricula.

### Ricardo Otheguy

Ricardo Otheguy received his Ph.D. in Linguistics from the City University of New York, where he is currently professor of Linguistics at the Graduate Center. He is also director of the Research Institute for the Study of Language in Urban Society (RISLUS) and coeditor of the research journal *Spanish in Context.* He has extensive experience with school-based research and has written on topics related to Spanish grammar, bilingual education, and Spanish in the United States. His work has been supported by private and government foundations, including the Rockefeller Brothers Fund and the National Science Foundation. He is coauthor of *Tu mundo: Curso para hispanohablantes,* and *Prueba de ubicación para hispanohablantes.*

### Barbara J. Rupert

Barbara Rupert completed her M.A. at Pacific Lutheran University. She has taught Level 1 through A.P. Spanish and has implemented a FLES program in her district. Barbara is the author of CD-ROM activities for the *¡Bravo!* series. She has presented at many local, regional, and national foreign language conferences. She has served as president of both the Pacific Northwest Council for Languages (PNCFL) and the Washington Association for Language Teaching, and was the PNCFL representative to ACTFL. In 1996, Barbara received the Christa McAuliffe Award for Excellence in Education, and in 1999, she was selected Washington's "Spanish Teacher of the Year" by the Juan de Fuca Chapter of the AATSP.

## John DeMado, Creative Consultant

John DeMado has been a vocal advocate for second-language acquisition in the United States for many years. He started his career as a middle/high school French and Spanish teacher, before entering the educational publishing profession. Since 1993, Mr. DeMado has directed his own business, John DeMado Language Seminars. Inc., a company devoted exclusively to language acquisition issues. He has authored numerous books in both French and Spanish that span the K–12 curriculum. Mr. DeMado wrote and performed the *¡AvanzaRap!* songs for Levels 1 and 2.

## Carl Johnson, Senior Program Advisor

Carl Johnson received degrees from Marietta College (OH), the University of Illinois, Université Laval, and a Ph.D. in Foreign Language Education from The Ohio State University, during which time he studied French, German, Spanish, and Russian. He has been a lifelong foreign language educator, retiring in 2003 after 27 years as a language teacher (secondary and university level), consultant, and Director of Languages Other Than English for the Texas Department of Education. He has completed many publications relating to student and teacher language proficiency development, language textbooks, and nationwide textbook adoption practices. He also served as president of the Texas Foreign Language Association, Chair of the Board of the Southwest Conference on Language Teaching, and president of the National Council of State Supervisors of Foreign Languages. In addition, he was named Chevalier dans l'Ordre des Palmes Académiques by the French government.

## Rebecca L. Oxford, Learning Strategy Specialist

Rebecca L. Oxford received her Ph.D. in educational psychology from The University of North Carolina. She also holds two degrees in foreign language from Vanderbilt University and Yale University, and a degree in educational psychology from Boston University. She leads the Second Language Education and Culture Program and is a professor at the University of Maryland. She has directed programs at Teachers College, Columbia University; the University of Alabama; and the Pennsylvania State University. In addition, she initiated and edited *Tapestry*, a series of student textbooks used around the world. Dr. Oxford specializes in language learning strategies and styles.

# Contributing Writers

**Louis G. Baskinger**
New Hartford High School
New Hartford, NY

**Jacquelyn Cinotti-Dirmann**
Duval County Public Schools
Jacksonville, FL

# Consulting Authors

**Dan Battisti**
**Dr. Teresa Carrera-Hanley**
**Bill Lionetti**
**Patty Murguía Bohannan**
**Lorena Richins Layser**

# ❖ Teacher Reviewers

## Middle School Reviewers

**Mary Jo Aronica**
Lincoln Hall Middle School
Lincolnwood, IL

**Suzanne M. Auffray**
The Overlake School
Redmond, WA

**Elizabeth M. Bossong**
Vestal High School
Vestal, NY

**Zahava Frymerman**
G. W. Carver Middle School
Miami, FL

**Ana Johnson**
Rising Star Middle School
Fayetteville, GA

**Sharon Larracoechea**
North Junior High
Boise, ID

**Deborah Tomkinson**
James Madison Middle School
Titusville, FL

**Elizabeth L. Torosian**
Lowell Community Charter Public
　School
Lowell, MA

**Heather T. Walker**
Chester Middle School
Chester, VA

**Mari Zimmerman**
James C. Wright Middle School
Madison, WI

## High School Reviewers

**Sue Arandjelovic**
Dobson High School
Mesa, AZ

**Susan K. Arbuckle**
Mahomet-Seymour High School
Mahomet, IL

**Kristi Ashe**
Amador Valley High School
Pleasanton, CA

**Shaun A. Bauer**
Olympia High School, *retired*
Orlando, FL

**Sheila Bayles**
Rogers High School
Rogers, AR

**Robert L. Bowbeer**
Detroit Country Day Upper School
Beverly Hills, MI

**Hercilia Bretón**
Highlands High School
San Antonio, TX

**Adrienne Chamberlain-Parris**
Mariner High School
Everett, WA

**Mike Cooperider**
Truman High School
Independence, MO

**Susan B. Cress**
Sheridan High School
Sheridan, IN

**Michèle S. de Cruz-Sáenz, Ph.D.**
Strath Haven High School
Wallingford, PA

**Lizveth Dague**
Park Vista Community High School
Lake Worth, FL

**Parthena Draggett**
Jackson High School
Massillon, OH

**Rubén D. Elías**
Roosevelt High School
Fresno, CA

**Phillip Elkins**
Lane Tech College Prep High School
Chicago, IL

**Maria Fleming Alvarez**
The Park School
Brookline, MA

**Michael Garber**
Boston Latin Academy
Boston, MA

**Marco García**
Derry University Advantage Academy
Chicago, IL

**David Gonzalez**
Hollywood Hills High School
Hollywood, FL

**Raquel R. González**
Odessa Senior High School
Odessa, TX

**Neyda Gonzalez-Droz**
Ridge Community High School
Davenport, FL

**Becky Hay de García**
James Madison Memorial
　High School
Madison, WI

**Fatima Hicks**
Suncoast High School, *retired*
Riviera Beach, FL

**Gladys V. Horford**
William T. Dwyer High School
Palm Beach Gardens, FL

**Pam Johnson**
Stevensville High School
Stevensville, MT

**Richard Ladd**
Ipswich High School
Ipswich, MA

**Patsy Lanigan**
Hume Fogg Academic Magnet
　High School
Nashville, TN

**Kris Laws**
Palm Bay High School
Melbourne, FL

**Kristen M. Lombardi**
Shenendehowa High School
Clifton Park, NY

**Elizabeth Lupafya**
North High School
Worcester, MA

**David Malatesta**
Niles West High School
Skokie, IL

**Patrick Malloy**
James B. Conant High School
Hoffman Estates, IL

**Brandi Meeks**
Starr's Mill High School
Fayetteville, GA

**Kathleen L. Michaels**
Palm Harbor University High School
Palm Harbor, FL

**Linda Nanos**
Brook Farm Business Academy
West Roxbury, MA

**Nadine F. Olson**
School of Teaching and Curriculum
  Leadership
Stillwater, OK

**Pam Osthoff**
Lakeland Senior High School
Lakeland, FL

**Nicholas Patterson**
Davenport Central High School
Davenport, IA

**Carolyn A. Peck**
Genesee Community College
Lakeville, NY

**Daniel N. Richardson**
Concord High School, *retired*
Concord, NH

**Rita E. Risco**
Palm Harbor University High School
Palm Harbor, FL

**Miguel Roma**
Boston Latin Academy
West Roxbury, MA

**Lauren Schultz**
Dover High School
Dover, NH

**Nona M. Seaver**
New Berlin West Middle/High
  School
New Berlin, WI

**Susan Seraphine-Kimel**
Astronaut High School
Titusville, FL

**Mary Severo**
Thomas Hart Middle School
Pleasanton, CA

**Clarette Shelton**
WT Woodson High School, *retired*
Fairfax, VA

**Maureen Shiland**
Saratoga Springs High School
Saratoga Springs, NY

**Irma Sprague**
Countryside High School
Clearwater, FL

**Mary A. Stimmel**
Lincoln High School
Des Moines, IA

**Karen Tharrington**
Wakefield High School
Raleigh, NC

**Alicia Turnier**
Countryside High School
Clearwater, FL

**Roberto E. del Valle**
The Overlake School
Redmond, WA

**Todd Wagner**
Upper Darby High School, *retired*
Drexel Hill, PA

**Ronie R. Webster**
Monson Junior/Senior High School
Monson, MA

**Cheryl Wellman**
Bloomingdale High School
Valrico, FL

**Thomasina White**
School District of Philadelphia
Philadelphia, PA

**Jena Williams**
Jonesboro High School
Jonesboro, AR

# Program Advisory Council

**Louis G. Baskinger**
New Hartford High School
New Hartford, NY

**Linda M. Bigler**
James Madison University
Harrisonburg, VA

**Flora Maria Ciccone-Quintanilla**
Holly Senior High School
Holly, MI

**Jacquelyn Cinotti-Dirmann**
Duval County Public Schools
Jacksonville, FL

**Desa Dawson**
Del City High School
Del City, OK

**Robin C. Hill**
Warrensville Heights High School
Warrensville Heights, OH

**Barbara M. Johnson**
Gordon Tech High School, *retired*
Chicago, IL

**Ray Maldonado**
Houston Independent School
  District
Houston, TX

**Karen S. Miller**
Friends School of Baltimore
Baltimore, MD

**Dr. Robert A. Miller**
Woodcreek High School
  Roseville Joint Union High School
  District
Roseville, CA

**Debra M. Morris**
Wellington Landings Middle School
Wellington, FL

**Maria Nieto Zezas**
West Morris Central High School
Chester, NJ

**Rita Oleksak**
Glastonbury Public Schools
Glastonbury, CT

**Sandra Rosenstiel**
University of Dallas, *retired*
Grapevine, TX

**Emily Serafa Manschot**
Northville High School
Northville, MI

# La Telehistoria

VIDEO DVD

Hi! My name is Alicia. My family and I live in Miami, Florida. My favorite thing to do is play soccer. At the Pan-American Youth Games, my team took second place. I made a lot of great friends from all over the world. I also met Trini Salgado, the best soccer player ever!

I got a T-shirt like hers, but I never got her to autograph it. She is always traveling to different countries, so maybe I can send my shirt to some of my soccer friends to try to get it signed.

Follow along in the *¡Avancemos!* Telehistoria to find out what happens to Alicia's T-shirt as it travels from country to country.

SALGAD
10

*Trini Salgado*

En Parque de la

Próximo Sábado, 15 de Jun

Sandra - San Antonio ✓
Pablo - México
Rodrigo - Puerto Rico ✓
Maribel - España ✓
Manuel - Ecuador ✓
Mario - República ✓
         Dominicana
Florencia - Argentina
Jorge - Costa Rica ✓

# Level 1a

**1** San Antonio
Sandra

**2** Mexico
Pablo

**3** Puerto Rico
Rodrigo

**4** Spain
Maribel

# Level 1b

**5** Ecuador
Manuel

**6** Dominican Republic
Mario

**7** Argentina
Florencia

**8** Costa Rica
Jorge

*Key Words to Know*

*el autógrafo*  autograph

*la camiseta*  T-shirt

*el jugador (la jugadora) de fútbol*  soccer player

# Why Study Spanish?

## Discover the world

Deciding to learn Spanish is one of the best decisions you can make if you want to travel and see the world.

More than 400 million people around the globe speak Spanish. After Chinese, English and Spanish are tied as the two most frequently spoken languages worldwide. Spanish is now the third most-used language on the Internet. In Europe, Spanish is the most popular foreign language after English. People who speak both Spanish and English can communicate with people from all around the globe, no matter where they find themselves.

# Explore your community

**Inside the United States, Spanish is by far the most widely spoken language after English.**

There are currently about 30 million Spanish speakers in the U.S. When you start to look and listen for it, you will quickly realize that Spanish is all around you—on the television, on the radio, and in magazines and newspapers. You may even hear your neighbors speaking it. Learning Spanish will help you communicate and interact with the rapidly growing communities of Spanish speakers around you.

 # Experience a new perspective

**Learning a language is more than just memorizing words and structures.**

When you study Spanish, you learn how the people who speak it think, feel, work, and live. Learning a language can open your eyes to a whole new world of ideas and insights. And as you learn about other cultures, you gain a better perspective on your own.

 # Create career possibilities

**Knowing Spanish opens many doors.**

If you speak Spanish fluently, you can work for international and multinational companies anywhere in the Spanish-speaking world. You can create a career working as a translator, an interpreter, or a teacher of Spanish. And because the number of Spanish speakers in the U.S. is growing so rapidly, being able to communicate in Spanish is becoming important in almost every career.

# What is Vocabulary?

## Building Your Spanish Vocabulary

Vocabulary is a basic building block for learning a foreign language. By learning just a few words, you can start to communicate in Spanish right away! You will probably find that it is easier to understand words you hear or read than it is to use them yourself. But with a little practice, you will start to produce the right words in the right context. Soon you will be able to carry on conversations with other Spanish speakers.

# How Do I Study Vocabulary?

## First Steps

- Read all of the new words in **blue** on the Vocabulary presentation page in your textbook.
- Point to each word as you say it out loud.

## Be Creative

- Make flashcards with your new vocabulary words. You could also draw pictures of the words on the back of the flashcards.
- Group vocabulary words by theme. Add other words that fit the categories you've learned.
- Imagine a picture of the word.
- Create a rhyme or song to help you remember the words.

## Make It Personal

- Use vocabulary words to write original sentences. Make them funny so you'll be sure to remember!
- Label everyday items in Spanish.
- Create reminders for difficult words. Put note cards inside your locker door, or on your mirror at home.
- See it, and say it to yourself! For example, if you are learning colors and clothing words, think of the Spanish word to describe what your friends are wearing.

el cuaderno

## Practice Makes Perfect

- Say your vocabulary words out loud and repeat each word several times.
- Write each word five times, keeping its meaning in mind.
- Use Spanish words with your classmates outside of class—if you're having lunch in the cafeteria, use the words you know for food. Greet your classmates in the hallway in Spanish!

## Create Your Own System

- Practice a little bit every day. Many short sessions are better than one long one.
- Focus on the words that are the hardest for you.
- Find a buddy. Quiz one another on the vocabulary words.
- Keep a vocabulary notebook and update it regularly.
- Use the study sheets in the back of your workbook to review vocabulary.

# What is Grammar?

Some people think of grammar as the rules of a language, rules that tell you the "correct" way to speak a language. For instance, why do you say *big red house*, not *red big house*? Why do you say *how much money do you have* instead of *how many money*? If English is your first language, you probably don't think about the rule. You make the correct choice instinctively because it *sounds right*. Non-native speakers of English have to learn the rules. As you begin your study of Spanish, you will need to learn the grammar rules of Spanish.

# Why Should I Study Grammar?

### Grammar helps you to communicate.

For instance, using the past tense or future tense makes it clear when something happens. (*I did my homework* versus *I will do my homework.*) Using subject pronouns lets you know who is performing the action. (*I gave the book to her* versus *She gave the book to me.*) Using correct grammar when speaking Spanish will help you communicate successfully with native speakers of Spanish.

# How Do I Study Grammar?

### Read the English Grammar Connection before each grammar explanation.

Think about how you use the same type of grammar in English. Understanding your own language will help you to better understand Spanish.

> **English Grammar Connection:** A **verb tense** is the form of the verb that shows *when* an action is happening. The **present tense** shows that an action is happening *now*. The Spanish present-tense verb form **estudiamos** can be expressed in English in three different ways: *we study, we are studying,* or *we do study.*
>
> We **study** Spanish.      **Estudiamos** español.
>
> ↑                ↑
>
> **present-tense verb**    **present-tense verb**

### Practice the new forms that you are learning.

Completing the practice activities in your student book and workbook will help you to learn the correct way to say things.

### Use the Spanish you know as often as you can.

After all, that's how you learned to speak English, by hearing and speaking it every day.

# What Is Culture?

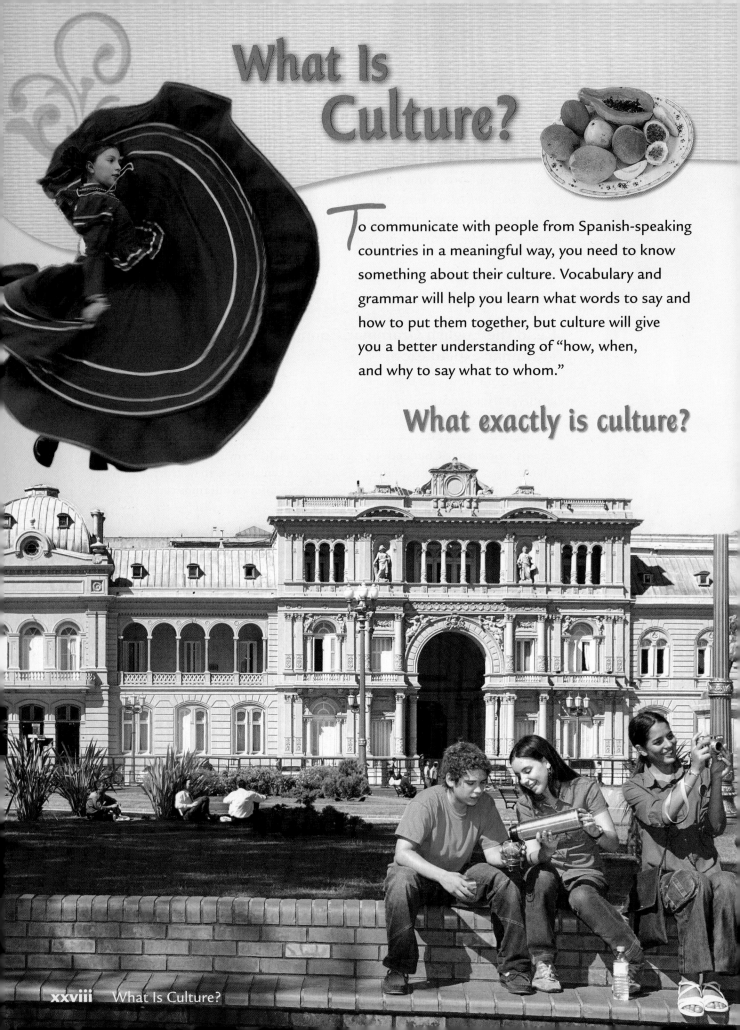

To communicate with people from Spanish-speaking countries in a meaningful way, you need to know something about their culture. Vocabulary and grammar will help you learn what words to say and how to put them together, but culture will give you a better understanding of "how, when, and why to say what to whom."

## What exactly is culture?

# Culture includes . . .

Art

History

Traditions

Relationships

Music

Holidays

Food

Architecture

Pastimes

   and more!

## How can I learn about another culture?

- Read the **Comparación cultural** information to find out more about the cultures that you are studying.
- Think about the answers to the questions in the **Comparación cultural.**
- Think about the perspectives and practices that shape and influence the culture.
- Compare your own culture with the cultures you are studying.

# El mundo

OCÉANO ÁRTICO

*Mar de Siberia Oriental*

*Mar de Beaufort*

*Bahía de Baffin*

**GROENLANDIA (DINAMARCA)**

**RUSIA**

Alaska (EE.UU.)

*Mar de Bering*

*Bahía de Hudson*

*Mar del Labrador*

**CANADÁ**

**ESTADOS UNIDOS**

OCÉANO ATLÁNTICO

*Golfo de México*

**REP. DOMINICANA**

**ISLAS BAHAMAS**

**PUERTO RICO (EE.UU.)**

**SAN CRISTÓBAL Y NEVIS**

**HAITÍ**

**ANTIGUA Y BARBUDA**

**CUBA**

**GUADALUPE (FRANCIA)**

Islas Hawai (EE.UU.)

**JAMAICA**

**DOMINICA**

**MÉXICO**

*Mar Caribe*

**MARTINICA (FRANCIA)**

**BELICE**

**SANTA LUCÍA**

**SAN VICENTE Y GRANADINA**

OCÉANO PACÍFICO

**GUATEMALA**

**GRANADA**

**BARBADOS**

**ISLAS MARSHALL**

**EL SALVADOR**

**PANAMÁ**

**TRINIDAD Y TOBAGO**

**HONDURAS**

**NICARAGUA**

**VENEZUELA**

**GUAYANA FRANCESA (FRANCIA)**

**COSTA RICA**

**COLOMBIA**

**NAURU**

**KIRIBATI**

Islas Galápagos (Ecuador)

**ECUADOR**

**GUYANA**

**SURINAM**

**ISLAS SALOMÓN**

**ISLAS TUVALU**

**SAMOA**

Samoa Americana (EE.UU.)

**BRASIL**

**VANUATÚ**

**PERÚ**

**FIDJI**

**TONGA**

**BOLIVIA**

**NUEVA CALEDONIA (FRANCIA)**

**PARAGUAY**

**CHILE**

**URUGUAY**

**NUEVA ZELANDA**

**ARGENTINA**

*Islas Malvinas (R.U.)*

OCÉANO ÁRTICO

Mar de Kara

Mar de Laptev

Mar de Barents

RUSIA

Mar de
Noruega

SUECIA   FINLANDIA

ESTONIA
LETONIA
LITUANIA
BIELORRUSIA

| 1 | DINAMARCA | 9 | ESLOVENIA |
| 2 | HOLANDA | 10 | CROACIA |
| 3 | BÉLGICA | 11 | BOSNIA Y HERZEGOVINA |
| 4 | LUXEMBURGO | 12 | SERBIA Y MONTENEGRO |
| 5 | SUIZA | 13 | ALBANIA |
| 6 | REPÚBLICA CHECA | 14 | MACEDONIA |
| 7 | ESLOVAQUIA | 15 | BULGARIA |
| 8 | HUNGRÍA | | |

NORUEGA

REINO
UNIDO

IRLANDA

Mar del
Norte

ALEMANIA   POLONIA

UCRANIA

MOLDAVIA

KAZAKSTÁN

MONGOLIA

FRANCIA

AUSTRIA

ANDORRA

RUMANIA

ITALIA

Mar Negro

GEORGIA

Mar de
Aral

UZBEKISTÁN   KIRGUISTÁN

COREA
DEL NORTE

Mar de
Japón

ESPAÑA

PORTUGAL

GRECIA

TURQUÍA

ARMENIA

Mar Caspio

TURKMENISTÁN

TADJIKISTÁN

CHINA

COREA
DEL SUR

JAPÓN

(R.U.)

MARRUECOS

TÚNEZ

MALTA

Mar Mediterráneo

CHIPRE
LÍBANO

SIRIA

IRAQ

AZERBAIYÁN

IRÁN

AFGANISTÁN

BHUTÁN

Canarias
(sp.)

ISRAEL

JORDANIA

KUWAIT
QATAR

PAQUISTÁN

NEPAL

BANGLADESH

TAIWÁN

Trópico de Cáncer

OCÉANO
PACÍFICO

AHARA
ENTAL

ARGELIA

LIBIA

EGIPTO

BAHREIN

E.Á.U

OMÁN

INDIA

MYANMAR

FILIPINAS

GUAM
(EE.UU.)

MAURITANIA

ARABIA
SAUDITA

LAOS

MALÍ

NÍGER

CHAD

SUDÁN

ERITREA

YEMEN

Mar
Arábigo

Golfo
de
Bengala

TAILANDIA

CAMBOYA

VIETNAM

Mar de
China

MICRONESIA

NEGAL

BURKINA
FASO

JIBUTI

BRUNEI

PALAU

GUINEA

COSTA
DE
MARFIL

BENIN

NIGERIA

TOGO

REP. CENTRO-
AFRICANA

ETIOPÍA

ISLAS
MALDIVAS

SRI
LANKA

MALASIA

LIBERIA

GHANA

CAMERÚN

UGANDA

SOMALIA

ERRA
EONA

GUINEA
ECUATORIAL

GABÓN

CONGO

KENIA

SINGAPUR

INDONESIA

PAPUASIA
NUEVA GUINEA

SANTO TOMÉ
Y PRÍNCIPE

CABINDA
(ANGOLA)

REP. DEM.
DEL CONGO

BURUNDI

RUANDA

TANZANÍA

SEYCHELLES

TIMOR
ORIENTAL

ANGOLA

COMORES

ZAMBIA

MALAWI

Ecuador 0°

SUECIA

NAMIBIA

MOZAMBIQUE

ZIMBABWE

MADAGASCAR

MAURICIO

OCÉANO ÍNDICO

BOTSWANA

Trópico de Capricornio

AUSTRALIA

SUAZILANDIA

SUDÁFRICA   LESOTHO

30°S

| 0 | 1,000 | 2,000 millas |

| 0 | 1,000 | 2,000 kilómetros |

N

O        E

S

60°S

ANTÁRTIDA

60°N

30°N

Mar de
Ojotsk

Lago
Baikal

# México y Centroamérica

Washington, D.C. ✪

**ESTADOS UNIDOS**

*OCÉANO ATLÁNTICO*

Tijuana
Mexicali
Ciudad Juárez

Hermosillo
Chihuahua
Nuevo Laredo

SIERRA MADRE OCCIDENTAL
SIERRA MADRE ORIENTAL

Baja California

**MÉXICO**

*Golfo de México*

**ISLAS BAHAMAS**

Nassau ✪

Monterrey

Durango
San Luis Potosí

Tampico

*Trópico de Cáncer*

La Habana ✪

**CUBA**

Guadalajara

Mérida

20°N

México, D.F. ✪
Puebla

Veracruz

**JAMAICA**

Kingston ✪

Acapulco

Oaxaca

Belice
**BELICE**
Belmopan

*Mar Caribe*

**HONDURAS**

Guatemala ✪   Tegucigalpa ✪

**GUATEMALA**

San Salvador ✪

**EL SALVADOR**

**NICARAGUA**

Managua ✪

San José ✪

Colón   Panamá

**COSTA RICA**

10°N

**PANAMÁ**

**COLOMBIA**

*OCÉANO PACÍFICO*

N
O   E
S

*Ecuador*

Quito ✪

**ECUADOR**

0°

250   500 millas
0
250   500 kilómetros

110°O   100°O   90°O   80°O

**PERÚ**

# El Caribe

ESTADOS UNIDOS

OCÉANO ATLÁNTICO

Estrecho de Florida

Nassau

ISLAS BAHAMAS

25°N

Trópico de Cáncer

La Habana

Santa Clara

CUBA

Nueva Gerona

Camagüey

Holguín

Manzanillo

Guantánamo

Santiago de Cuba

ISLAS DE TURCOS Y CAICOS (R.U.)

REPÚBLICA DOMINICANA

20°N

HAITÍ

La Española

Arecibo

San Juan

Mayagüez

A N T I L L A S

Puerto Príncipe

Santo Domingo

Ponce

Humacao

JAMAICA

Kingston

M A Y O R E S

PUERTO RICO

HONDURAS

Mar Caribe

15°N

NICARAGUA

Aruba (Hol.)

Curaçao (Hol.)

Bonaire (Hol.)

San José

Caracas

10°N

COSTA RICA

Panamá

PANAMÁ

Golfo de Panamá

VENEZUELA

OCÉANO PACÍFICO

N
O    E
S

5°N

Bogotá

COLOMBIA

0    150    300 millas
0    150    300 kilómetros

# Sudamérica

Mar Caribe

**OCÉANO ATLÁNTICO**

Barranquilla
Cartagena
Maracaibo
**TRINIDAD Y TOBAGO**
Puerto España
Lago Maracaibo
Caracas
Río Orinoco
**VENEZUELA**
Georgetown
Paramaribo
**GUYANA**
Cayena
**SURINAM**
**GUAYANA FRANCESA (FRANCIA)**
Medellín
Manizales
Bogotá
**COLOMBIA**
Cali
Río Negro
Río Amazonas
Ecuador 0°
Otavalo
Quito
**ECUADOR**
Guayaquil
Cuenca
**PERÚ**
Río Madeira
Río Tapajóz
Río Xingú
Río Tocantins
**BRASIL**
Río São Francisco
Trujillo
C O R D I L L E R A
Callao
Lima
10°S
Lago Titicaca
**BOLIVIA**
La Paz
Cochabamba
Santa Cruz
Sucre
Brasilia
20°S

**OCÉANO PACÍFICO**
*Islas Galápagos (Ecuador)*
**Bogotá**
**COLOMBIA**
Quito
**ECUADOR**
**PERÚ**
0   200   400 millas
0   200   400 kilómetros

GRAN CHACO
**PARAGUAY**
Salta
Asunción
San Miguel de Tucumán
Resistencia
Trópico de Capricornio
**CHILE**
D E   L O S
Córdoba
30°S
Valparaíso
Mendoza
Rosario
**URUGUAY**
Santiago
Buenos Aires
Montevideo
**ARGENTINA**
La Plata
Concepción
A N D E S
PAMPAS
Mar del Plata
Temuco
Bahía Blanca
40°S
**OCÉANO PACÍFICO**
**OCÉANO ATLÁNTICO**

PATAGONIA
N
O      E
S
0   250   500 millas
0   250   500 kilómetros

Estrecho de Magallanes
Islas Malvinas (R.U.)
50°S
Tierra del Fuego
Cabo de Hornos

100°O   90°O   80°O   70°O   50°O   40°O   30°O   20°O

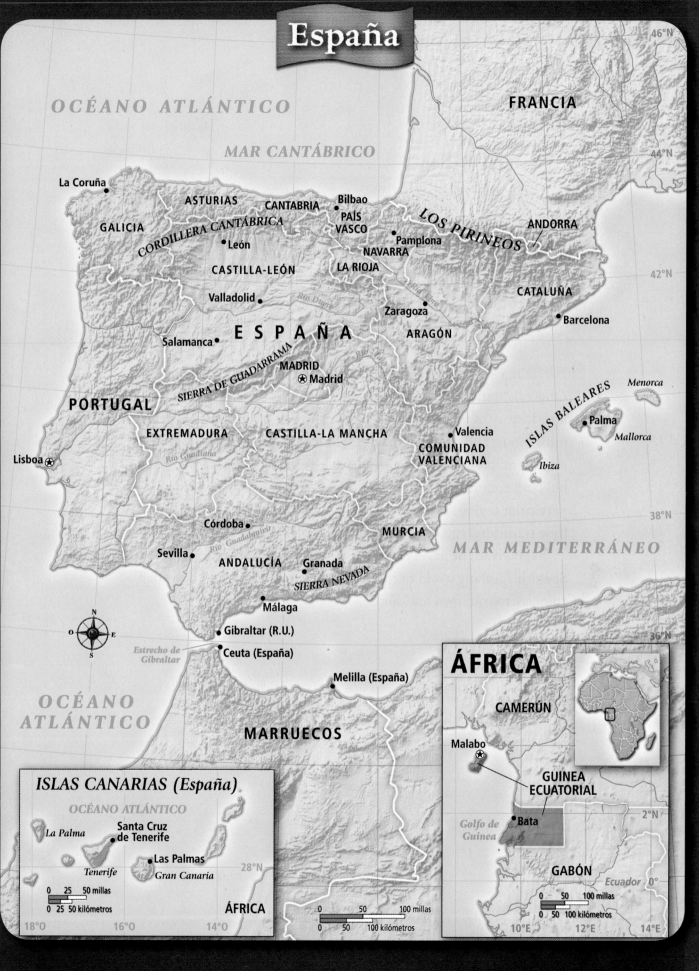

# España

OCÉANO ATLÁNTICO

FRANCIA

MAR CANTÁBRICO

La Coruña

ASTURIAS
CANTABRIA
Bilbao
PAÍS
VASCO

LOS PIRINEOS
ANDORRA

GALICIA
CORDILLERA CANTÁBRICA
León
Pamplona
NAVARRA
LA RIOJA

CASTILLA-LEÓN
Río Duero

CATALUÑA

Valladolid

Zaragoza
ARAGÓN
Barcelona

E S P A Ñ A

Salamanca
Río Tajo

Menorca

MADRID
Madrid
SIERRA DE GUADARRAMA

ISLAS BALEARES
Palma

PORTUGAL

Mallorca

EXTREMADURA
CASTILLA-LA MANCHA
Valencia
COMUNIDAD
VALENCIANA

Ibiza

Lisboa
Río Guadiana

Córdoba
Río Guadalquivir

MURCIA

MAR MEDITERRÁNEO

Sevilla

ANDALUCÍA
Granada
SIERRA NEVADA

Málaga

N
O      E
S

Gibraltar (R.U.)
Estrecho de
Gibraltar
Ceuta (España)

Melilla (España)

OCÉANO
ATLÁNTICO

MARRUECOS

**ÁFRICA**

CAMERÚN

Malabo

GUINEA
ECUATORIAL

## ISLAS CANARIAS (España)

OCÉANO ATLÁNTICO

La Palma

Santa Cruz
de Tenerife

Tenerife

Las Palmas
Gran Canaria

28°N

ÁFRICA

0   25   50 millas

0   25   50 kilómetros

18°O          16°O          14°O

0        50       100 millas

0      50     100 kilómetros

Golfo de
Guinea

Bata

2°N

GABÓN

Ecuador          0°

0      50     100 millas

0     50    100 kilómetros

10°E       12°E       14°E

46°N

44°N

42°N

38°N

36°N

# Las celebraciones

The following lessons about holidays are provided for your personal enjoyment. You may choose to read them on your own, or your teacher may present them throughout the year.

*Countries in the Spanish-speaking world* often share the same celebrations and holidays. The celebrations are a result of a long history of traditions that reflect the mix of primarily Spanish, indigenous, and African cultures. Holidays celebrating religious events and beliefs are often similar between countries. Other holidays commemorate events or people that are important to a particular region. Many holidays, though celebrated on the same day, have traditions and customs that differ between countries.

As you read the pages of Celebraciones, you will discover how the Spanish-speaking world celebrates important holidays and how they compare to your own traditions.

# Contenido

# FERIA DE MÁLAGA

**La Feria de Málaga** celebrates King Ferdinand and Queen Isabella's triumphant entrance into the coastal city of Málaga on August 19, 1487. The pair claimed the city for the crown of Castile, an event this Spanish city has been celebrating for over 500 years. The *Feria de Málaga* now lasts for nine days and takes place in two parts of the city. Each day at noon the downtown fills with fairgoers. In the *Real,* a separate fairground, participants in *flamenco* dress or riding clothes ride on horseback or in horse-drawn carriages, or stroll, in a tradition known as *el paseo.* This daytime *feria* unfolds against a backdrop of music, singing, and dancing and ends at 6:00 p.m., when everyone goes home to rest. The celebration starts again at night in the *Real* and continues into the early morning hours. For this nightly *feria,* people gather in public and private *casetas,* to enjoy concerts, theatrical presentations, music, dance, and food. The last night of the *feria* ends with a city-sponsored concert followed by a spectacular fireworks display.

***Feria de caballos*** More than a thousand riders and over a hundred horse-drawn carriages and carts participate in *el paseo.*

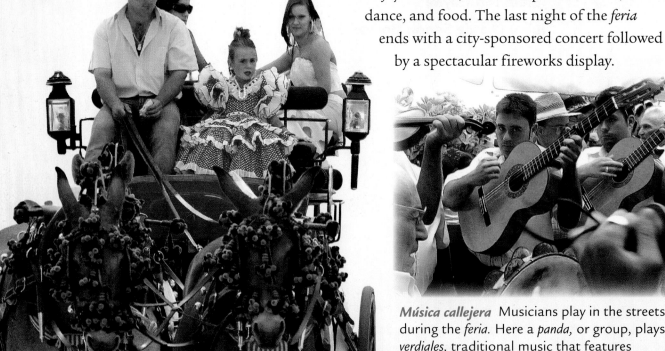

***Música callejera*** Musicians play in the streets during the *feria.* Here a *panda,* or group, plays *verdiales,* traditional music that features guitars, tambourines, and tiny cymbals.

*Una caseta* offers free samples of *paella*, a rice and seafood dish that is a regional specialty from the coastal cities of Spain.

*Bailando flamenco* Fairgoers perform folkloric dances such as *flamenco* and *sevillanas* in the streets, plazas, and *casetas,* wherever there is music.

*Una entrada a la feria* Riders pass in front of one of the decorative entrances to a street in the historic downtown of Málaga.

*Vocabulario para celebrar*

| | |
|---|---|
| *los caballos* | horses |
| *las carretas* | horse-drawn carriages |
| *las casetas* | small houses or tents |
| *la feria* | fair |
| *el paseo* | a walk, stroll, or ride |

## Comparación cultural

1. Does your town or city celebrate its beginnings or inauguration as a community, or is there a special "town day"? What events take place during the celebration?

2. What events in your community or region are similar to those of the *Feria de Málaga*? Describe them and then compare them to the *Feria de Málaga*.

Celebraciones **C3**

# DÍA DE LA INDEPENDENCIA

**El Día de la Independencia** falls in September for many of the Spanish-speaking countries in the Americas. Mexico celebrates on September 15 and 16, with the *Grito de la Independencia,* music, fireworks, and parades. The first *Grito* occurred at dawn on September 16, 1810, when Padre Miguel Hidalgo de Costilla called to the people of Dolores to rise up against the Spanish crown. That rebellion led to the Mexican War of Independence.

Just two days later, on September 18, 1810, Chile declared its independence from Spain. Today Chile celebrates the date during a week of *fiestas patrias* that include parades, rodeos, dance competitions, and special foods.

Eleven years later, on September 15, 1821, a large part of Central America also proclaimed its independence from Spain, becoming El Salvador, Nicaragua, Guatemala, Costa Rica, and Honduras. These countries celebrate their independence on the 14 and 15 with a focus on students: parades, assemblies, and sports competitions.

### México

*El Grito de la Independencia* On the night of September 15, the president of Mexico commemorates *el Grito* by ringing a bell, proclaiming *¡Que viva México!*, and waving the Mexican flag from a balcony above the Zócalo. Crowds gather below to participate in the *Grito*.

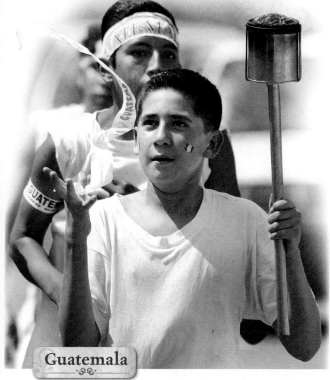

*Fiestas patrias* Costa Rican schoolchildren, dressed in colors of their country, dance in a parade.

## Costa Rica

## Guatemala

*El recorrido de la antorcha* Runners carrying a flaming torch start in Guatemala and end in Costa Rica. All along the route, uniformed schoolchildren wait expectantly for the torch to pass.

### Vocabulario para celebrar

| | |
|---|---|
| *la antorcha* | torch |
| *la banda* | band |
| *las fiestas patrias* | patriotic holidays |
| *el grito* | shout |
| *el recorrido* | run, journey |
| *proclamar* | to declare |

## Comparación cultural

1. Compare the way your town or city celebrates Independence Day with the celebrations in Mexico and Central America. How are they similar? Are there any differences?

2. How do you celebrate Independence Day? Do you participate in community events or have a special tradition?

# El 12 de Octubre

*El 12 de Octubre* has many different meanings in the Spanish-speaking world. For some people it is *el Día de Colón,* the day Christopher Columbus arrived in the Americas. For some, it is *el Día de la Hispanidad,* a day to celebrate one's connection with all other Spanish-speaking people, regardless of their country. And for others, it is *el Día de la Raza,* a day when indigenous people come together as a community and celebrate their heritage. Other Spanish speakers celebrate their mixed heritage of indigenous, African, and European cultures. How you celebrate depends very much on you and your family's origin and on the community where you live. For all Spanish-speaking groups, *el 12 de octubre* marks a key turning point in the lives and cultures of the people in Spain and those living in the Americas.

## Vocabulario para celebrar

| | |
|---|---|
| *Cristóbal Colón* | Christopher Columbus |
| *el Día Nacional* | National Day |
| *la hispanidad* | the cultural community of Spanish speakers |
| *la raza* | race |

México

**Día de la Raza** Indigenous groups gather in Mexico City dressed in their community's traditional outfits, some wearing pre-Columbian clothing and headdresses.

### Chile

*Día de la Raza*  A woman from the Pehuenche indigenous community gathers with other indigenous groups in downtown Santiago.

### Nueva York

*Día de la Hispanidad*  High school students carry flags representing all the American countries as they march in a parade down Fifth Avenue.

### España

*Día Nacional de España*  The Spanish government celebrates with a parade in Madrid.

## Comparación cultural

1. How do you celebrate October 12 in your community or school? Is it similar to or different from the celebrations in Spanish-speaking countries? How so?

2. What does October 12 mean to you? Which of the Spanish names for the holiday has the most meaning for you? How would you rename the holiday to celebrate your heritage?

*noviembre*

# ¡Día de los Muertos!

*Las mojigangas* People parade through the Pilsen-Little Village neighborhood of Chicago. Some carry *mojigangas*, giant papier-mâché puppets typically carried in Mexican processions.

**On Día de los Muertos** families visit the cemeteries and gravesites of their loved ones. They clean the sites and leave flowers and candles and, in many countries, they bring entire meals with special drinks and traditional breads to share with the deceased. Displays are set up next to the gravesite that include flowers, hand-crafted skeletons, colorful paper cutouts, candy skulls, personal items, and photos. Family members pass the night sharing food and conversation as they keep vigil for their ancestors.

The celebration of *Día de los Muertos* spans two days, November 1 and 2. Also known as *Día de los Difuntos*, the traditions originate in the centuries-old religious holiday *Día de Todos los Santos*. In the Americas, this holiday coincided with pre-Columbian festivals that celebrated the harvest, the new year, and honored the dead. The mix of cultures and traditions resulted in the celebration *Día de los Muertos*.

**México**

*Las calaveras* A display of dressed-up skulls and skeletons on a street in Mexico City

## Ecuador

*El pan de muertos* This bread is made only for *Día de los Muertos*. In Ecuador, these breads are called *guaguas de pan*. *Guagua* is the Quechua word for "baby" and refers to the bread's shape. The *guaguas* are served with *colada morada,* a warm, purple-colored drink made from blueberries and raspberries.

## México

*El papel picado* These tissue paper cutouts are a common holiday decoration. To celebrate *Día de los Muertos,* the cutouts form images of skeletons.

## Guatemala

*Los barriletes* Guatemalans celebrate by flying *barriletes,* or colorful kites, to which they attach messages for the deceased. The town of Santiago Sacatepéquez celebrates with a *barrilete* contest.

### Vocabulario para celebrar

| | |
|---|---|
| *las calaveras* | skulls |
| *el cementerio* | cemetery |
| *los difuntos* | deceased |
| *el esqueleto* | skeleton |
| *el pan de muertos* | special bread made for *Día de los Muertos* |
| *el papel picado* | paper cutouts |
| *los santos* | saints |

## Comparación cultural

1. Does your family or community have a special day or specific traditions to remember the deceased? How are they similar to or different from the traditions of *Día de los Muertos*?

2. Centuries ago in Europe, the night of October 31, before All Saint's Day, was known as "All Hallowed's Eve." According to ancient beliefs, on this night the dead join the world of the living. Today we call this night Halloween. How would you compare the celebrations of Halloween and *Día de los Muertos*?

# Las Navidades

**Las Navidades** are celebrated throughout the Spanish-speaking world with family gatherings and special meals. Celebrations start in mid-December and, in some countries, extend to January 6.

Many families gather the night of December 24, or *la Nochebuena,* to share a special meal of traditional foods and drinks that vary depending on the country. *Tamales, empanadas,* and *buñuelos* are served in many countries. In Spain, there is turkey, or *pavo,* and *turrón.* In Argentina and Chile, where it is summer, people eat cold foods and salads.

The tradition of giving and receiving gifts also forms a part of *las Navidades.* In some countries, families exchange gifts at midnight on *la Nochebuena,* while in others children receive gifts the morning of December 25, and in other countries the gifts appear the morning of January 6. Often gifts are given primarily to children.

**Panamá**

*Un desfile navideño* The holiday parade in Panama City takes place in mid-December.

**México**

*La noche de rábanos* On the night of December 23, elaborate carvings made from radishes, or *rábanos,* are on display in Oaxaca's central plaza. The figures include people, animals, and even entire scenes. This unique tradition has been celebrated for over 100 years.

**Argentina**

*Las empanadas* Dancers dress as *empanadas* in Buenos Aires. These meat-filled pies are especially enjoyed during *las Navidades.*

## Perú

*El Día de los Reyes Magos* In Peru, Argentina, the Dominican Republic, Paraguay, and Spain, children receive presents on January 6 from *los Reyes Magos*. In anticipation, children leave out a snack for the Three Kings, carrots or grass for the camels, and a pair of empty shoes for the gifts.

## España

*Un desfile navideño* Circus elephants take part in Madrid's holiday parade on January 5. In Spain, parades on January 5 or 6 celebrate the arrival of *los Reyes Magos*.

### Vocabulario para celebrar

| | |
|---|---|
| la Nochebuena | Christmas Eve |
| los Reyes Magos | Three Kings |
| la rosca de reyes | sweet bread eaten on January 6 |
| el turrón | almond nougat candy |
| los villancicos | seasonal Christmas songs |

## Comparación cultural

1. Do you and your family celebrate a holiday in December? If so, compare the traditions of your family to the traditions of *las Navidades*.

2. What special meals and foods do you associate with certain holidays? Describe the foods you traditionally enjoy on a holiday you celebrate.

3. What time of the year do you give or receive gifts and for what reason?

# ¡Año Nuevo!

**El Año Nuevo** celebrates the arrival of the New Year and *la Nochevieja* says goodbye to the old. In much of the Spanish-speaking world, traditions include making a toast, exchanging a kiss or hug, or eating twelve grapes—one for each stroke of midnight—to ensure your wishes come true for the New Year. Other good luck traditions include wearing yellow or red, eating a tablespoon of lentils, or carrying a suitcase around the block if you hope to take a trip. To wish someone a happy New Year, say *¡Feliz año nuevo!* or *¡Próspero año nuevo!*

On *Nochevieja,* there are also traditions for saying goodbye to the old year. Some people dress in masks representing *el año viejo.* Others build satirical figures called *los años viejos* that represent famous people or politicians. Adorned with poems or messages that poke fun at *el año viejo,* and filled with shavings and firecrackers, these figures are lit on fire at midnight, to burn and explode on street corners, as a final *despedida,* or farewell, to the old year.

### Perú

*La buena suerte* In Lima, people believe touching a Chinese Lion brings happiness, good luck, and prosperity in the New Year. Ten percent of Peru's population is of Chinese descent.

### España

*La medianoche* In Madrid, people gather in the Puerta del Sol, holding bags of 12 grapes as they wait for the 12 strokes of midnight from the Puerta del Sol clock, the city's official timekeeper.

*Paseo de los años viejos* In Popayán, families and neighbors take their *año viejo* figures out for a final ride before the *Nochevieja* celebration. Later on, at midnight, they will burn the figures.

Guatemala

*Baile de los Gigantes* In Antigua, people celebrate the New Year with the folkloric "Dance of the Giants." These giant heads, or *cabezudos,* are similar to costumes used since the medieval period in Spain.

*Vocabulario para celebrar*

| | |
|---|---|
| el Año Nuevo | New Year |
| el brindis | toast |
| las doce uvas | twelve grapes |
| las lentejas | lentils |
| la medianoche | midnight |
| la Nochevieja | New Year's Eve |

## Comparación cultural

1. How do you celebrate the New Year? Does your family or community have any special traditions? Are any of the traditions similar to the ones in Spanish-speaking countries? How are they similar or different?

2. If you were to build an *año viejo* representing the past year, what figure or event would you portray? Explain your choice.

# ¡Carnaval!

**Carnaval** marks a period of festivity prior to the beginning of Lent. Lent was, and for some still is, a 40-day period of solemnity and fasting with the removal of meat from the diet being a key feature. You can see the word *carne* (meat) in *Carnaval*; traditionally, this was the last chance to eat meat before the Lenten fast. Today, *Carnaval* often resembles a lively, multi-day party.

Falling in either February or March, *Carnaval* is typically celebrated during the five days that precede Ash Wednesday, the first day of Lent. In some countries, *Carnaval* lasts longer, overlapping other local celebrations. In many regions, traditions such as throwing water and eggs can start over a month before the actual holiday. The planning for the next year's parades, parties, and dance groups often starts as soon as the current *Carnaval* ends!

**España**

**Disfraces** Elaborate costumes are central to the *Carnaval* celebration. This costume, entitled "África soy yo," appeared in Las Palmas, in the Canary Islands.

*Carnaval* Revelers dance in Encarnación, site of the largest celebration in Paraguay.

**Paraguay**

**México**

*Cascarones* Breaking *cascarones* on the heads of friends and other party-goers is a *Carnaval* tradition. The sprinkling of confetti from these hollowed-out eggs is said to bring good luck, as seen here in Mazatlán.

**Bolivia**

*Máscaras* are a *Carnaval* tradition dating back to medieval Spain. This masked dancer is from the parade in Oruro, where some 40,000 folkloric dancers and musicians participate.

*Bailarines folklóricos* Dancers from the Mestizaje dance group perform in Barranquilla. The Colombian government proclaimed this city's *Carnaval* celebration, which combines indigenous, African, and European traditions, a National Cultural Heritage. UNESCO declared it a "Masterpiece" for its cultural uniqueness.

**Colombia**

*Vocabulario para celebrar*

| | |
|---|---|
| *los bailarines* | dancers |
| *la banda* | musical band |
| *Carnaval* | Carnival |
| *los cascarones* | confetti-filled eggs |
| *el disfraz* | costume |
| *las máscaras* | masks |

## Comparación cultural

1. The ways in which *Carnaval* is celebrated in the Spanish-speaking world differ depending on the region. Why do you think the celebrations have evolved differently?

2. Compare the traditions of *Carnaval* to any holiday that you celebrate. Which one(s) are similar? How are they similar?

# Las Fallas

**Las Fallas** is a weeklong festival in March that engulfs the city of Valencia, Spain. Tens of thousands of visitors from all over the world come to the city to experience *Las Fallas,* a week of pageants, music, flowers, and creative displays. Each day, the deafening explosions of thousands of firecrackers, *la mascletà,* fills the city at 2:00 p.m. and each night's celebration ends in fireworks.

The main characters of the celebration are the *ninots,* gigantic figures built of wood, plaster, and cardboard. The largest are up to several stories tall. Neighborhood organizations build these enormous figures during the preceding year. Then, during the week of *Las Fallas,* they display them in intersections, parks, and plazas throughout the city. The public visits the more than 400 *fallas* and votes for their favorite one. On the last night at midnight, all but the favorite are burned in enormous bonfires. Then one final, brilliant display of fireworks explodes over the city.

**Los ninots** These gigantic figures poke fun at well-known people or current events from the preceding year.

**Las falleras** During the festival, women dress in traditional outfits that include lace dresses, veils, jewelry, and colorful sashes.

**Una falla iluminada** Thousands of visitors come at night to see the illuminated *fallas*. This display was entered into a special contest, *la Sección Especial,* where a committee judges the *fallas* for creativity, gracefulness and charm, originality, and lighting.

**La Cremà** At midnight on the last night, the *fallas* are burned throughout the city. At the same time there are huge displays of colorful fireworks, which include explosions of roman candles and thousands of firecrackers.

*Vocabulario para celebrar*

| | |
|---|---|
| *La Cremà* | burning of the *fallas* |
| *las fallas* | displays of figures |
| *los falleros* | celebrants of *Las Fallas* |
| *los fuegos artificiales* | fireworks |
| *la mascletà* | rhythmic explosion of large and small firecrackers |
| *los ninots* | large papier-mâché figures |
| *quemar* | to burn |

## Comparación cultural

1. Fireworks are a major part of *Las Fallas*. Does your community or region have fireworks displays? When and for what reasons?

2. Are there any other traditions in the festival of *Las Fallas* that are similar to traditions you follow in your community? What are they? Are they part of a specific celebration or season?

# Semana Santa

*La Semana Santa* is one holiday during the year where in most Spanish-speaking countries entire towns, businesses, schools, and government close for at least four days, Thursday through Sunday. People that have relocated to other places often go back to their hometowns. Others take advantage of the long break to go to the countryside or beach. Entire communities come together for *Semana Santa* celebrations. In some places, religious processions fill the streets each day of the week from Palm Sunday to Easter; in others, Thursday and Friday are the most important days. Most *Semana Santa* traditions are hundreds of years old and originated in Spain, but many now have a unique twist due to the mix of cultures in each country.

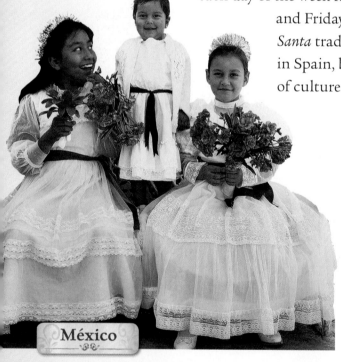

**México**

***Vestidos blancos*** Girls from San Miguel de Allende dress in white for the procession on *Viernes Santo*. In this town, the celebrations extend for two weeks, ending on *el Domingo de Pascua* with an explosion of papier-mâché figures in the center of town.

**El Salvador**

***Alfombras de aserrín*** Rugs traditionally made of colored sawdust or sand, flowers, and fruits cover the streets where processions will pass in Sonsonate. Artisans also now use modern industrial paints and sprays.

**Ecuador**

*La fanesca* Ecuadorians eat *fanesca*, a bean and grain soup with a fish base, only during *Semana Santa*. The soup is traditionally served with *bolitas de harina* (fritters), *plátano verde* (fried green plantain), fresh cheese, and *ají*, a spicy sauce.

**Perú**

*Decoraciones de flores* Flowers fill the city of Tarma for the *Semana Santa* celebrations. In preparation for the processions that begin on Thursday, arches and rugs made of flowers decorate the streets and remain on display until Sunday.

**Vocabulario para celebrar**

| | |
|---|---|
| *las alfombras* | rugs |
| *las flores* | flowers |
| *las procesiones* | processions |
| *Semana Santa* | Holy Week |

**México**

*Una procesión* Young boys carry streamers during the processions in Cadereyta.

## Comparación cultural

1. What holidays do you celebrate with special parades or processions? What kinds of decorations do people use?

2. In what kind of event would most of the people in your community participate? Compare the event to *Semana Santa*.

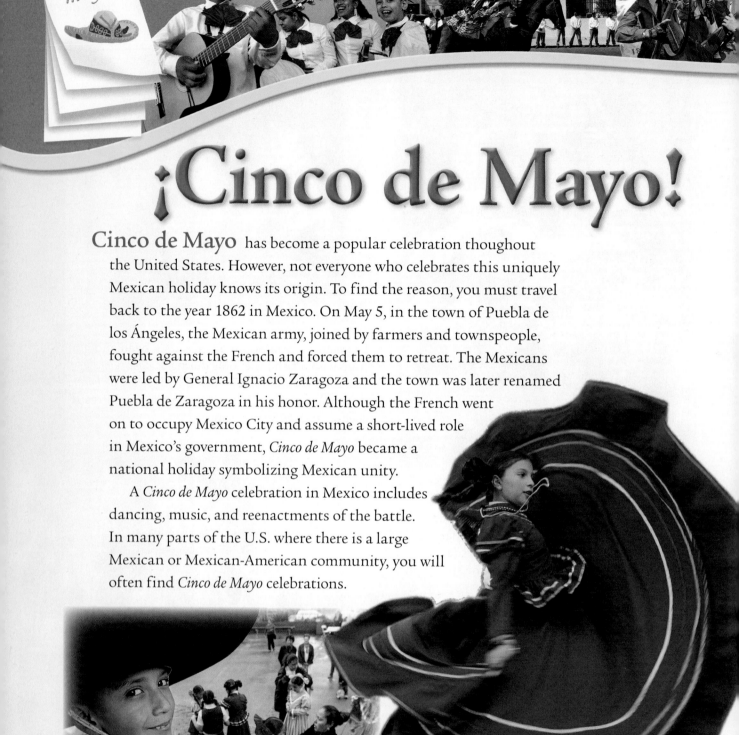

# ¡Cinco de Mayo!

**Cinco de Mayo** has become a popular celebration thoughout the United States. However, not everyone who celebrates this uniquely Mexican holiday knows its origin. To find the reason, you must travel back to the year 1862 in Mexico. On May 5, in the town of Puebla de los Ángeles, the Mexican army, joined by farmers and townspeople, fought against the French and forced them to retreat. The Mexicans were led by General Ignacio Zaragoza and the town was later renamed Puebla de Zaragoza in his honor. Although the French went on to occupy Mexico City and assume a short-lived role in Mexico's government, *Cinco de Mayo* became a national holiday symbolizing Mexican unity.

A *Cinco de Mayo* celebration in Mexico includes dancing, music, and reenactments of the battle. In many parts of the U.S. where there is a large Mexican or Mexican-American community, you will often find *Cinco de Mayo* celebrations.

Los Ángeles

*Mariachis y bailarines* Folkloric dancers and musicians perform throughout the day in the Plaza Olvera during the *Cinco de Mayo* celebrations.

## México

***Reconstrucción de la batalla***
A reenactment of the historic battle in Puebla commemorates Mexico's victory over the French.

### Vocabulario para celebrar

| | |
|---|---|
| *los bailarines* | dancers |
| *la batalla* | battle |
| *el ejército* | army |
| *los franceses* | French |
| *los músicos* | musicians |
| *la reconstrucción* | reenactment |

## Washington, D.C.

***Bailarín folklórico*** A dancer performs in a traditional Mexican costume at the White House.

## Comparación cultural

1. Do you know of a *Cinco de Mayo* celebration in your community or region? If so, how or where is it celebrated?

2. What important battles or historic events are celebrated in your community or state? How are they celebrated? Are they local or national holidays? Compare one of these holiday celebrations with the *Cinco de Mayo* celebrations.

# Inti Raymi

***Inti Raymi,*** or the "Festival of the Sun," falls on June 21 or 22, the date of the southern hemisphere's winter solstice, the shortest day of the year. Indigenous communities throughout the Andean highland countries of South America celebrate the winter solstice with ceremonies designed to bring the Sun back and shorten the longest night. Incan in origin, *Inti Raymi* honored the sun as the source of light, heat, and life, and celebrated the start of a new planting season. The name *Inti Raymi* comes from the Quechua language: *inti* means "sun" and *raymi* means "festival." The largest festival takes place in Cuzco, Peru, the ancient capital of the Incan civilization and empire. In Cuzco, *Inti Raymi* has grown into a major tourist attraction. Thousands of people visit the city to enjoy the performances by folkloric groups and to watch the theatrical presentation of the Incan ceremony, the focal point of the celebration.

Perú

***Presentación cultural de Inti Raymi***
In Cuzco, professional actors and actresses interpret the roles of the Incan emperor and others.
*Above:* A woman carries offerings.
*Right:* The Incan emperor passes through the streets of Cuzco to the ruins of the Incan fortress, Sacsayhuaman.

**C22**   Celebraciones

## Ecuador

**Indígenas ecuatorianas** A dance group from the Paktarinmi cultural organization forms a "sacred circle" with grains of corn, a pre-Incan rite. In Ecuador, which lies on the equator, this date is considered the summer solstice, rather than the winter.

### Vocabulario para celebrar

*el aymara*  language of indigenous group from Bolivia and Peru

*los incas*  Incas, an ancient South American people

*el quechua*  language common to many South American indigenous groups and adopted and spread by Incas

*el sol*  sun

## Bolivia

**Los aymaras** In the pre-Columbian ruins of Tihuanaku, an Aymara priest blows on a shell to celebrate the winter solstice, which marks the new year. The Aymara are one of two dominant indigenous groups in Bolivia, comprising 25 percent of the population. The other group, Quechua, makes up 30 percent.

## Comparación cultural

1. In North America, June 21 is the summer solstice, or the longest day of the year, and December 21 is the winter solstice, or the shortest day of the year. What important holidays or events occur during this time of year?

2. In ancient civilizations, the appearance of the sun and moon were important events that helped mark the passing of time and the seasons. If you were to celebrate the winter or summer solstice, what would you include in your celebration?

# Día de Simón Bolívar

*Simón Bolívar,* known as *El Libertador,* envisioned a united South America, a union for which he fought, but never attained. Despite this, he was instrumental in bringing about much of South America's independence from Spain and became one of its most revered leaders. His birthday is a national holiday in Venezuela, Ecuador, and Bolivia, and many cities and towns have plazas or monuments in his honor.

Born on July 24, 1783, in Caracas, Venezuela, Simón Bolívar strongly believed in freedom from Spanish rule and worked toward that goal as a political leader, writer, and military commander. With his troops, he liberated present-day Venezuela, then Colombia. He was then named president of Gran Colombia, a federation comprised of what is now Venezuela, Colombia, Panama, and Ecuador. He went on to lead his troops into Peru, aiding in the final defeat of Spain. For two more years, Bolívar maintained his leadership, writing the constitution of Bolivia, a country named in his honor. By 1827, his dream of unification dissolved amidst growing rivalries between the South American military leaders. Three years later Bolívar died, on December 17, 1830.

**Colombia**

**Monumento a Simón Bolívar** This monument marks the location of the Battle of Boyacá, where Bolívar's forces defeated the Spanish resulting in the liberation of Gran Colombia. To celebrate the anniversary of the battle, students form the colors of the Colombian flag.

**Bolívares** Venezuela's currency carries both Bolívar's name and image.

**Venezuela**

**C24** Celebraciones

### Ecuador

*Líder de la Batalla de Pichincha* Each year, the city of Quito commemorates the Battle of Pichincha, where Simón Bolívar sent troops under the command of Antonio José de Sucre to defeat the Spanish in one of the crucial battles in the fight for independence.

*Simón Bolívar (1830), José Gil de Castro*
José Gil de Castro, renowned painter of Chilean society and of the independence leaders, painted this portrait of Bolívar in the early 1800s.

### Venezuela

*Plaza de Bolívar* This statue of Bolívar is located in the Plaza Bolívar, the historic, political, and commercial center of Caracas.

**Vocabulario para celebrar**

*la batalla*       battle
*la independencia*
      independence
*El Libertador*
      the liberator

## Comparación cultural

1. What famous leader in U.S. history would you compare with Simón Bolívar? Why? What do both leaders have in common?

2. What U.S. holidays are in honor of famous leaders? How are they celebrated? What other ways do we honor our important leaders?

# Nueva York

**Tema:**

## ¡Hola!

¡AVANZA!

### Let's get started

- greet people and say goodbye
- introduce yourself and others
- ask and say how to spell names
- say where you are from
- exchange phone numbers
- say what day of the week it is
- describe the weather
- respond to classroom instructions

*A performer wearing the colors of the Puerto Rican flag*

*Dominican dancers in colorful costumes*

**Nueva York** New York City has the largest Hispanic population of any city in the nation. During its annual Hispanic Day Parade, colorful floats, bands, costumed dancers, and flags from Spanish-speaking countries fill Fifth Avenue. *What cultural celebrations are there in your area?*

**A view of Lower Manhattan from the East River**

*New York, New York*

# Hola, ¿qué tal?

¡AVANZA!

**Goal:** Learn how various Spanish speakers greet each other. Then practice what you have learned to greet and say goodbye to others. *Actividades 1–3*

AUDIO

**A**

Hola. ¿Cómo estás?

Bien. ¿Y tú?

Mal.

**B** **Juan:** ¡Hola, Miguel! ¿Qué tal?
**Miguel:** Hola, ¿qué pasa?

**C** **Juan:** ¡Hasta luego, Ana!
**Ana:** Hasta luego.

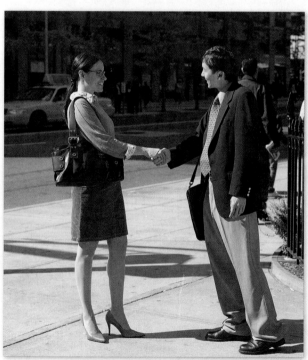

**D** **Srta. Daza:** Adiós.
**Sr. Ortega:** Adiós, señorita.

**E** **Sr. Martínez:** Buenos días, señora Ramos.
¿Cómo está usted?
**Sra. Ramos:** Regular. ¿Y usted?
**Sr. Martínez:** Más o menos.

**F** **Juan:** Buenas tardes. ¿Cómo estás?
**Esteban:** Muy bien.

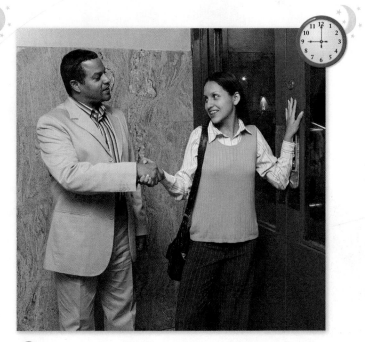

**G** **Sra. Acevedo:** Hola, **buenas noches.**
**Diana:** Buenas noches, señora.

**H** **Sr. García:** Buenas noches, Diana.
**Diana:** **Hasta mañana, señor** García.

**¡A responder!** Escuchar

Listen to these people greeting and saying goodbye. Wave toward the
front of the room if you hear a greeting or toward the back of the room
if you hear a goodbye.

# 1 | Muy bien

Leer Complete each expression.

1. ¿Cómo está...
2. Buenas...
3. ¿Qué...
4. Muy bien...
5. Hasta...

a. tal?
b. mañana.
c. usted?
d. tardes.
e. ¿Y usted?

# 2 | ¿Cómo estás?

Escribir   Create a conversation to complete the speech bubbles of this cartoon strip.

**Manuel**

## NOMBRES DE CHICOS

| | |
|---|---|
| Alejandro | Juan |
| Andrés | Luis |
| Carlos | Manuel |
| Cristóbal | Mateo |
| Daniel | Miguel |
| David | Nicolás |
| Eduardo | Pablo |
| Esteban | Pedro |
| Felipe | Ramón |
| Guillermo | Ricardo |
| Jaime | Roberto |
| Jorge | Tomás |
| José | Vicente |

## NOMBRES DE CHICAS

| | |
|---|---|
| Alejandra | Juana |
| Alicia | Luisa |
| Ana | María |
| Bárbara | Marta |
| Carmen | Natalia |
| Carolina | Patricia |
| Cristina | Raquel |
| Diana | Rosa |
| Elena | Sofía |
| Emilia | Susana |
| Florencia | Teresa |
| Gabriela | Verónica |
| Isabel | Yolanda |

**Isabel**

¿**Cómo estás?** and ¿**Cómo está usted?** both mean *How are you?*

| ¿**Cómo estás?** and ¿**Y tú?** are familiar phrases used with: | ¿**Cómo está usted?** and ¿**Y usted?** are formal phrases used with: |
| --- | --- |
| • a person your own age<br>• a relative<br>• a person you call by his or her first name<br><br>Other familiar greetings:<br>¿**Qué tal?** and ¿**Qué pasa?** | • a person you don't know<br>• someone older<br>• a person to whom you want to show respect |

# 3 | Buenos días

Hablar

According to the time of day, greet your partner as if he or she were the following people. Use a formal greeting or a familiar greeting depending on whom you address.

**modelo:** Sr. (Sra.) Vargas / 7 a.m.

**A** Buenos días, señor (señora) Vargas. ¿Cómo está usted?

**B** Muy bien.

1. your best friend / 10 p.m.
2. the school principal / 2 p.m.
3. Sr. (Srta.) López / 7 p.m.
4. your mother/father / 9 a.m.
5. Sr. (Sra.) Santos / 4 p.m.
6. your brother/sister / 9 p.m.
7. your coach / 11 a.m.
8. your Spanish teacher / 10 a.m.

AUDIO

## Pronunciación    La letra h

In Spanish, the letter **h** is always silent.

Listen and repeat.

| **ha** | **he** | **hi** | **ho** | **hu** |
| --- | --- | --- | --- | --- |
| **hace** | **helado** | **hispano** | **hola** | **humano** |

¡**Hola, Hugo!**

**Hasta mañana, Héctor.**

PARA Y PIENSA

**Did you get it?**
1. Tell a friend good morning.
2. Ask a friend how he or she is.
3. Say goodbye to your teacher.

**Get Help Online**
ClassZone.com

# ¡Mucho gusto!

AUDIO

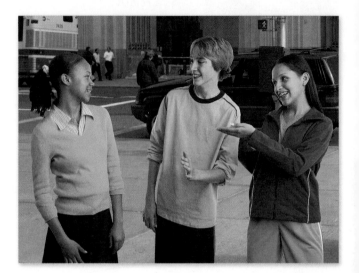

**A** **Esteban:** Hola. **Me llamo** Esteban. **¿Y tú? ¿Cómo te llamas?**

   **Diana:** Me llamo Diana.

   **Esteban:** **Encantado,** Diana.

   **Diana:** **Igualmente.**

**B** **Diana:** **Te presento a** Esteban.

   **Ana:** **Encantada.**

   **Esteban:** Igualmente.

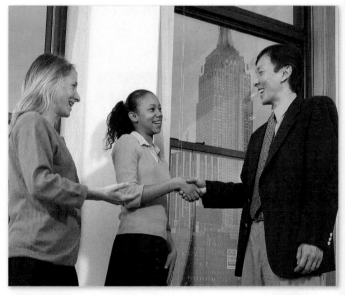

**C** **Srta. Machado:** **Perdón.** **¿Cómo se llama?**

   **Srta. Daza:** Me llamo Raquel Daza.

**D** **Srta. Machado:** **Le presento a** Ana Vega.

   **Sr. Ortega:** **Mucho gusto.**

   **Ana:** **El gusto es mío.**

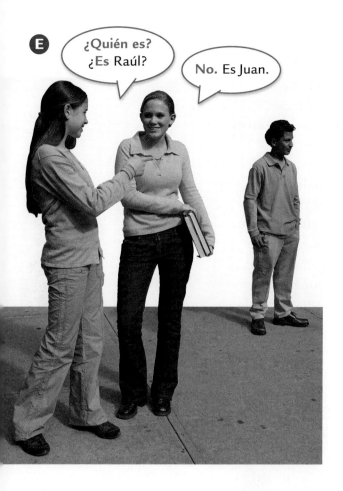

**E**

¿Quién es? ¿Es Raúl?

No. Es Juan.

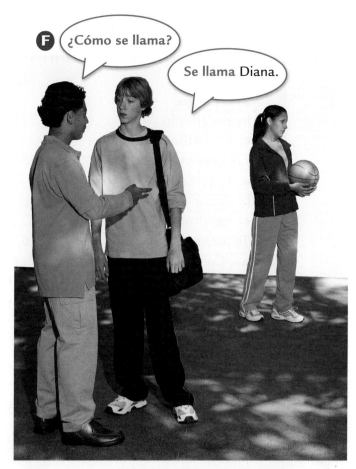

**F**

¿Cómo se llama?

Se llama Diana.

**G** **Rosa:** ¿Se llama Miguel?

**Esteban:** **Sí.** Se llama Miguel Luque.

**¡A responder!** Escuchar

Listen to four people make introductions. Point to yourself if you hear someone introducing themselves. Point to the person next to you if you hear someone introducing someone else.

# 4 | ¿Cómo te llamas?

**Leer** | Choose the correct response to each question or statement.

1. ¿Quién es?
   a. Es Hugo.
   b. Encantado.
   c. Me llamo Carlos.

2. Encantada.
   a. Le presento a Sergio.
   b. ¿Y tú?
   c. Igualmente.

3. Te presento a Joaquín.
   a. ¿Cómo se llama?
   b. Mucho gusto.
   c. Igualmente.

4. ¿Cómo te llamas?
   a. Perdón.
   b. Me llamo Isabel.
   c. Bien.

5. Me llamo Gabriel.
   a. Igualmente.
   b. Encantado.
   c. El gusto es mío.

6. Mucho gusto.
   a. Buenas tardes.
   b. ¿Quién es?
   c. El gusto es mío.

# 5 | Conversación

**Leer**
**Escribir** | Complete the conversation with the correct words.

**Carlos:** Hola. Me __1.__ Carlos. ¿ __2.__ te llamas?

**Beatriz:** Me __3.__ Beatriz.

**Carlos:** __4.__ , Beatriz.

**Beatriz:** __5.__ .

# 6 | Mucho gusto

**Hablar** | Work in a group of four. Introduce yourself to each member of the group.

¿**Cómo te llamas?** and ¿**Cómo se llama?** both are used to ask *What is your name?*
**Te presento a...** and **Le presento a...** both mean *I'd like you to meet . . .*

| ¿**Cómo te llamas?** and **Te presento a...** are familiar phrases used with: | ¿**Cómo se llama?** and **Le presento a...** are formal phrases used with: |
|---|---|
| • a person your own age<br>• a relative<br>• a person you call by his or her first name | • a person to whom you want to show respect<br>• a person you don't know<br>• someone older |

# 7 | Te presento a...

Hablar | Work in a group of three. Take turns introducing each other.

**A** Te presento a Tomás.

**B** Encantado(a), Tomás.

**C** Igualmente.

## Comparación cultural

### Un mural en Nueva York

*How can artists give back to their neighborhood through their work?* Artist Manuel Vega moved with his family from Puerto Rico to **New York** at a young age. He grew up in East Harlem and his works often depict neighborhood scenes inspired by his childhood. Vega was commissioned to restore this image, originally created by Hank Prussing in 1973, on a multi-story building in East Harlem.

The Spirit of East Harlem,
*Manuel Vega*

**Compara con tu mundo** *What childhood memory would you paint if you were creating a neighborhood mural? Compare it with the scene in Vega's mural.*

PARA Y PIENSA

**Did you get it?** Complete each statement.

1. Me llamo...       **a.** a Maricela.
2. Te presento...    **b.** gusto, señor.
3. Mucho...          **c.** Walter.

**Get Help Online**
ClassZone.com

# El abecedario

**¡AVANZA!** **Goal:** Learn to say the Spanish alphabet. Then practice how to say the letters to spell different things. *Actividades 8–10*

AUDIO

**A** (a) — **a**lfombra

**B** (be, be grande) — **b**ate

**C** (ce) — **c**ine

**D** (de) — **d**inero

**E** (e) — **e**ntrada

**F** (efe) — **f**ruta

**G** (ge) — **g**ato

**H** (hache) — **h**elado

**I** (i) — **i**glú

**J** (jota) — **j**abón

**K** (ka) — **k**arate

**L** (ele) — **l**ápiz

**M** (eme) — **m**ochila

**N** (ene) — **n**ariz

**Ñ** (eñe) — **ñ**u

**O** (o) — **o**reja

**P** (pe) — **p**atines

**Q** (cu) — **q**ueso

**R** (ere) — **r**egalo

**S** (ese) — **s**ofá

**T** (te) — **t**iza

**U** (u) — **u**vas

**V** (uve, ve chica) — **v**entana

**W** (doble uve, doble ve) — **w**afle

**X** (equis) — **x**ilófono

**Y** (i griega) — **y**ogur

**Z** (zeta) — **z**apato

**Dos letras con un sonido**

**CH** (che) — **ch**aqueta

**LL** (elle) — **ll**ave

**RR** (erre) — guita**rr**a

---

**¡A responder!** Escuchar

Listen to letters of the Spanish alphabet. Write each letter that you hear on a piece of paper and hold it up.

## 8 | Lista

**Escuchar Escribir**

Listen to someone dictate an invitation list for a party. Write down each name as it is spelled.

> **modelo:** You hear: de, a, ene, i, e, ele
>
> You write: Daniel

## 9 | Me llamo...

**Hablar**

Work in a group of three. Ask each person his or her name and write down the name as he or she spells it.

**A** ¿Cómo te llamas?

**B** Me llamo Shawna, S - H - A - W - N - A. (ese, hache, a, doble uve, ene, a)

## 10 | ABC

**Hablar**

Spell aloud the following things for a partner. He or she will write the word. Then verify that your partner spelled the word correctly.

**your middle name**    **your favorite singer**    **the name of your town**

**the name of your school**    **your favorite sports team**    ¿?

---

**AUDIO**

### Pronunciación  Las vocales

In Spanish, the vowels are **a, e, i, o,** and **u.** Each vowel is always pronounced the same way. Spanish vowels are always short and crisp.

Listen to and repeat these words.

| | | | | |
|---|---|---|---|---|
| **a** → | as in *father* | encantada | mal | mañana |
| **e** → | as in *hey* | menos | señor | presento |
| **i** → | sounds like *meet* | igualmente | adiós | bien |
| **o** → | as in *woke* | hola | noches | cómo |
| **u** → | sounds like *boot* | usted | mucho | tú |

---

**PARA Y PIENSA**

**Did you get it?** Recite the Spanish alphabet.

**Get Help Online**
ClassZone.com

# ¿De dónde eres?

¡AVANZA! **Goal:** Look at the Spanish-speaking world and how Spanish speakers say where someone is from. Then practice what you have learned to ask where people are from. *Actividades 11–13*

AUDIO

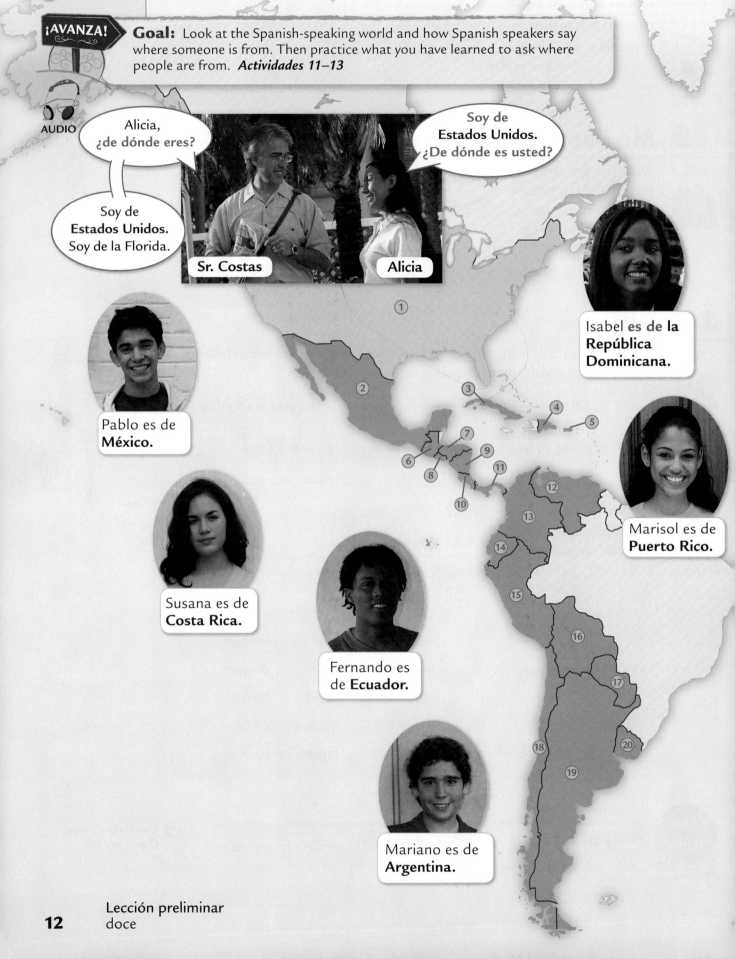

Alicia, ¿de dónde eres?

Soy de **Estados Unidos.** Soy de la Florida.

Soy de **Estados Unidos.** ¿De dónde es usted?

**Sr. Costas**

**Alicia**

Isabel **es de la República Dominicana.**

Pablo es de **México.**

Marisol es de **Puerto Rico.**

Susana es de **Costa Rica.**

Fernando es de **Ecuador.**

Mariano es de **Argentina.**

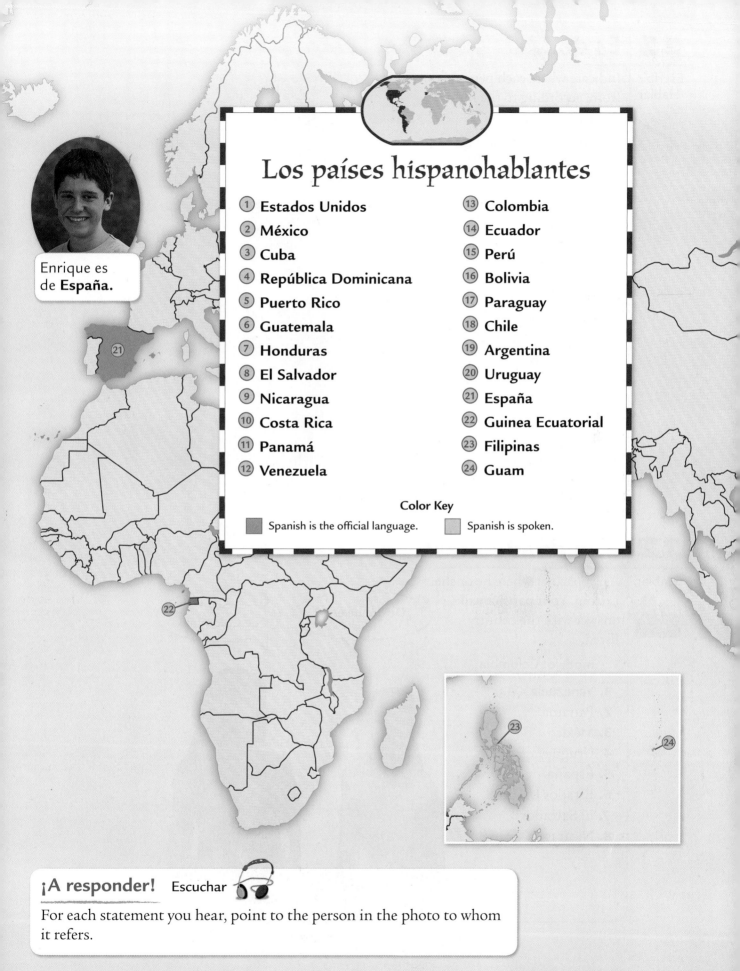

Enrique es de **España.**

# Los países hispanohablantes

1. **Estados Unidos**
2. **México**
3. **Cuba**
4. **República Dominicana**
5. **Puerto Rico**
6. **Guatemala**
7. **Honduras**
8. **El Salvador**
9. **Nicaragua**
10. **Costa Rica**
11. **Panamá**
12. **Venezuela**
13. **Colombia**
14. **Ecuador**
15. **Perú**
16. **Bolivia**
17. **Paraguay**
18. **Chile**
19. **Argentina**
20. **Uruguay**
21. **España**
22. **Guinea Ecuatorial**
23. **Filipinas**
24. **Guam**

**Color Key**

Spanish is the official language.    Spanish is spoken.

**¡A responder!**   Escuchar

For each statement you hear, point to the person in the photo to whom it refers.

## 11 | Es de...

Indicate where each person is from, according to the number on the map.

**modelo:** Guillermo / ⑦

Guillermo es de **Uruguay.**

1. Andrea / ⑤
2. Tomás / ⑧
3. Nicolás / ④
4. Sofía / ②
5. Verónica / ③
6. Mateo / ⑨
7. Consuelo / ①
8. Pablo / ⑥

## 12 | ¿De dónde eres?

Ask a partner where he or she is from. Your partner will answer with the country listed.

**modelo: Colombia**

1. Venezuela
2. Panamá
3. México
4. Uruguay
5. España
6. Estados Unidos
7. El Salvador
8. Nicaragua

**A** ¿De dónde eres?

**B** Soy de Colombia.

Lección preliminar
catorce

# 13 | ¿Eres de Honduras?

**Hablar**

Ask a partner if he or she is from the country indicated. He or she will answer according to the number.

modelo: ① / ⑩

**A** ¿Eres de **México**?

**B** No. Soy de **Panamá.**

| Estudiante **A** | | Estudiante **B** | |
|---|---|---|---|
| **1.** ⑨ | **4.** ⑩ | **1.** ③ | **4.** ⑩ |
| **2.** ④ | **5.** ⑤ | **2.** ④ | **5.** ⑤ |
| **3.** ⑥ | **6.** ⑧ | **3.** ② | **6.** ⑦ |

**PARA Y PIENSA**

**Did you get it?** Match each question with the correct response.

1. ¿De dónde eres?     **a.** Es de Puerto Rico.
2. ¿De dónde es Hugo?     **b.** Soy de Colombia.
3. ¿Eres de México?     **c.** Sí, soy de México.

**Get Help Online**
ClassZone.com

# Mi número de teléfono

**Goal:** Learn how to say the numbers from zero to ten and how to exchange phone numbers. Then use what you have learned to say your home (or cellular) phone number. *Actividades 14–16*

AUDIO

¿Cuál es tu número de teléfono?

Es 7-6-4-9-0-8-1.

Perdón. ¿Cuál es su número de teléfono?

Mi número de teléfono es 2-5-3-7-1-0-9.

---

## ¡A responder!   Escuchar

Listen to these numbers. If you hear an even number, raise your right hand. If you hear an odd number, raise your left hand.

## 14 | Matemáticas

**Hablar Escribir**

Give the answers to the following math problems using words.

**modelo:** 2 + 4
       seis

**1.** 8 − 3      **3.** 3 + 6      **5.** 1 + 9      **7.** 6 − 5      **9.** 10 − 8

**2.** 4 + 4      **4.** 7 − 7      **6.** 5 − 2      **8.** 7 + 0      **10.** 1 + 3

## 15 | Teléfono

**Hablar**

Work in a group of five. Whisper a phone number to the person at your right. He or she will repeat it to the person at his or her right, and so on. Verify that the phone number you gave was repeated accurately.

**A** Mi número de teléfono es cinco - dos - uno - nueve - ocho - siete - uno.

**B** Cinco - dos - uno - nueve - ocho - siete - uno.

**C** Cinco - dos - uno...

## 16 | ¿Quién es?

**Hablar**

Work with a partner. Look at this Buenos Aires phone directory and read a phone number at random. Your partner will say whose phone number it is.

**A** Cuatro - tres - cero - tres - ocho - siete - cuatro - cero.

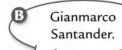

**B** Gianmarco Santander.

**Santander Gemma**
Lauerbach 3472 Pb 11- Capital Federal
Ciudad de Buenos Aires.....................4301-9203

**Santander Genoveva**
Löschner 244- Capital Federal
Ciudad de Buenos Aires.....................4921-4808

**Santander Geraldo**
López de Padilla 12 Pb 4- Capital Federal
Ciudad de Buenos Aires.....................4704-5960

**Santander Giancarlo**
Filippozzi 9903 Pb Casa- Capital Federal
Ciudad de Buenos Aires.....................4638-3123

**Santander Gianmarco**
Filippozzi 1099- Capital Federal
Ciudad de Buenos Aires.....................4303-8740

**Santander Gregorio**
Sta Marta 374 Pb 7- Capital Federal
Ciudad de Buenos Aires.....................4941-7819

**PARA Y PIENSA**

**Did you get it?** Say these phone numbers.

**1.** 6251-4209      **2.** 3708-9263      **3.** 4185-2760

**Get Help Online**
ClassZone.com

# Los días de la semana

**Goal:** Learn to talk about the days of the week. Then practice what you have learned to say what day of the week it is. *Actividades 17–19*

**AUDIO**

la semana

| lunes | martes | miércoles | jueves | viernes | sábado |
|-------|--------|-----------|--------|---------|--------|

el día

hoy    mañana

domingo

**Nota**

In Spanish, the days of the week are never capitalized: **domingo** (*Sunday*). Use **el** and **los** to talk about what you do on a certain day or days.

| **el lunes** | *on Monday* |
|--------------|-------------|
| **los lunes** | *on Mondays* |

**A** **Ana:** ¿Qué día es hoy?
**Rosa:** Hoy es jueves.

**B** **Juan:** ¿Hoy es viernes?
**Esteban:** No. Mañana es viernes.

**¡A responder!** Escuchar

Listen to the days of the week. If you hear a day that you have Spanish class, stand up. If you hear a day that you don't have Spanish class, remain seated.

## 17 | Los días

Complete each list with the missing day of the week.

1. lunes, _____, miércoles, jueves
2. viernes, _____, domingo, lunes
3. _____, martes, miércoles, jueves
4. lunes, martes, miércoles, _____

5. _____, jueves, viernes, sábado
6. domingo, _____, martes, miércoles
7. sábado, _____, lunes, martes
8. martes, miércoles, jueves, _____

## 18 | ¿Lógico o ilógico?

Listen to these statements about the days of the week. Write **L** if the statement you hear is **lógico** (*logical*) or **I** if it is **ilógico** (*not logical*).

**modelo:** You hear: Hoy es viernes. Mañana es domingo.
You write: I

## 19 | ¿Qué día es?

Ask a partner what day of the week it is. He or she will tell you what day of the week today is and what tomorrow is.

modelo: 6

**A** ¿Qué día es hoy?

**B** Hoy es **martes.** Mañana es **miércoles.**

1. 2
2. 12
3. 28
4. 15

5. 18
6. 3
7. 20
8. 16

**SEPTIEMBRE**

| L | M | M | J | V | S | D |
|---|---|---|---|---|---|---|
| | | | 1 | 2 | 3 | 4 |
| 5 | 6 | 7 | 8 | 9 | 10 | 11 |
| 12 | 13 | 14 | 15 | 16 | 17 | 18 |
| 19 | 20 | 21 | 22 | 23 | 24 | 25 |
| 26 | 27 | 28 | 29 | 30 | | |

**PARA Y PIENSA**

**Did you get it?**
1. Tell someone that today is Monday.  Hoy es _____.
2. Ask what day tomorrow is.  ¿Qué día es _____?

**Get Help Online**
ClassZone.com

# ¿Qué tiempo hace?

**Goal:** Learn how to describe the weather. Then practice what you have learned to describe a sunny day, a rainy day, and a windy day. *Actividades 20–22*

AUDIO

¿Qué tiempo hace?

**A Luis:** Hace calor.

**B Natalia:** Hace sol.

**C Jorge:** Llueve.

**D Andrea:** Hace frío.

**E Diego:** Hace viento.

**F Mariana:** Nieva.

## ¡A responder! Escuchar

Listen to weather descriptions. Point to the photo of the person that corresponds to the description you hear.

## 20 | El tiempo

Escuchar

Listen to four meteorologists describe the weather in their region. Write the letter of the photo that corresponds to the weather description you hear.

a.   b.    c.    d.

## 21 | ¿Hace calor o hace frío?

Hablar

Work with a partner. Say whether it is cold or hot, according to the temperature given.

modelo: 32°F / 0°C
       Hace frío.

1. 15°F / –9°C
2. 94°F / 35°C
3. 20°F / –6°C
4. 4°F / –16°C
5. 88°F / 32°C
6. 104°F / 40°C

## 22 | ¿Qué tiempo hace?

Hablar

Tell what city you are from, and ask a partner what the weather is like. He or she will give you the weather conditions for that city.

| Buenos Aires | Bogotá | Madrid | México | Nueva York |
|---|---|---|---|---|
| 86° | 53° | 45° | 65° | 30° |

A  Soy de la Ciudad de México. ¿Qué tiempo hace?

B  Hace viento.

**PARA Y PIENSA**

**Did you get it?** Match each question with the correct response.

1. ¿Qué tiempo hace?
2. ¿Hace calor?
3. ¿Llueve?

a. No. Hace frío.
b. Hace viento.
c. No. Hace sol.

**Get Help Online**
ClassZone.com

# En la clase

AUDIO

**¡AVANZA!** **Goal:** Learn some useful phrases used by teachers and students. Then practice what you have learned to use classroom phrases with others. *Actividades 23–25*

Maestro, ¿cómo se dice *Wednesday*?

Se dice *miércoles*.

la clase

## En la clase

| | |
|---|---|
| Abran los libros (en la página...) | *Open your books (to page . . .)* |
| Cierren los libros. | *Close your books.* |
| ¿Cómo se dice...? | *How do you say . . . ?* |
| Se dice... | *You say . . .* |
| ¿Cómo se escribe (tu nombre)? | *How do you spell (your name)?* |
| Se escribe... | *It is spelled . . .* |
| ¿Comprendes? | *Do you understand?* |
| Levanten la mano. | *Raise your hand.* |
| Más despacio, por favor. | *More slowly, please.* |
| No sé. | *I don't know.* |
| ¿Qué quiere decir...? | *What does . . . mean?* |
| Quiere decir... | *It means . . .* |
| Repitan, por favor. | *Please repeat.* |
| Saquen una hoja de papel. | *Take out a piece of paper.* |
| Siéntense. | *Sit down.* |
| ¿Tienen preguntas? | *Do you have questions?* |
| ¿Verdad? | *Right?* |

Muchas gracias.

De nada.

el maestro de español

# Otras instrucciones

| | |
|---|---|
| Completa la conversación. | *Complete the conversation.* |
| Contesta las preguntas. | *Answer the questions.* |
| Escoge la palabra / la respuesta... | *Choose the word / answer . . .* |
| Escribe... | *Write . . .* |
| Escucha... | *Listen . . .* |
| Explica... | *Explain . . .* |
| Indica si es cierto o falso. | *Indicate whether it is true or false.* |
| Lee... | *Read . . .* |
| Pregúntale a otro(a) estudiante. | *Ask another student.* |
| Trabaja con otro(a) estudiante. | *Work with another student.* |
| Trabaja en un grupo de... | *Work in a group of . . .* |

Perdón, ¿qué quiere decir *número*?

Quiere decir *number*.

la maestra de español

## ¡A responder! Escuchar

Listen to each classroom instruction and respond appropriately.

## 23 | Instrucciones

**Leer** | Match each picture with the correct instruction.

**1.**

**2.**

a. Abran los libros en la página 7.
b. Levanten la mano.
c. Repitan, por favor.
d. Siéntense.

**3.**

**4.**

## 24 | ¿Qué dices?

**Escribir Hablar**  | Indicate what you would say in each situation. Refer to the expressions on pages 22–23.

1. You want to thank your Spanish teacher.
2. Your teacher is speaking too fast.
3. You want to know how to say *book* in Spanish.
4. You want to know what **página** means.
5. You must admit that you don't have the answer to a question.
6. You wonder if your friend understands the lesson.

## 25 | ¿Cómo se dice?

**Hablar**  | Ask a partner to say the following words in Spanish and how to spell them.

**modelo:** Tuesday

1. Spanish
2. week
3. Thank you very much.
4. male teacher
5. See you later.
6. Friday
7. It's raining.

**A** ¿Cómo se dice *Tuesday*?

**B** Se dice *martes*.

¿Cómo se escribe *martes*?

Se escribe eme, a, ere, te, e, ese.

**PARA Y PIENSA**

**Did you get it?**
1. Ask how to say the word *please*.
2. Ask a friend if he or she understands.

**Get Help Online**
ClassZone.com

# *En resumen*
## Vocabulario

*¡AvanzaRap!*
DVD
**Sing and Learn**

## Vocabulario

### Greet People and Say Goodbye

**Greetings**

| | |
|---|---|
| Buenos días. | *Good morning.* |
| Buenas tardes. | *Good afternoon.* |
| Buenas noches. | *Good evening.* |
| Hola. | *Hello./Hi.* |

**Say Goodbye**

| | |
|---|---|
| Adiós. | *Goodbye.* |
| Buenas noches. | *Good night.* |
| Hasta luego. | *See you later.* |
| Hasta mañana. | *See you tomorrow.* |

**Say How You Are**

| | |
|---|---|
| ¿Cómo estás? | *How are you? (familiar)* |
| ¿Cómo está usted? | *How are you? (formal)* |
| ¿Qué tal? | *How is it going?* |
| Bien. | *Fine.* |
| Mal. | *Bad.* |
| Más o menos. | *So-so.* |
| Muy bien. | *Very well.* |
| Regular. | *Okay.* |
| ¿Y tú? | *And you? (familiar)* |
| ¿Y usted? | *And you? (formal)* |
| ¿Qué pasa? | *What's up?* |

### Make Introductions

| | |
|---|---|
| ¿Cómo se llama? | *What's his/her/ your (formal) name?* |
| Se llama... | *His/Her name is . . .* |
| ¿Cómo te llamas? | *What's your (familiar) name?* |
| Me llamo... | *My name is . . .* |
| Te/Le presento a... | *Let me introduce you (familiar/ formal) to . . .* |
| El gusto es mío. | *The pleasure is mine.* |
| Encantado(a). | *Delighted./Pleased to meet you.* |
| Igualmente. | *Same here./ Likewise.* |
| Mucho gusto. | *Nice to meet you.* |
| ¿Quién es? | *Who is he/she/it?* |
| Es... | *He/She/It is . . .* |

### Say Which Day It Is

| | |
|---|---|
| ¿Qué día es hoy? | *What day is today?* |
| Hoy es... | *Today is . . .* |
| Mañana es... | *Tomorrow is . . .* |
| el día | *day* |
| hoy | *today* |
| mañana | *tomorrow* |
| la semana | *week* |

**Days of the week** *p. 18*

### Exchange Phone Numbers

| | |
|---|---|
| ¿Cuál es tu/su número de teléfono? | *What's your (familiar/ formal) phone number?* |
| Mi número de teléfono es... | *My phone number is . . .* |

**Numbers from zero to ten** *p. 16*

### Other Words and Phrases

| | |
|---|---|
| la clase | *class* |
| el (la) maestro(a) de español | *Spanish teacher (male/female)* |
| el país | *country* |
| Perdón. | *Excuse me.* |
| por favor | *please* |
| (Muchas) Gracias. | *Thank you (very much).* |
| De nada. | *You're welcome.* |
| el señor (Sr.) | *Mr.* |
| la señora (Sra.) | *Mrs.* |
| la señorita (Srta.) | *Miss* |
| sí | *yes* |
| no | *no* |

### Describe the Weather

| | |
|---|---|
| ¿Qué tiempo hace? | *What is the weather like?* |
| Hace calor. | *It is hot.* |
| Hace frío. | *It is cold.* |
| Hace sol. | *It is sunny.* |
| Hace viento. | *It is windy.* |
| Llueve. | *It is raining.* |
| Nieva. | *It is snowing.* |

### Say Where You Are From

| | |
|---|---|
| ¿De dónde eres? | *Where are you (familiar) from?* |
| ¿De dónde es? | *Where is he/she from?* |
| ¿De dónde es usted? | *Where are you (formal) from?* |
| Soy de... | *I am from . . .* |
| Es de... | *He/She is from . . .* |

**Spanish-speaking countries** *p. 13*

# Repaso de la lección

 ¡LLEGADA!

¡AvanzaRap! DVD
Sing and Learn

@HomeTutor
ClassZone.com

## Now you can
- greet people and say goodbye
- introduce yourself and others
- ask and say how to spell names
- say where you are from
- exchange phone numbers
- say what day of the week it is
- describe the weather
- respond to classroom instructions

**To review**
- introductions pp. 6–7
- classroom instructions pp. 22–23

## 1 Listen and understand

You will hear four separate conversations. Put the drawings in order according to what you hear.

a.   b.   c.   d.

**To review**
- greet people pp. 2–3
- introductions pp. 6–7
- weather p. 20

## 2 Introduce yourself and others

Complete Enrique's e-mail message to his new e-pal.

Adiós    Hace    Hoy    calor

Hola    Soy    Cómo    tiempo    llamo

**1.** ,

¿ **2.** estás? Me **3.** Enrique. **4.** de Panamá. **5.** es sábado y hace **6.** . ¿Qué **7.** hace en Estados Unidos? ¿ **8.** frío?

**9.** ,

Enrique

**To review**
· origin pp. 12–13
· numbers p. 16

## **3** | Say where you are from

Look at these students' ID cards from the International Club.
Then complete the sentences that follow.

**Club Internacional**

NOMBRE:
**Cristina Villaveces**
PAÍS DE ORIGEN:
**Venezuela**
DOMICILIO:
**332 Avenida de las Américas**
TELÉFONO:
**241-0976**

**Club Internacional**

NOMBRE:
**Yolanda Hoyos**
PAÍS DE ORIGEN:
**Chile**
DOMICILIO:
**1902 Rúa Mayor**
TELÉFONO:
**397-2261**

**Club Internacional**

NOMBRE:
**Alejandro Cruz**
PAÍS DE ORIGEN:
**México**
DOMICILIO:
**214 Paseo Suárez**
TELÉFONO:
**898-1035**

**Club Internacional**

NOMBRE:
**Guillermo Morales**
PAÍS DE ORIGEN:
**España**
DOMICILIO:
**38 Calle Toro, 3°D**
TELÉFONO:
**460-1853**

1. _____ es de España.
2. El número de teléfono es ocho - nueve - ocho - uno - cero - tres - cinco. Se llama _____ .
3. Se llama Cristina. El número de teléfono es _____ .
4. La señorita de Chile se llama _____ .
5. Se llama Guillermo. El número de teléfono es _____ .
6. _____ es de México.

**To review**
· alphabet p. 10
· numbers p. 16
· days of the week p. 18

## **4** | Answer personal questions

Answer these questions using complete sentences.

1. ¿Cómo te llamas?
2. ¿Cómo se escribe tu nombre?
3. ¿De dónde eres?
4. ¿Cuál es tu número de teléfono?
5. ¿Quién es el (la) maestro(a) de español? ¿De dónde es?
6. ¿Cómo se llama el libro de español?
7. ¿Qué día es mañana?
8. ¿Qué tiempo hace hoy?
9. ¿Cómo se dice *country* en español?

**Get Help Online**
ClassZone.com

# UNIDAD 1

# Estados Unidos

## Un rato con los amigos

### Lección 1
*Tema:* **¿Qué te gusta hacer?**

### Lección 2
*Tema:* **Mis amigos y yo**

Alaska

Islas Hawai

**«¡Hola!**
**Nosotras somos Alicia y Sandra.**
**Somos de Estados Unidos.»**

Chicago · Filadelfia · Nueva York

· San José    Denver ·    **Estados Unidos**

Los Ángeles
· Phoenix · Albuquerque

San Diego · Tucson
· El Paso · Dallas
· Houston

San Antonio

Miami ·

*Océano Atlántico*

**Cuba**

*Golfo de México*

**México**

*Mar Caribe*

**Honduras**
**Nicaragua**

**Costa Rica**

*Océano Pacífico*

**Guatemala**
**El Salvador**

**Panamá**

**Población:** 304.059.724

**Población de ascendencia hispana:** 43.168.000

**Ciudad con más latinos:** Nueva York (más de 2.000.000)

**Ciudad con mayor porcentaje de latinos:** El Paso, Texas (77%)

**Comida latina:** el sándwich cubano, burritos, fajitas

**Gente famosa:** Sandra Cisneros (escritora), Gloria Estefan (cantante), Eva Mendes (actriz), Eloy Rodríguez (bioquímico)

*El sándwich cubano*

*Hispanic teens gather for a celebration in Miami, Florida*

◀ **La ascendencia hispana**  The over 40 million Hispanics living in the United States trace their roots to more than 20 nations. From September 15 to October 15, Hispanic Heritage Month celebrates the diverse backgrounds and cultures of these Americans. *Do you know anyone from a Spanish-speaking country?*

**La comunidad cubana de Miami**  The Cuban American community thrives in Miami's Little Havana. **Calle Ocho** is known for its Cuban restaurants, cafés, and shops, and the nearby Freedom Tower houses the Cuban American Museum. *How have people from other countries shaped your community?* ▶

*Miami's Freedom Tower, home to the Cuban American Museum*

*Dancers in traditional dress during the Fiesta San Antonio*

**LA VILLITA**
LITTLE VILLAGE
of
SAN ANTONIO

◀ **Las celebraciones**  San Antonio is proud of its unique multicultural history. The **Fiesta San Antonio,** a ten-day celebration with food, music, and parades, honors the heroes of the Alamo and the Battle of San Jacinto. La Villita, the city's oldest neighborhood, hosts many of the festival events. *How do people celebrate history and culture where you live?*

# Estados Unidos

## Lección 1

**Tema:**

## ¿Qué te gusta hacer?

¡AVANZA!

### In this lesson you will learn to
- talk about activities
- tell where you are from
- say what you like and don't like to do

### using
- subject pronouns and **ser**
- **de** to describe where you are from
- **gustar** with an infinitive

♻ *¿Recuerdas?*
- weather expressions

## Comparación cultural

### In this lesson you will learn about
- *Los Premios Juventud,* an awards show in Miami
- Cuban-American artist Xavier Cortada
- free-time activities of students at a Florida school

### Compara con tu mundo
This group of teenagers is spending the day at a beach. In southern Florida, beaches are open year-round and are popular places to do many different activities. *Where do you like to go with your friends in your free time? What do you like to do?*

### ¿Qué ves?

*Mira la foto*
What is the weather like?

Do you think that these teenagers are friends?

What activities do they like to do?

## Una playa de Miami Beach
*Miami Beach, Florida*

# Presentación de VOCABULARIO

**¡AVANZA!**

**Goal:** Learn about what Alicia and her friends like to do. Then use what you have learned to talk about activities. *Actividades 1–2*

VIDEO
DVD

AUDIO

**A** ¡Hola! Me llamo Teresa. **Después de las clases, me gusta pasar un rato con los amigos.** Me gusta **escuchar música o tocar la guitarra.**

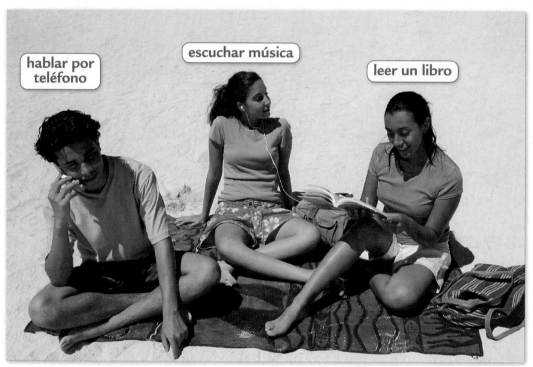

hablar por teléfono

escuchar música

leer un libro

Miguel          Teresa          Alicia

dibujar

tocar la guitarra

**B** ¡Hola! Me llamo Miguel. A mí me gusta **hablar por teléfono, dibujar** y **estudiar.** Me gusta **pasear, pero** me gusta **más correr.** A ti, ¿qué te gusta hacer?

estudiar

pasear

correr

**C** ¡Hola! Me llamo Alicia. A mí me gusta **montar en bicicleta** y **jugar al fútbol. También** me gusta **andar en patineta.**

montar en bicicleta

jugar al fútbol

andar en patineta

**D** Hoy hace calor en Miami. **Antes de practicar deportes** me gusta **comprar agua.**

comprar

las papas fritas

la fruta

el agua

la pizza

el refresco

el helado

las galletas

Continuará...

**E** Me gusta **beber** agua o **jugo** pero no me gusta beber **refrescos**.

preparar la comida

comer

beber

el jugo

### Más vocabulario

**la actividad** *activity*

**alquilar un DVD** *to rent a DVD*

**aprender el español**
*to learn Spanish*

**la escuela** *school*

**hacer la tarea** *to do homework*

*Expansión de vocabulario* p. R2

**F** No me gusta **trabajar** los sábados y domingos. Me gusta **escribir correos electrónicos** y **descansar**. También me gusta **mirar la televisión**. ¿Te gusta pasar un rato con los amigos?

escribir correos electrónicos

descansar

mirar la televisión

---

## ¡A responder! Escuchar

Listen to the list of activities. As you listen, act out the activities.

**@HomeTutor** VideoPlus
**Interactive Flashcards**
ClassZone.com

# Práctica de VOCABULARIO

## 1 | El sábado

Leer
Escribir

Miguel, Teresa, and Alicia are talking about the activities they like to do. Complete the conversation with the appropriate words.

**un libro**

**la tarea**

**deportes**

**bicicleta**

**un DVD**

**música**

**la comida**

**Alicia:** Miguel, ¿te gusta escuchar __1.__ los sábados?

**Miguel:** Sí, pero me gusta más practicar __2.__ .
Teresa, ¿te gusta montar en __3.__ ?

**Teresa:** No, no me gusta. Me gusta más leer __4.__ .

**Alicia:** Teresa, ¿te gusta hacer __5.__ los sábados?

**Teresa:** ¿Los sábados? No, sólo me gusta preparar __6.__ , alquilar __7.__ y descansar.

## 2 | ¿Te gusta?

Hablar
Escribir

Tell whether you like or don't like to eat or drink these foods and beverages.

**modelo:** beber
(No) Me gusta beber refrescos.

**1.** comer

**2.** beber

**3.** comer

**4.** comer

**5.** beber

**6.** comer

*Más práctica*   Cuaderno *pp. 1–3*  Cuaderno para hispanohablantes *pp. 1–4*

**PARA Y PIENSA**

**Did you get it?**
1. Tell someone that you like to listen to music.
2. Ask a friend if he or she likes to do homework.

Me gusta _____.
¿Te gusta _____?

**Get Help Online**
ClassZone.com

# VOCABULARIO *en contexto*

**Goal:** Listen to the words Alicia and Sandra use to talk about activities. Then practice what you have heard to talk about the activities you and others like to do. *Actividades 3–5*

 *¿Recuerdas?* Weather expressions p. 20

## Telehistoria escena 1

@*HomeTutor* VideoPlus
**View, Read and Record**
ClassZone.com

### STRATEGIES

**Cuando lees**

**Search for clues** Look for clues in the picture before starting to read. Who's in the photos? What are they doing?

**Cuando escuchas**

**Listen for intonation** The way people speak, not just what they say, often reflects how they feel. Listen for Alicia's intonation. How does she feel about the activities mentioned?

VIDEO DVD

AUDIO

Sandra

Papá

Alicia

**Alicia:** *(on phone, to Sandra, a friend in San Antonio, Texas)* En Miami, hace calor. ¿Te gusta andar en patineta?

**Sandra:** No, me gusta más pasear o montar en bicicleta. Los sábados me gusta hacer la tarea.

**Alicia:** ¿Sí? Los sábados me gusta pasar un rato con amigos... ¡y dibujar! Y los domingos, ¡jugar al fútbol! Los viernes me gusta alquilar un DVD y comer pizza.

**Sandra:** Sí, sí. Mmm. Me gusta comer pizza y hablar por teléfono.

**Alicia:** ¿Hablar por teléfono? No me gusta hablar por teléfono. *(Father gives a look of disbelief.)*

**Continuará...** p. 42

### También se dice

**Miami** To talk about riding bicycles, Sandra uses the phrase **montar en bicicleta.** In other Spanish-speaking countries you might hear:

· **muchos países** andar en bicicleta

## 3 | A Alicia y a Sandra les gusta... *Comprensión del episodio*

Escuchar
Leer

Tell if what Alicia and Sandra say is true or false. Correct the false statements.

> **modelo:** **Alicia:** Los viernes no me gusta comer pizza.
> **Falso. Los viernes me gusta comer pizza.**

1. **Alicia:** Llueve en Miami.
2. **Sandra:** Me gusta correr los sábados.
3. **Alicia:** Me gusta pasar un rato con los amigos.
4. **Sandra:** Me gusta hacer la tarea los domingos.
5. **Alicia:** Los sábados me gusta alquilar un DVD.
6. **Sandra:** Me gusta hablar por teléfono.

## 4 | ¡Hace frío! ♻ *¿Recuerdas?* Weather expressions p. 20

Hablar

Tell a partner what you like to do in each situation.

| beber agua | leer un libro | jugar al fútbol | montar en bicicleta |

| correr | descansar | pasear | mirar la televisión | ¿ ? |

> **modelo:** Hace viento.

**A** Hace viento. ¿Qué te gusta hacer?

**B** Me gusta mirar la televisión o descansar.

1. Hace frío y llueve.
2. Hace sol.
3. Hace viento y hace frío.
4. Hace calor.
5. Nieva y hace sol.
6. Llueve y hace calor.

## 5 | ¡Me gusta!

Escribir
Hablar

Write a list of your after-school activities and then compare them with other students' activities.

> — escribir correos electrónicos
> — practicar deportes
> — dibujar
> — andar en patineta

**A** ¿Te gusta pasear después de las clases?

**B** Sí, me gusta pasear.

**C** No, me gusta pasear antes de las clases.

**PARA Y PIENSA**

**Did you get it?** Fill in Alicia's sentences with the appropriate vocabulary word.

1. Me gusta _____ al fútbol.
2. ¿Te gusta escuchar _____ ?
3. También me gusta _____ pizza.

🔊 **Get Help Online** ClassZone.com

# Presentación de GRAMÁTICA

**Goal:** Learn how to use subject pronouns and the verb **ser.** Then practice the forms of **ser** with **de** to talk about where you and others are from.
*Actividades 6–11*

**English Grammar Connection: Pronouns** are words that take the place of nouns. **Subject pronouns** indicate who is being described or who does the action in a sentence.

**We** are friends.                **Nosotros** somos amigos.

## Subject Pronouns and ser

**Animated** Grammar
ClassZone.com

**Ser** means *to be*. Use **ser** to identify a person or say where he or she is from. How do you use this verb with **subject pronouns**?

*Here's how:*

| Singular | | | Plural | | |
|---|---|---|---|---|---|
| yo | **soy** | *I am* | nosotros(as) | **somos** | *we are* |
| tú | **eres** | *you are* | vosotros(as) | **sois** | *you are* |
| usted | **es** | *you are* | ustedes | **son** | *you are* |
| él, ella | **es** | *he, she is* | ellos(as) | **son** | *they are* |

*familiar* → tú                vosotros(as) ← *familiar*
*formal* → usted

**Yo soy** de Buenos Aires.        **Ellas son** de Venezuela.
*I am* from Buenos Aires.        *They are* from Venezuela.

**Singular**

Use **tú** with
- a friend
- a family member
- someone younger

Use **usted** with
- a person you don't know
- someone older
- someone to whom you want to show respect

**Plural**

- Use **vosotros(as)** with friends, family, and younger people only in Spain.

- Use **ustedes** with people you don't know, older people, and people to whom you want to show respect in Spain; use it in Latin America with any group of people.

- Use **nosotras, vosotras,** and **ellas** when all the people you are talking about are female.

*Más práctica*
Cuaderno *pp. 4–6*
Cuaderno para hispanohablantes *pp. 5–7*

**Conjuguemos.com**

**@HomeTutor**
Leveled Practice
ClassZone.com

# Práctica de GRAMÁTICA

## 6 | ¿Quién?

Write the corresponding pronoun.

**modelo:** ella

**1.**    **2.**    **3.**

**4.**    **5.**    **6.**

---

**Nota gramatical**

Use **de** with the verb **ser** to talk about where someone is from.

Daniela y Sonia **son de** Miami.          Martín **es de** Honduras.
*Daniela and Sonia **are from** Miami.*     *Martín **is from** Honduras.*

---

## 7 | ¿De dónde son?

Lucía's friends and teachers are from different places. Write the correct form of **ser** to learn where they are from.

> Hola, me llamo Lucía. Mi amigo Andrés y yo **1.** de la
> República Dominicana. Yo **2.** de Santo Domingo y él **3.**
> de San Pedro de Macorís. La señora Muñoz y el señor
> Vázquez **4.** de Puerto Rico. Son mis maestros favoritos.
> Mis amigas Laura y Ana **5.** de Colombia. Laura **6.** de
> Bogotá y Ana **7.** de Cartagena. Y tú, ¿de dónde **8.** ?

## 8 | Ella es de...

Hablar
Escribir

Choose the correct form of **ser** to say where each person is from.
Some forms may be used more than once.

> **modelo:** Ella _____ de Uruguay.
> Ella **es** de Uruguay.

1. Nosotros _____ de Bolivia.
2. Ellos _____ de Chile.
3. Usted _____ de Paraguay.
4. Yo _____ de El Salvador.
5. Él _____ de Nicaragua.
6. Tú _____ de Cuba.
7. Nosotras _____ de Venezuela.
8. Ustedes _____ de Panamá.

**a.** eres
**b.** es
**c.** somos
**d.** son
**e.** soy

## 9 | Los amigos de Alicia

Escribir

Alicia has a lot of friends that you are going to meet in the following
chapters. Write where they are from.

> **modelo:** Maribel y Enrique / España
> Maribel y Enrique son de España.

**1.** yo /
Miami

**2.** Claudia y Pablo /
México

**3.** Marisol /
Puerto Rico

**4.** papá y yo /
Miami

**5.** Fernando /
Ecuador

**6.** Mario / la República
Dominicana

## 10 | De muchos países

**Hablar**

Ask another student where Miguel's friends are from. Your partner should use pronouns to answer.

**modelo:** Luis

**A** ¿De dónde es Luis?

**B** Él es de Colombia.

1. Leticia
2. Álvaro y Linda
3. Isabel y Ángela
4. Andrés y Jorge
5. Ana Sofía y Elena
6. Y tú, ¿ ?

## 11 | Mis amigos

**Escribir**

Write five sentences telling where your friends are from.

**modelo:** Amy es de Minnesota. Mike es de Indiana...

*Más práctica*   Cuaderno *pp. 4–6*   Cuaderno para hispanohablantes *pp. 5–7*

**PARA Y PIENSA**

**Did you get it?** Match the phrases to make a complete sentence.

1. Cristóbal y yo
2. Tomás
3. Yo

a. soy de México.
b. somos de Honduras.
c. es de la República Dominicana.

**Get Help Online**
ClassZone.com

# GRAMÁTICA *en contexto*

**¡AVANZA!** **Goal:** Notice how Alicia and her friends say where they are from. Then use **ser** with **de** to tell where people are from. *Actividades 12–14*

## Telehistoria escena 2

@*HomeTutor* VideoPlus
**View, Read and Record**
ClassZone.com

### STRATEGIES

**Cuando lees**
**Scan for details** Quickly look ahead for certain details before you read the scene. Scan for names and people. What do you think this scene is about?

**Cuando escuchas**
**Listen for guesses** Listen as Mr. Costas guesses where Teresa and Miguel are from. What does he guess? What does Miguel guess about where Mr. Costas is from?

VIDEO
DVD

AUDIO

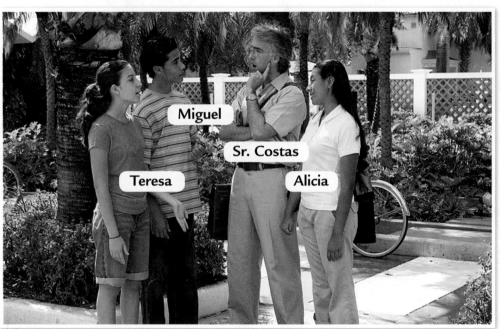

Miguel

Sr. Costas

Teresa

Alicia

**Alicia:** ¡Hola! Señor Costas, le presento a dos amigos... Teresa y Miguel. Ellos son de...

*Mr. Costas stops her because he wants to guess.*

**Sr. Costas:** Tú eres de... ¿Puerto Rico? ¿Panamá? ¿Costa Rica?

**Teresa:** No, yo soy de...

*Mr. Costas interrupts and gestures toward Miguel.*

**Sr. Costas:** ¿Él es de México? ¿El Salvador? ¿Colombia?

**Miguel:** No, nosotros somos de *(pointing to himself)* Cuba y *(pointing to Teresa)* de Honduras. Y usted, ¿de dónde es?

**Sr. Costas:** Soy de...

**Miguel:** ¿Argentina? ¿Chile? ¿Cuba?

**Sr. Costas:** Soy de la Florida.

**Continuará...** p. 48

## 12 | Los orígenes  *Comprensión del episodio*

Answer the questions about the episode.

**1.** Teresa y Miguel son los amigos de
   **a.** Alicia.
   **b.** el señor Costas.
   **c.** el señor Díaz.

**2.** ¿De dónde es Miguel?
   **a.** Es de Puerto Rico.
   **b.** Es de Cuba.
   **c.** Es de la República Dominicana.

**3.** ¿De dónde es Teresa?
   **a.** Es de Puerto Rico.
   **b.** Es de Costa Rica.
   **c.** Es de Honduras.

**4.** ¿Quién es de la Florida?
   **a.** Miguel
   **b.** el señor Costas
   **c.** Teresa

---

## 13 | Los famosos en Miami

Leer
Hablar

**Comparación cultural**

### Los Premios Juventud

*How have Latino performers and athletes affected popular culture in the United States? Los Premios Juventud is an awards show held in **Miami** and broadcast on Spanish-language television. Teens vote for their favorite stars in music, film, and sports. Past nominees include Shakira and Juanes (Colombia), Paulina Rubio and Gael García Bernal (Mexico), Miguel Cabrera (Venezuela), and Jennifer Lopez (New York).*

*Juanes*

*Paulina Rubio*

**Compara con tu mundo**  *Who are your favorite figures in music, film, and sports, and why?*

Talk with a partner about where the nominees are from.

**A** ¿De dónde es Juanes?

**B** Juanes es de Colombia.

---

## 14 | ¿De dónde somos?

Hablar

Ask other students where they are from.

**A** Nora, ¿de dónde eres?

**B** Soy de Miami. ¿Y tú?

También soy de Miami.

---

**PARA Y PIENSA**

**Did you get it?**  Create sentences to tell where the people are from.

1. el Sr. Costas / la Florida
2. Alicia / Miami
3. Teresa y Miguel / Honduras y Cuba

**Get Help Online**
ClassZone.com

# Presentación de GRAMÁTICA

 **Goal:** Learn how to express what people like to do using the verb **gustar.** Then use **gustar** to say what you and others like to do. *Actividades 15–19*

**English Grammar Connection:** An **infinitive** is the basic form of a **verb,** a word that expresses action or a state of being. In English, most infinitives include the word *to*. In Spanish, infinitives are always one word that ends in **-ar, -er,** or **-ir.**

I like **to run.**          Me gusta **correr.**

infinitive          infinitive

 **Gustar with an Infinitive**

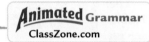 **Animated** Grammar
ClassZone.com

Use **gustar** to talk about what people like to do.

*Here's how:* Use phrases like **me gusta + infinitive.**

| | |
|---|---|
| **Me gusta dibujar.** | *I like to draw.* |
| **Te gusta dibujar.** | *You (familiar singular) like to draw.* |
| **Le gusta dibujar.** | *You (formal singular) like to draw.* <br> *He/She likes to draw.* |
| **Nos gusta dibujar.** | *We like to draw.* |
| **Os gusta dibujar.** | *You (familiar plural) like to draw.* |
| **Les gusta dibujar.** | *You (plural) like to draw.* <br> *They like to draw.* |

When you want to really emphasize or identify the person that you are talking about, add **a + noun/pronoun.**

**A Sonia le gusta leer.**          **A ella le gusta leer.**
*Sonia likes to read.*          *She likes to read.*

These are the **pronouns** that follow **a.**

A mí **me gusta** dibujar.          A nosotros(as) **nos gusta** dibujar.

A ti **te gusta** dibujar.          A vosotros(as) **os gusta** dibujar.

A usted **le gusta** dibujar.          A ustedes **les gusta** dibujar.

A él, ella **le gusta** dibujar.          A ellos(as) **les gusta** dibujar.

*Más práctica*
Cuaderno *pp. 7–9*
Cuaderno para hispanohablantes *pp. 8–11*

*@HomeTutor*
**Leveled Practice**
ClassZone.com

# Práctica de GRAMÁTICA

## 15 | ¿Les gusta o no?

**Escribir**

Write what these people like and don't like to do.

modelo: a Luisa / preparar la comida
No le gusta preparar la comida.

**1.** a nosotras /  comer pizza

**5.** a Alicia y a Miguel /  aprender el español

**2.** a ustedes / estudiar

**6.** a usted / trabajar

**3.** a ti / montar en bicicleta

**7.** a Teresa / tocar la guitarra

**4.** a mí / escuchar música

**8.** a ellos / hacer la tarea

## Comparación cultural

### El arte de Miami

*How would being Cuban American influence an artist's work?* Growing up in **Miami**, artist Xavier Cortada learned about his Cuban heritage through his family and community around him. Many of his paintings reflect his identity as a Cuban American. His colorful painting *Music* presents a variety of instruments found in traditional Cuban music *(son, rumba, mambo, Afro-Latin jazz)* as well as American music. How many instruments can you identify?

*Music (2005), Xavier Cortada*

**Compara con tu mundo** *What would you paint to represent your community? Where would you display your painting?*

## 16 | ¿Qué les gusta hacer?

**Hablar**

With a partner, use the photos to say what Alicia and others like to do.

Teresa

A ¿Qué le gusta hacer a Teresa?

B Le gusta leer un libro.

**1.** Alicia

**2.** ella

**3.** él

**4.** Alicia y Miguel

**5.** Teresa

**6.** ustedes

## 17 | En el parque

**Hablar**
**Escribir**

Look at the drawing and say whether the people like or don't like what they are doing.

**modelo:** Le gusta jugar al fútbol.

## 18 | Las actividades

Escuchar
Escribir

Copy this chart on a piece of paper. Listen to Mariana's description of what she and her friends like to do on Saturdays, and complete your chart with **sí** or **no.** Then answer the questions.

| ¿Le gusta...? | descansar | pasear | mirar la televisión | tocar la guitarra |
|---|---|---|---|---|
| A Mariana | sí | | | |
| A Jorge | | no | | |
| A Federico | | | | |

**1.** ¿Qué le gusta hacer a Jorge?

**2.** ¿Qué le gusta hacer a Mariana?

**3.** ¿Qué le gusta hacer a Federico?

**4.** ¿Qué no le gusta hacer a Mariana?

**5.** ¿Qué no les gusta hacer a Jorge y a Federico?

**6.** ¿Qué les gusta hacer a los tres amigos?

## 19 | A mi amigo(a) le gusta

Hablar

Ask a classmate what he or she likes to do on Saturdays and Sundays. Then tell the class.

¿**T**e gusta mon**t**ar en biclcle**t**a?

### Pronunciación ░ Las letras p y t

AUDIO

When you pronounce the **p** and **t** in English, a puff of air comes out of your mouth. In Spanish, there is no puff of air. Listen and repeat.

| pasar | por favor | Puerto Rico |
|---|---|---|
| pizza | pero | papas |

**Pepe prepara las papas fritas.**

| fruta | televisión | practicar |
|---|---|---|
| tocar | estudiar | tarea |

*Más práctica*  Cuaderno *pp. 7–9*  Cuaderno para hispanohablantes *pp. 8–11*

**PARA Y PIENSA**

**Did you get it?** Complete each sentence with the correct **gustar** phrase.

1. _____ correr. (a ella)
2. ¿_____ andar en patineta? (a ti)
3. _____ tocar la guitarra. (a nosotros)

Get Help Online
ClassZone.com

# Todo junto

¡AVANZA!

**Goal:** *Show what you know* Pay attention to Alicia and her friends as they describe the activities they like to do. Then use **ser** and **gustar** to say where you are from and what you like to do. *Actividades 20–24*

## Telehistoria completa

@*HomeTutor* VideoPlus
**View, Read and Record**
ClassZone.com

### STRATEGIES

**Cuando lees**

**Unlock the main idea** Find repeated phrases that can unlock the overall meaning. Find all the phrases that contain the verb **gustar.** What is this scene about?

**Cuando escuchas**

**Listen for cognates** A cognate is a Spanish word that sounds like an English word and means the same thing. For example, *telephone* and **teléfono.** In the video, listen for at least three cognates.

**Escena 1** *Resumen*

A Alicia y a Sandra les gusta hacer muchas actividades. Les gusta dibujar, comer pizza y más.

**Escena 2** *Resumen*

Miguel es de Cuba y Teresa es de Honduras. El señor Costas es de la Florida.

VIDEO
DVD

AUDIO

**Escena 3**

**Alicia:** ¿Qué les gusta hacer?

**Miguel:** Me gusta mirar la televisión.

**Teresa:** No me gusta mirar la televisión. Me gusta más tocar la guitarra o escuchar música.

**Miguel:** Me gusta comer.

**Teresa:** Sí, me gusta comer.

**Alicia:** ¡Nos gusta comer!

*They stand to go eat.*

**Alicia:** ¿Qué les gusta comer? ¿Pizza? ¿Les gusta comer helado? ¿Fruta? ¿Beber jugos?

*Both say no, and they all sit. Teresa shows them the paper.*

**Alicia:** ¿Trini Salgado? ¿En San Antonio? *(She quickly takes out her cell phone.)* ¡Sandra!

## 20 | ¿Quiénes son? *Comprensión de los episodios*

Escuchar
Leer

Write the name(s) of the character(s) according to the descriptions.

1. No le gusta andar en patineta.
2. Es de Honduras.
3. Les gusta comer.
4. Es de la Florida.
5. Le gusta tocar la guitarra.
6. Es de San Antonio, Texas.
7. Le gusta hablar por teléfono.
8. Le gusta escuchar música.

## 21 | Los amigos *Comprensión de los episodios*

Escuchar
Leer

Answer the questions according to the episodes.

1.
a. ¿Cómo se llama?
b. ¿Qué le gusta hacer?
c. ¿Qué no le gusta hacer?

2.
a. ¿Cómo se llama?
b. ¿De dónde es?
c. ¿Qué le gusta hacer?

## 22 | Nuevos amigos

Hablar

> **STRATEGY Hablar**
> **Boost your "speaking self-confidence" with positive statements**
> To increase your speaking self-confidence, say something positive to yourself like:
> *I learn from my mistakes. I can say things now that I couldn't say last week.* Create your own
> positive statement. Say it to yourself before the speaking activity below.

You are a new student at school. Talk with other students about where you are from and what you like and don't like to do. Make a list of the things you have in common.

**A** Hola, me llamo Víctor. Soy de Chicago. Me gusta escuchar música y correr.

**B** Hola, me llamo Carolina y soy de Chicago también. No me gusta escuchar música pero me gusta practicar deportes.

**C** Hola. Me llamo Alex...

## 23 | Integración

Leer
Escuchar
Hablar

Read the e-mail from Vanessa, then listen to Carmen and take notes.
Say what both of them like and don't like.

### Fuente 1  Correo electrónico

¡Hola, Carmen! Soy Vanessa. Soy de Morelos, México. Me gusta mucho practicar deportes. También me gusta andar en patineta. No me gusta escuchar música. Después de las clases me gusta pasar un rato con los amigos y comer pizza. Los sábados y domingos no me gusta hacer la tarea. Me gusta más alquilar un DVD o descansar. ¿Y a ti? ¿Qué te gusta hacer?

### Fuente 2  Escucha a Carmen

**Listen and take notes**
- ¿Qué le gusta hacer a Carmen?
- ¿Qué no le gusta hacer?

**modelo:** A las chicas les gusta...

## 24 | Un correo electrónico

Escribir

Write to your new e-pal in Puebla, Mexico. Introduce yourself and tell him or her where you are from and what you like and don't like to do. Also write three questions for him or her to answer.

**modelo:** Hola, Eva. Me llamo Ana, y soy de la Florida. Me gusta leer un libro, pero no me gusta mirar la televisión. ¿Te gusta hablar por teléfono?

| Writing Criteria | Excellent | Good | Needs Work |
|---|---|---|---|
| **Content** | Your e-mail includes a lot of information and questions. | Your e-mail includes some information and questions. | Your e-mail includes little information and not enough questions. |
| **Communication** | Most of your e-mail is organized and easy to follow. | Parts of your e-mail are organized and easy to follow. | Your e-mail is disorganized and hard to follow. |
| **Accuracy** | Your e-mail has few mistakes in grammar and vocabulary. | Your e-mail has some mistakes in grammar and vocabulary. | Your e-mail has many mistakes in grammar and vocabulary. |

*Más práctica*  Cuaderno *pp. 10–11*  Cuaderno para hispanohablantes *pp. 12–13*

**PARA Y PIENSA**

**Did you get it?** Tell where these people are from and what they like to do, based on the Telehistoria.

1. Teresa / Honduras / tocar la guitarra
2. Alicia / Miami / comer
3. Miguel / Cuba / mirar la televisión

**Get Help Online**
ClassZone.com

# Juegos y diversiones

Review the verb **ser** by playing a game.

## The Setup

Your teacher will hand you a card with the name of a country on it. This will be your country of origin for use in the game. Do not show your card to anyone. The object of the game is to find another person in your class with the same country card.

Colombia    Perú    Honduras

## Playing the Game

You will go around asking your classmates where they are from in order to find the person who has the same country card as you. You must use the correct Spanish phrasing and answer in complete sentences.

## The Winners!

The first two students to match country cards and say the word **¡Ganamos!** (we win) are the winners.

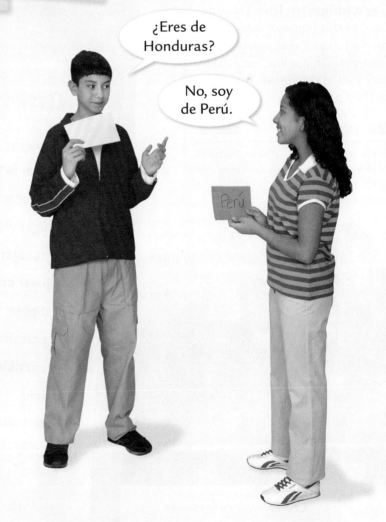

¿Eres de Honduras?

No, soy de Perú.

# Lectura

¡AVANZA! **Goal:** Read about what students in a dual-language school in Florida like to do in their free time. Then compare the activities they like to do with what you like to do.

AUDIO

# ¿Qué te gusta hacer?

This is a survey about what students like to do in their free time. It was conducted among students at a dual-language school in Florida.

**STRATEGY Leer**

**Use a judgment line** Draw a line like this one with *least popular* on the left and *most popular* on the right. On the line, list all the activities in the survey according to their popularity.

leer estudiar          dibujar
_____
least popular     most popular

## ¿Qué te gusta hacer?

Me gusta...
- mirar la televisión ☐
- pasar un rato con los amigos ✓
- jugar videojuegos [1] ☐
- trabajar ✓
- jugar con los amigos ☐
- dibujar ✓
- practicar deportes ☐
- escribir ☐
- leer ✓
- estudiar ☐
- otras [2] actividades _tocar la guitarra_
  _____

[1] videogames     [2] other

*Una encuesta en la escuela*

# Resultados de la encuesta[3]

25 estudiantes respondieron[4] a las 11 categorías o actividades.

*Actividades*

| mirar la tele | pasar un rato | videojuegos | trabajar | jugar | dibujar | deportes | escribir | leer | estudiar | otras |

*Número de estudiantes*

[3] survey    [4] replied

**PARA Y PIENSA**

## ¡Interpreta!

Based on the chart and survey, answer the following questions.

1. How many students took the survey?
2. What are the three most popular activities and the three least popular activities?
3. Would you get the same results if you used the survey with your classmates? Give specific reasons why or why not.

## ¿Y tú?

Record your answers to the survey on the previous page and compare them to the results of these students.

# Conexiones   *La geografía*

## La expedición de Hernando de Soto

*Hernando de Soto*

The map below shows one account of the expedition of Hernando de Soto, a sixteenth-century Spanish explorer. It is believed that de Soto's team traveled through ten present-day U.S. states, and through many Native American villages. The following table gives the latitude and longitude of four U.S. cities, as well as the villages that were close to these locations. Use the coordinates to find the city that corresponds to each Native American village.

| NATIVE AMERICAN VILLAGE | LOCATION OF CITY | NAME OF CITY |
|---|---|---|
| Ucita | 27° 56' N 82° 27' O | |
| Casqui | 35° 15' N 90° 34' O | |
| Mabila | 30° 41' N 88° 02' O | |
| Anhayca | 30° 26' N 84° 16' O | |

**La expedición (1539–1543)**

OKLAHOMA · Parkin · TENNESSEE · CAROLINA DEL NORTE · 35°N · CAROLINA DEL SUR · ARK. · MISISIPÍ · TEXAS · Río Misisipí · ALA. · GEORGIA · Mobile · Tallahassee · 30°N · LUISIANA · Tampa · FLORIDA · Golfo de México · 0 100 200 millas · 0 100 200 kilómetros · N O E S · 25°N · 95°O · 90°O · 85°O · 80°O

### Proyecto 1 *Las matemáticas*

A common form of measurement during the time of de Soto was the league (**legua**). A league was based on the distance an average person could walk in an hour: 3.5 miles. Calculate what these distances would be in leagues.

| | |
|---|---|
| Ucita to Anhayca: | 204 miles |
| Anhayca to Mabila: | 224 miles |
| Mabila to Casqui: | 347 miles |

### Proyecto 2 *El lenguaje*

Many places in the United States have Spanish names. **Florida,** for instance, means *full of flowers.* Use an atlas or the Internet to find three places in the United States with Spanish names. Then write the meaning of each place.

### Proyecto 3 *La música*

The term "Tex–Mex" also describes music that blends elements of Mexico and the southwestern U.S. Most Tex–Mex music features the accordion, brought to Texas in the 1890s by German immigrants. Find an example of Tex–Mex music—such as Selena or Los Tigres del Norte—and listen to it. Then write a paragraph describing the instruments and the music and list the Spanish names of the instruments.

*Los Tigres del Norte*

**Animated** Grammar
**Interactive Flashcards**
ClassZone.com

## Vocabulario

### Talk About Activities

| | | | |
|---|---|---|---|
| alquilar un DVD | to rent a DVD | hacer la tarea | to do homework |
| andar en patineta | to skateboard | jugar al fútbol | to play soccer |
| aprender el español | to learn Spanish | leer un libro | to read a book |
| beber | to drink | mirar la televisión | to watch television |
| comer | to eat | montar en bicicleta | to ride a bike |
| comprar | to buy | pasar un rato con los amigos | to spend time with friends |
| correr | to run | | |
| descansar | to rest | pasear | to go for a walk |
| dibujar | to draw | practicar deportes | to practice / play sports |
| escribir correos electrónicos | to write e-mails | preparar la comida | to prepare food / a meal |
| escuchar música | to listen to music | tocar la guitarra | to play the guitar |
| estudiar | to study | trabajar | to work |
| hablar por teléfono | to talk on the phone | | |

### Say What You Like and Don't Like to Do

| | | | |
|---|---|---|---|
| ¿Qué te gusta hacer? | What do you like to do? | Me gusta... | I like . . . |
| ¿Te gusta...? | Do you like . . . ? | No me gusta... | I don't like . . . |

### Snack Foods and Beverages

| | |
|---|---|
| el agua (fem.) | water |
| la fruta | fruit |
| la galleta | cookie |
| el helado | ice cream |
| el jugo | juice |
| las papas fritas | French fries |
| la pizza | pizza |
| el refresco | soft drink |

### Other Words and Phrases

| | |
|---|---|
| la actividad | activity |
| antes de | before |
| después (de) | afterward, after |
| la escuela | school |
| más | more |
| o | or |
| pero | but |
| también | also |

## Gramática

**Nota gramatical:** **de** to describe where you are from *p. 39*

### Pronouns and ser

**Ser** means *to be.* Use **ser** to identify a person or say where he or she is from.

| Singular | | Plural | |
|---|---|---|---|
| yo | soy | nosotros(as) | somos |
| tú | eres | vosotros(as) | sois |
| usted | es | ustedes | son |
| él, ella | es | ellos(as) | son |

### Gustar with an Infinitive

Use **gustar** to talk about what people like to do.

A mí **me gusta** dibujar.
A ti **te gusta** dibujar.
A usted **le gusta** dibujar.
A él, ella **le gusta** dibujar.
A nosotros(as) **nos gusta** dibujar.
A vosotros(as) **os gusta** dibujar.
A ustedes **les gusta** dibujar.
A ellos(as) **les gusta** dibujar.

# Repaso de la lección

**¡LLEGADA!**

@HomeTutor
ClassZone.com

**Now you can**
- talk about activities
- tell where you are from
- say what you like and don't like to do

**Using**
- subject pronouns and **ser**
- **de** to describe where you are from
- **gustar** with an infinitive

---

**To review**
- **gustar** with an infinitive p. 44
- **de** to describe where you are from p. 39

AUDIO

## 1 | Listen and understand

Listen to Pablo and Sara talk about their activities. Then match the descriptions with the name or names.

1. Es de Puerto Rico.
2. Es de Miami.
3. Le gusta escuchar música.
4. No le gusta andar en patineta.
5. No le gusta comer frutas.
6. Le gusta comer helado.

a. Pablo
b. Sara
c. Pablo y Sara

---

**To review**
- **gustar** with an infinitive p. 44

## 2 | Say what you like and don't like to do

Write sentences describing the activities you like and don't like to do.

**modelo:** alquilar un DVD
(No) Me gusta alquilar un DVD.

1. beber refrescos
2. preparar la comida
3. hacer la tarea
4. descansar
5. escribir correos electrónicos
6. pasar un rato con los amigos
7. practicar deportes
8. trabajar
9. comprar libros
10. comer pizza

# 3 | Tell where you are from

**To review**
- subject pronouns and **ser** p. 38
- **de** to describe where you are from p. 39

Complete the e-mail with the appropriate form of **ser.**

Hola, me llamo Eduardo. Yo __1.__ de Miami. Y tú, ¿de dónde __2.__? Mis amigos y yo __3.__ de diferentes países. Roberto __4.__ de Chile y Yolanda __5.__ de Perú. Nosotros __6.__ estudiantes. El señor Santana y la señora Zabala __7.__ maestros. Ellos __8.__ de Cuba.

# 4 | Talk about activities

**To review**
- **gustar** with an infinitive p. 44

Tell what activities these people like to do, according to the photos.

**modelo:** a José
A José le gusta tocar la guitarra.

**1.** a Sonia

**2.** a ellos

**3.** a usted

**4.** a nosotras

**5.** a ustedes

**6.** a ti

# 5 | United States

**To review**
- Miami's Freedom Tower p. 29
- Fiesta San Antonio p. 29
- Comparación cultural pp. 43, 45

### Comparación cultural

Answer these culture questions.

**1.** What is inside Miami's Freedom Tower?
**2.** What occurs during Fiesta San Antonio?
**3.** Who votes for the winners of **Los Premios Juventud**?
**4.** What is Xavier Cortada's heritage?

*Más práctica* Cuaderno *pp. 12–23* Cuaderno para hispanohablantes *pp. 14–23*

**Get Help Online**
ClassZone.com

# Estados Unidos

# 2

**Tema:**

## Mis amigos y yo

**¡AVANZA!**

### In this lesson you will learn to
- describe yourself and others
- identify people and things

### using
- **ser** to describe what someone is like
- definite and indefinite articles
- noun-adjective agreement

### ♻ ¿Recuerdas?
- snack foods, after-school activities
- **ser, gustar** with an infinitive

## Comparación cultural

### In this lesson you will learn about
- Latin-American and Tex-Mex food
- the tradition of making **cascarones**
- after-school activities in Miami and San Antonio
- students from Miami, Colombia, and Mexico

### Compara con tu mundo
These Texas teens are exploring the Paseo del Río, one of San Antonio's main attractions. In this refreshing city retreat, people eat in restaurants, ride riverboats, or stroll along the river. *Does your city or town have a park or place of interest? What do people do there?*

### ¿Qué ves?

*Mira la foto*
¿Son amigos?
¿Qué les gusta hacer?
¿Llueve o hace sol?

**Paseo del Río**
*San Antonio, Texas*

# Presentación de VOCABULARIO

**Goal:** Learn how Sandra describes herself and her friends. Then practice what you have learned to describe yourself and others. *Actividades 1–2*

♻ *¿Recuerdas?* The verb **ser** p. 38

VIDEO
DVD

AUDIO

**A** ¡Hola! Soy Sandra.
Soy **artística** y **tengo pelo castaño.**
A mi **amigo** Ricardo le gusta practicar
deportes **porque** es **atlético.**

artística

atlético

**B** Alberto es **trabajador** y **estudioso.** Le gusta estudiar. David es **un poco perezoso.** No es **un estudiante muy bueno.** No le gusta trabajar.

trabajador

perezoso

**C** Soy **una persona** muy **organizada.** Mi **amiga** Ana es **inteligente** pero un poco **desorganizada.**

organizada

desorganizada

**D** Rafael es muy **alto,** pero Laura es **baja.** Manuel es **grande,** pero Francisco es **pequeño.** La señora Santa Cruz es un poco **vieja,** pero Rosita es **joven.**

alto

baja

grande

pequeño

vieja

joven

### Más vocabulario

**bonito(a)** *pretty*
**guapo(a)** *good-looking*
**malo(a)** *bad*

*Expansión de vocabulario* p. R2

Continuará...

**E** La señora Guardado es **pelirroja** y el señor Guardado **tiene** pelo castaño. Marco y Laura son **chicos** muy buenos. Marco tiene **pelo rubio** y Laura tiene pelo castaño.

pelirroja

la mujer

pelo castaño

el hombre

pelo rubio

el chico

la chica

**F** Yo soy un poco **seria,** pero mi amigo Alberto es muy **cómico. Todos** mis amigos son muy **simpáticos.** ¿Y tú? **¿Cómo eres?**

cómico

seria

## ¡A responder! Escuchar

Listen to these descriptions of Sandra and her friends. Point to the person in the photo who matches each description you hear.

*@HomeTutor* VideoPlus
**Interactive Flashcards**
ClassZone.com

# Práctica de VOCABULARIO

## 1 | Los opuestos

**Leer**

Sandra describes her friends but Ricardo says the opposite. Match Sandra's description with Ricardo's response.

**Sandra**

1. Marco es pequeño.
2. Luisa es trabajadora.
3. Pablo es organizado.
4. Joaquín es malo.
5. Anabel es joven.
6. Francisco es cómico.

**Ricardo**

a. No, es bueno.
b. No, es grande.
c. No, es desorganizado.
d. No, es perezosa.
e. No, es serio.
f. No, es vieja.

---

**Nota gramatical**  **¿Recuerdas?** The verb **ser** p. 38

Use **ser** to describe what people are like.

| La mujer **es** alta. | Los chicos **son** organizados. |
| *The woman **is** tall.* | *The boys **are** organized.* |

---

## 2 | Porque...

**Hablar
Escribir**

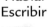

Explain why Ricardo and Alberto like or don't like the following activities.

| serio | atlético | artístico |

| estudioso | desorganizado | trabajador |

**modelo:** A Ricardo le gusta practicar deportes porque es atlético.

1. A Ricardo le gusta hacer la tarea.
2. A Ricardo le gusta dibujar.
3. A Alberto no le gusta ser cómico.
4. A Alberto le gusta correr.
5. A Alberto no le gusta ser perezoso.
6. A Alberto no le gusta ser organizado.

*Más práctica*   Cuaderno *pp. 24–26*   Cuaderno para hispanohablantes *pp. 24–27*

**PARA Y PIENSA**

**Did you get it?**
1. Say that Juan is short.
2. Say that David is artistic.
3. Say that Carlos is serious.

**Get Help Online**
ClassZone.com

# VOCABULARIO en contexto

**Goal:** Notice how Sandra and her friends describe themselves and each other. Then practice these words to describe others. *Actividades 3–4*

## Telehistoria escena 1

@**HomeTutor** VideoPlus
**View, Read and Record**
ClassZone.com

### STRATEGIES

**VIDEO DVD**

**AUDIO**

**Cuando lees**

**Skim** Find the main idea by skimming (rapidly glancing over) the text before reading it carefully. What is the main idea of the scene below?

**Cuando escuchas**

**Find the humor** Humor makes a scene fun and memorable. Listen for exaggeration, teasing, and jokes. What are some examples of humor in the following scene?

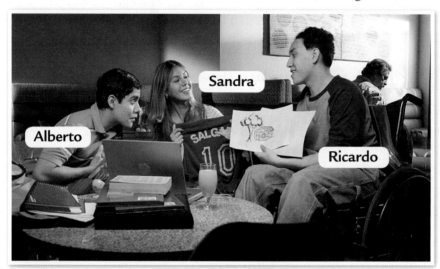

Alberto | Sandra | Ricardo

*Sandra, speaking to Alicia via webcam, holds up Alicia's T-shirt.*

**Sandra:** Es bonita. Pero te gusta más con el autógrafo de Trini Salgado, ¿no?

*Alberto and Ricardo join Sandra.*

**Sandra:** Alicia, te presento a mis amigos: Alberto y Ricardo.

**Alberto:** Hola, Alicia. Me llamo Alberto. Soy alto... no soy muy alto. Tengo pelo castaño, y soy muy trabajador. Pero me gusta mirar la televisión y escuchar música. *(He pulls CDs from his backpack.)*

**Sandra:** No, él no es perezoso pero es un poco desorganizado.

**Ricardo:** Hola, Alicia. ¿Qué tal? Me llamo Ricardo. Soy inteligente, simpático y estudioso. Me gusta practicar deportes porque soy atlético. Y me gusta dibujar porque soy muy artístico.

*Sandra shows one of Ricardo's drawings that is not very good.*

**Sandra:** Sí. Él es muy artístico.

**Ricardo:** Ella es cómica, ¿no?

**Alberto:** Ella no es muy seria.

**Sandra:** OK, OK. Adiós, Alicia. Hasta luego.    **Continuará...** p. 70

Escuchar
Leer

Copy the Venn diagram on a piece of paper and use it to compare Ricardo and Alberto. Write their differences below their names. In the center, write what they have in common.

Ricardo    Alberto

Le gusta dibujar.

4 **Una entrevista**

Leer
Hablar

Read the interview with Raúl López, a famous young soccer player. Then talk to another student about the article. Use at least three adjectives to ask him or her questions.

**A** ¿Es Raúl perezoso?

**B** No, es trabajador porque le gusta estudiar.

## ENTREVISTA

### ¡ESTRELLA DEL FUTURO!

*Revista Estrella:* Raúl, ¿cómo eres?

*Raúl:* Soy muy atlético. Me gusta mucho jugar al fútbol y practicar deportes. Pero también me gusta descansar.

*Revista Estrella:* Y eres un estudiante serio, ¿no?

*Raúl:* Sí, me gusta leer libros y estudiar.

*Revista Estrella:* ¿Te gusta escuchar música?

*Raúl:* Sí, me gusta escuchar música, pero me gusta más tocar la guitarra. También me gusta dibujar.

## Comparación cultural

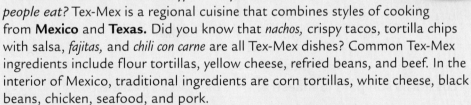

*Unas fajitas*

### La comida mexicana y Tex-Mex

*How does local environment affect the food that people eat?* Tex-Mex is a regional cuisine that combines styles of cooking from **Mexico** and **Texas.** Did you know that *nachos,* crispy tacos, tortilla chips with salsa, *fajitas,* and *chili con carne* are all Tex-Mex dishes? Common Tex-Mex ingredients include flour tortillas, yellow cheese, refried beans, and beef. In the interior of Mexico, traditional ingredients are corn tortillas, white cheese, black beans, chicken, seafood, and pork.

**Compara con tu mundo** *What are some restaurants in your community that serve foods from other countries? Have you eaten at any of them?*

PARA Y PIENSA

**Did you get it?** Fill in the appropriate adjective.
1. Alberto es trabajador. No es _____ .
2. A Ricardo le gusta practicar deportes. Es _____ .
3. A Ricardo le gusta hacer la tarea. Es _____ .

**Get Help Online**
ClassZone.com

# Presentación de GRAMÁTICA

**¡AVANZA!**

**Goal:** Learn about definite and indefinite articles. Then practice using these articles to identify people and things. *Actividades 5–11*

♻ *¿Recuerdas?* Snack foods p. 33, **gustar** with an infinitive p. 44

**English Grammar Connection: Definite articles** (in English, *the*) are used with nouns to indicate *specific* persons, places, or things. **Indefinite articles** (*a, an*) are used with nouns to indicate *nonspecific* persons, places, or things.

**The** boy is **a** friend.          **El** chico es **un** amigo.

| definite article | indefinite article |   | definite article | indefinite article |

## Definite and Indefinite Articles

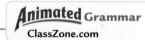
**Animated** Grammar
ClassZone.com

In Spanish, articles match nouns in gender and number.

*Here's how:* All Spanish nouns, even if they refer to objects, are either **masculine** or **feminine.**

- Nouns ending in **-o** are usually **masculine.**
- Nouns ending in **-a** are usually **feminine.**

|  |  | Definite Article | Noun | Indefinite Article | Noun |
|---|---|---|---|---|---|
| **Masculine** | Singular | **el** *the* | chico *boy* | **un** *a* | chico *boy* |
| | Plural | **los** *the* | chicos *boys* | **unos** *some* | chicos *boys* |
| **Feminine** | Singular | **la** *the* | chica *girl* | **una** *a* | chica *girl* |
| | Plural | **las** *the* | chicas *girls* | **unas** *some* | chicas *girls* |

*matches*          *matches*

**Los libros** son para **la maestra.**          ***The** books are for **the** teacher.*

To form the **plural** of a noun, add **-s** if the noun ends in a vowel. Add **-es** if the noun ends in a consonant.

vowel ⌐          consonant ⌐

estudiante → estudiant**es**          mujer → muj**eres**

*Más práctica*

Cuaderno *pp. 27–29*
Cuaderno para hispanohablantes *pp. 28–30*

**@HomeTutor**
**Leveled Practice**
ClassZone.com

# Práctica de GRAMÁTICA

## 5 | ¿Cómo son las personas en la oficina?

**Leer** | Miguel is describing various people in the school office. Complete his sentences with **el, la, los, las.**

1. ___ chicas son atléticas.
2. ___ maestra es inteligente.
3. ___ amigos son simpáticos.
4. ___ chico es pelirrojo.
5. ___ mujeres son artísticas.

6. ___ hombre es guapo.
7. ___ personas son organizadas.
8. ___ amigas son jóvenes.
9. ___ estudiantes son bajos.
10. ___ mujer es cómica.

## 6 | La lista de Sandra

**Escuchar Escribir** | Sandra likes to buy many things. Listen and write a list of what she likes to buy, using **el, la, los, las.**

## 7 | ¿Qué es? ♻ *¿Recuerdas?* Snack foods p. 33

**Hablar Escribir** | Identify these foods, using **un, una, unos, unas.**

**modelo:** Son unas galletas.

1.
2.
3.
4.

5.
6.
7.
8.

## 8 | ¿Son estudiosos?

**Hablar**
**Escribir**

Describe these people, using **ser** and **un, una, unos, unas.**

**modelo:** chico cómico
Daniel es un chico cómico.

1. chicas estudiosas
2. chicos serios
3. amigas trabajadoras
4. chico desorganizado

5. chica alta
6. chico alto
7. estudiante pelirroja
8. chico grande

## 9 | Después de las clases

**Escribir**

Describe what Marta likes to do after school. Combine elements from the three columns to create six different sentences. You may use each article more than once.

**modelo:** tocar / la / guitarra
Le gusta tocar la guitarra.

## 10 | ¿Qué te gusta más? ♻ *¿Recuerdas?* **gustar** with an infinitive p. 44

**Hablar**

Ask a partner what he or she likes more.

**modelo:** comprar

**A** ¿Te gusta más comprar una fruta o unas papas fritas?

**B** Me gusta más comprar una fruta.

**1.** leer

**2.** hablar con

**3.** pasar un rato con

**4.** comer

**5.** beber

**6.** comprar

## 11 | En una isla desierta

**Hablar**

Work in a group of five. Take turns naming some of the items you would wish for if you were stranded on a desert island. Repeat the items other group members wished for, and then add one of your own. Include the definite or indefinite article with each item.

**A** Una pizza.

**B** Una pizza, unos libros.

**C** Una pizza, unos libros, un refresco.

*Más práctica*    Cuaderno *pp. 27–29*    Cuaderno para hispanohablantes *pp. 28–30*

**PARA Y PIENSA**

**Did you get it?**
Match the article to its corresponding noun.

1. la
2. unas
3. el
4. unos

a. libro
b. hombres
c. televisión
d. frutas

 **Get Help Online** ClassZone.com

# GRAMÁTICA *en contexto*

**¡AVANZA!**

**Goal:** Listen to the conversation between Sandra and her friends. Then use definite and indefinite articles to talk about people. *Actividades 12–13*

♻ *¿Recuerdas?* After-school activities p. 32

## Telehistoria escena 2

**@HomeTutor** VideoPlus
**View, Read and Record**
ClassZone.com

### STRATEGIES

**Cuando lees**
**Answer questions related to context** Knowing the context helps you understand the meaning. Ask yourself: Where is the action taking place?

**Cuando escuchas**
**Listen for unstated wishes** People often reveal their wishes without saying them out loud. How do Alberto and Ricardo make it obvious that they want to meet Ana?

VIDEO
DVD

AUDIO

**Ricardo:** Un helado.

**Alberto:** Unas papas fritas y un refresco.

**Sandra:** Un jugo y una pizza. *(Alberto looks over at another table.)*

**Alberto:** ¿Son las chicas de la clase de la señora García?

**Ricardo:** Sí, son Marta, Carla y...

**Sandra:** Ana.

*Both boys look interested.*

**Alberto:** ¿Quién es ella?

**Sandra:** Ella es la amiga de Carla. Es muy inteligente. Le gusta leer y tocar la guitarra.

**Alberto:** Me gusta escuchar música. Ana, ¿no?

**Sandra:** Sí. Y le gusta practicar deportes.

**Ricardo:** Yo soy atlético. Soy muy bueno.

**Sandra:** ¡Ay, los chicos! *(Leaving, Alberto trips and lands in the seat next to Ana and her friends.)*

**Alberto:** Uh... hola. Perdón. **Continuará...** p. 76

### También se dice

**San Antonio** Alberto says **unas papas fritas** to talk about French fries. In other Spanish-speaking countries you might hear:
• **España** **las patatas fritas**
• **Colombia, México** **las papitas**
To talk about juice, Sandra says **un jugo.** In other Spanish-speaking countries you might hear:
• **España** **el zumo**

## 12 | A corregir  *Comprensión del episodio*

**Escuchar
Leer**

All of these sentences are false. Correct the errors.

1. Las chicas se llaman Marta, Beatriz y Ana.
2. Ana es la amiga de Sandra.
3. A Ricardo le gusta escuchar música.
4. Ana no es inteligente.
5. A Alberto le gusta tocar la guitarra.
6. Ricardo no es atlético.

## 13 | En el parque  ♻ *¿Recuerdas?* After-school activities p. 32

**Hablar**

Choose a person or a group of people from the drawings. Follow the model to give clues to another student, who will guess the people you describe. Change roles and describe everyone.

**A** Es una chica. Le gusta tocar la guitarra.

**B** Es la chica de San Antonio.

**San Antonio**

**Bogotá**

**AUDIO**

### ▶ Pronunciación ◀  La letra ñ

The **ñ** sounds like the /ny/ of the word *canyon*. The letter **ñ** does not exist in English, but the sound does. Listen and repeat.

**señor     España     mañana     pequeño     castaño**

**La señora es española.     El señor es de España y tiene pelo castaño.**

**PARA Y PIENSA**

**Did you get it?** Change the article to make the noun more or less specific.

1. Ricardo es el amigo de Alberto.
2. Marta y Carla son las chicas de la clase de español.
3. Ana es la chica muy inteligente.

**Get Help Online**
ClassZone.com

# Presentación de GRAMÁTICA

**Goal:** Learn how to use adjectives with nouns. Then practice using adjectives to describe people. *Actividades 14–19*

**English Grammar Connection: Adjectives** are words that describe **nouns**. In English, the adjective almost always comes before the noun. In Spanish, the adjective usually comes after the noun.

┌─ *before the noun*
the **serious** students

*after the noun* ─┐
los **estudiantes serios**

## Noun-Adjective Agreement

**Animated** Grammar
ClassZone.com

In Spanish, adjectives match the gender and number of the nouns they describe.

***Here's how:***

|  | Singular | Plural |
|---|---|---|
| **Masculine** | el chic**o** alt**o** <br> *the tall boy* | los chic**os** alt**os** <br> *the tall boys* |
| **Feminine** | la chic**a** alt**a** <br> *the tall girl* | las chic**as** alt**as** <br> *the tall girls* |

• Adjectives that end in **-e** match both genders.

el maestr**o** inteligent**e**
la maestr**a** inteligent**e**

• Many adjectives that end in a **consonant** match both genders.

el amig**o** jove**n**
la amig**a** jove**n**

• Some adjectives that end in a **consonant** add **-a** to form the feminine singular. These exceptions have to be memorized.

el chic**o** trabajado**r**
la chic**a** trabajado**ra**

• To make an adjective plural, add **-s** if it ends in a **vowel;** add **-es** if it ends in a **consonant.**

las chicas trabajador**as**
los chicos trabajador**es**

*Más práctica*
   Cuaderno *pp. 30–32*
   Cuaderno para hispanohablantes *pp. 31–34*

***@HomeTutor***
**Leveled Practice**
ClassZone.com

# *Práctica de* GRAMÁTICA

## 14 | Un correo electrónico

**Leer** | Help Sandra solve the puzzle in Alicia's e-mail by choosing the correct words in parentheses.

A: Sandra

Asunto: ¡Una persona famosa en Miami!

Hola, amiga. Te gusta jugar al fútbol y eres
 **1.** (inteligente / inteligentes), ¿no? ¿Quién es la
persona famosa en Miami? No es un chico **2.** (grande /
grandes). No es una chica **3.** (pequeño / pequeña). Tiene
pelo **4.** (castaño / castaña) y es una persona **5.**
(simpático / simpática). Es una mujer **6.** (serio / seria)
pero le gusta pasar un rato con los amigos. Los amigos de
ella son **7.** (atléticos / atlético) también y les gusta
practicar deportes. Ella se llama Trini...

Alicia

## 15 | Descripciones

**Escribir** | Write descriptions of the people in the drawing.

alto(a)    guapo(a)    cómico(a)    atlético(a)

estudioso(a)    desorganizado(a)    serio(a)    ¿?

la Sra. de Silva

Rafael

Mónica

Mario

## 16 | ¡No son iguales!

Laura and her brother Luis are almost total opposites. Change each statement about one to say what the other is like. Use an adjective in each answer. Be careful! Laura and Luis do have a few things in common.

> **modelo:** A Luis no le gusta practicar deportes.
> Laura es atlética.

1. Laura es alta.
2. Luis es desorganizado.
3. Laura es pelirroja.
4. Luis es serio.
5. Laura es joven.
6. A Luis no le gusta dibujar.
7. A Laura no le gusta estudiar.
8. Luis es guapo.

## 17 | Un amigo

Escribir

Write a short description of a friend. Be sure to describe what your friend looks like, his or her personality, and what he or she likes to do.

> **modelo:** Cristina tiene pelo rubio. Es baja. Le gusta leer libros.
> Ella es inteligente...

## 18 | ¿Cómo son los amigos de clase?

Escribir
Hablar

Write descriptions of three people in the class. Read the descriptions to a partner, who will guess the people being described.

**A** Es un chico. Es alto, inteligente y atlético. Es un poco serio también. Tiene pelo castaño.

**B** Es Felipe.

## 19 | La Fiesta San Antonio

Hablar

**Comparación cultural**

### Los cascarones

*How do cultural traditions influence an artist's work? Cascarones* are painted eggs filled with confetti. They are popular at Easter and events such as parties or graduations. They are also a common sight during Fiesta San Antonio, an annual citywide celebration that honors the history and culture of San Antonio, **Texas**. But *cascarones* are not meant for decoration. Children sneak up on their friends and try to crack the eggs over their heads. If a *cascarón* is broken over your head, it is supposed to bring you good luck. Artists are often influenced by traditions like these. Carmen Lomas Garza is a Mexican-American artist who depicts scenes of traditional celebration. In her 1989 painting *Cascarones,* Lomas Garza presents a family making the colorful eggs.

*Fiesta San Antonio*

**Compara con tu mundo** *What are some traditions in your family and why are they important to you? Which is your favorite tradition?*

Point to a person in the photo and ask a partner what he or she is like. Your partner will answer. Change roles. Describe all of the people.

**A** ¿Cómo es la chica?

**B** La chica es bonita.

*Más práctica*  Cuaderno *pp. 30–32*  Cuaderno para hispanohablantes *pp. 31–34*

**PARA Y PIENSA**

**Did you get it?** Give the correct ending for each adjective.
1. una estudiante desorganizad_____
2. unos chicos simpátic_____
3. unas mujeres trabajador_____
4. un hombre grand_____

**Get Help Online**
ClassZone.com

# Todo junto

**Goal:** *Show what you know* Pay attention to how Sandra and her friends describe specific people. Then use definite and indefinite articles and adjectives to tell what someone is like. *Actividades 20–24*

## Telehistoria completa

@*HomeTutor* VideoPlus
**View, Read and Record**
ClassZone.com

### STRATEGIES

**Cuando lees**

**Discover a problem** Scenes often reveal problems that the characters must solve. While reading the text below, search for a problem. What is it? Can it be solved?

**Cuando escuchas**

**Listen for the parts** Even a short scene can have parts, each with a somewhat different topic or action. These can be keys to meaning. How would you divide this scene?

**Escena 1** *Resumen*

Alberto y Ricardo son amigos de Sandra. Alberto es un poco desorganizado. Ricardo es artístico.

**Escena 2** *Resumen*

Ana es la amiga de Carla. A Ricardo y a Ana les gusta practicar deportes, y a Alberto y a Ana les gusta escuchar música.

### Escena 3

VIDEO
DVD

AUDIO

*The group enters a store where Trini Salgado will be signing autographs.*

**Alberto:** Ana es bonita, inteligente, simpática... y nosotros somos inteligentes y simpáticos, ¿no?

**Sandra:** Sí, sí, ustedes son inteligentes, atléticos, cómicos. Ricardo, tú eres estudioso y Alberto, tú eres trabajador.

*Ricardo notices a woman in the store.*

**Ricardo:** ¿Es Trini Salgado?

**Alberto:** ¿Quién?

**Ricardo:** La mujer seria. Tiene pelo castaño.

**Sandra:** No es ella. Es un poco baja. Trini es alta y más joven.

*Ricardo finds the sign announcing Trini Salgado and points to the date.*

**Sandra:** Pero... es el sábado. Hoy es domingo.

**Ricardo:** Sí, el sábado en San Antonio y el lunes en México.

**Sandra:** ¿México? ¿Puebla, México? Pablo, un amigo muy simpático de Alicia, es de México.

*Sandra thinks of a plan to send the T-shirt to Pablo.*

## 20 ¿Cómo son? *Comprensión de los episodios*

Escuchar
Leer

Combine phrases from the two columns to make sentences about the people in the Telehistoria.

**1.** Alberto y Ricardo son     **a.** un poco baja.

**2.** Sandra es     **b.** una amiga de Ricardo y Alberto.

**3.** Ana es     **c.** un amigo de Alicia.

**4.** Ricardo es     **d.** jóvenes.

**5.** Alberto es     **e.** alto y trabajador.

**6.** Todos los chicos son     **f.** cómicos.

**7.** La mujer seria es     **g.** inteligente y le gusta leer.

**8.** Pablo es     **h.** artístico y atlético.

## 21 Los amigos *Comprensión de los episodios*

Escuchar
Leer

Write descriptions of the Telehistoria characters, based on the three episodes.

## 22 Las personas famosas

Escribir
Hablar

> **STRATEGY Hablar**
>
> **Practice pronunciation** To speak more fluently and accurately, practice the sounds of words you need to use in your descriptions. Paying attention to pronunciation will help you with cognates.

Write descriptions of three famous people. Include what they like and don't like to do. Read your descriptions to a partner, who will guess the people being described.

**A** Es un hombre. Tiene pelo rubio. Es muy atlético. Le gusta montar en bicicleta. No es muy joven y no es muy viejo. Es de Estados Unidos. ¿Quién es?

**B** Es Lance Armstrong.

## 23 | Integración

Leer
Escuchar
Hablar

Read the Web page and listen to the boys' messages. Describe the two boys.

**Fuente 1 Página Web**

Amigos por correspondencia

Buscar en la Web [ ] Buscar   Busca Imágenes

**Alejandro**
¡Hola! Soy de San José, Costa Rica. Soy un estudiante muy bueno. Soy inteligente y me gusta estudiar. Soy un poco serio pero también soy simpático.
*¡Escucha!*

**Édgar**
Soy de Colombia. Soy alto y tengo pelo castaño. Soy cómico y simpático. Soy inteligente pero no soy muy trabajador. No me gusta estudiar. ;-)
*¡Escucha!*

**Fuente 2 Audio en Internet**

**Listen and take notes**
• ¿Cómo es Alejandro? ¿Qué le gusta hacer?
• ¿Cómo es Édgar? ¿Qué le gusta hacer?

**modelo:** Alejandro es un poco serio, pero Édgar es cómico...

## 24 | Un(a) amigo(a) perfecto(a)

Escribir

Describe the perfect friend for a special page in the yearbook. What is this person like? What does he or she like to do? Why?

**modelo:** Ella se llama Megan. Es bonita, inteligente y artística. Es una chica muy simpática. Le gusta escuchar música y...

| Writing Criteria | Excellent | Good | Needs Work |
|---|---|---|---|
| **Content** | Your description includes a lot of information. | Your description includes some information. | Your description includes little information. |
| **Communication** | Most of your description is organized and easy to follow. | Parts of your description are organized and easy to follow. | Your description is disorganized and hard to follow. |
| **Accuracy** | Your description has few mistakes in grammar and vocabulary. | Your description has some mistakes in grammar and vocabulary. | Your description has many mistakes in grammar and vocabulary. |

*Más práctica*   Cuaderno *pp. 33–34*   Cuaderno para hispanohablantes *pp. 35–36*

PARA Y PIENSA

**Did you get it?** Create sentences with the following information.

1. Alberto / chico(a) / simpático(a)
2. Ricardo / estudiante / trabajador(a)
3. Sandra / persona / organizado(a)

**Get Help Online**
ClassZone.com

# Juegos y diversiones

Review descriptive adjectives, noun-adjective agreement, and indefinite articles by playing a game.

# 20 preguntas

## The Setup

Get a good look at your classmates, as you will need to identify them based on descriptions used in the game. Form two teams.

### Palabras útiles
equipo *team*
puntos *points*

## Playing the Game

**First:** One person from each team will go to the board and face the class, with his or her back to the board.

**Then:** Your teacher will write on the board the name of someone in the class. Each player at the board will alternate asking a yes/no question to his or her teammates about the mystery person. The player at the board who correctly identifies the mystery person first gets a point for his or her team.

Two new players go to the board, and the game continues.

## The Winner!

The team with the most points at the end wins.

# Lectura cultural

¡AVANZA!

**Goal:** Read about things to do in San Antonio and Miami. Then compare what teens do in those cities with what you like to do where you live.

Comparación cultural

AUDIO

# Saludos desde[1]
## San Antonio y Miami

**STRATEGY Leer**

**Make a comparison chart**
Create a chart like the one below to compare San Antonio and Miami.

|  | San Antonio | Miami |
|---|---|---|
| sitios de interés |  |  |
| actividades |  |  |
| comida |  |  |

En San Antonio, Texas, hay[2] parques de diversiones[3], museos[4], el Paseo del Río y el Álamo. Después de las clases, a los chicos y a las chicas les gusta pasar un rato con los amigos en El Mercado, donde es posible escuchar música de los mariachis y comer comida típica mexicana.

---

[1] **Saludos...** Greetings from  [2] there are
[3] amusement parks  [4] museums

San Antonio

*El Álamo en San Antonio, Texas*

En Miami, Florida, si[5] hace buen tiempo, a los chicos y a las chicas les gusta andar en patineta o montar en bicicleta. Después de las clases, a muchos chicos les gusta pasear con los amigos por la Calle Ocho, en la Pequeña Habana de Miami. ¡Es una pequeña Cuba en la Florida! Allí[6] es posible comer sándwiches cubanos y beber jugo de mango.

---

[5] if    [6] There

Miami

*Andar en patineta en Miami, Florida*

**PARA Y PIENSA**

## ¿Comprendiste?
**1.** ¿Qué hay en San Antonio?
**2.** ¿Qué les gusta hacer a muchos chicos en Miami?
**3.** ¿Qué hay en la Pequeña Habana de Miami?

## ¿Y tú?
¿De dónde eres? ¿Qué te gusta hacer después de las clases?

# Proyectos culturales

## Platos tradicionales de México y Cuba

*Why do traditional dishes change when they are brought from one country to another?* In the U.S. we enjoy foods from many different Spanish-speaking countries. In many parts of the U.S. you can easily find dishes from Mexico, the Caribbean, Central America, and South America. Yet you might be surprised that those dishes aren't exactly the same as they are in their countries of origin. Here are two traditional recipes. The original list of ingredients for both has been modified to include foods more readily available in the U.S. They also reflect the widespread cooking practices and tastes that were already in place when the recipes were brought to this country.

### Proyecto 1 *Salsa fresca*

**México** This is a common sauce in Mexico and all Central America. It is made from scratch and can be eaten as a dip with tortilla chips.

**Ingredients for salsa fresca**
4–5 fresh tomatoes, diced
1 onion, diced
1 green chile, diced
1 clove of garlic, crushed
Juice of 1 fresh lime

**Instructions**
Combine the ingredients in a bowl. Cover and let stand for an hour in the refrigerator so that the flavors mix. Serve with tortilla chips.

### Proyecto 2 *Sándwich cubano*

**Cuba** This is a traditional Cuban lunch dish found throughout Florida. The sandwich is pressed in a special grill or on a skillet.

**Ingredients for sándwich cubano**
1 long sandwich roll
Slices of roast pork, ham, turkey, or bacon
Slice of Swiss or monterey jack cheese
Mustard or mayonnaise
Olive oil

**Instructions**
First brush the outside of the roll with olive oil. Then split it open and lay meat, cheese, and mustard or mayonnaise as desired. Put the sandwich in a hot skillet, placing a small, heavy skillet on top and pressing lightly. Cook three minutes or until cheese melts and bread is toasted.

### En tu comunidad

Check the Internet or your phone book for local restaurants that serve foods from Mexico, Cuba, or other Spanish-speaking countries. Do any of the restaurants in your area serve **salsa fresca** or **sándwiches cubanos**?

# Lección 2

# *En resumen*
## Vocabulario y gramática

**Animated** Grammar
**Interactive Flashcards**
ClassZone.com

## Vocabulario

### Describe Yourself and Others

| ¿Cómo eres? | What are you like? |
|---|---|

**Personality**

| | |
|---|---|
| artístico(a) | artistic |
| atlético(a) | athletic |
| bueno(a) | good |
| cómico(a) | funny |
| desorganizado(a) | disorganized |
| estudioso(a) | studious |
| inteligente | intelligent |
| malo(a) | bad |
| organizado(a) | organized |
| perezoso(a) | lazy |
| serio(a) | serious |
| simpático(a) | nice |
| trabajador(a) | hard-working |

**Appearance**

| | |
|---|---|
| alto(a) | tall |
| bajo(a) | short (height) |
| bonito(a) | pretty |
| grande | big, large; great |
| guapo(a) | good-looking |
| joven (pl. jóvenes) | young |
| pelirrojo(a) | red-haired |
| pequeño(a) | small |
| viejo(a) | old |
| Tengo... | I have . . . |
| Tiene... | He / She has . . . |
|   pelo rubio | blond hair |
|   pelo castaño | brown hair |

### People

| | |
|---|---|
| el (la) amigo(a) | friend |
| la chica | girl |
| el chico | boy |
| el (la) estudiante | student |
| el hombre | man |
| la mujer | woman |
| la persona | person |

### Other Words and Phrases

| | |
|---|---|
| muy | very |
| un poco | a little |
| porque | because |
| todos(as) | all |

## Gramática

**Nota gramatical: ser** to describe what someone is like *p. 63*

### Definite and Indefinite Articles

In Spanish, articles match nouns in gender and number.

| | | Definite Article | Noun | Indefinite Article | Noun |
|---|---|---|---|---|---|
| **Masculine** | Singular | el | chico | un | chico |
| | Plural | los | chicos | unos | chicos |
| **Feminine** | Singular | la | chica | una | chica |
| | Plural | las | chicas | unas | chicas |

### Noun-Adjective Agreement

In Spanish, adjectives match the gender and number of the nouns they describe.

| | Singular | Plural |
|---|---|---|
| **Masculine** | el chico alto | los chicos altos |
| **Feminine** | la chica alta | las chicas altas |

# Repaso de la lección

¡AvanzaRap!
DVD
Sing and Learn

@HomeTutor
ClassZone.com

**Now you can**
• describe yourself and others
• identify people and things

**Using**
• **ser** to describe what someone is like
• definite and indefinite articles
• noun-adjective agreement

**To review**
• definite and indefinite articles p. 66
• **ser** to describe what someone is like p. 63
• noun-adjective agreement p. 72

## 1 Listen and understand

AUDIO

Listen to Carlos talk about himself and his teacher. Then write a description of Carlos and Mrs. Pérez, according to what Carlos says.

**To review**
• definite and indefinite articles p. 66

## 2 Identify people and things

Identify the people in the drawing.

modelo: señor viejo / hombre
El señor viejo es un hombre de Honduras.

México  Honduras  Uruguay  Panamá  Bolivia  Argentina  Estados Unidos

1. chica pelirroja / estudiante
2. hombre grande / maestro
3. chicos pelirrojos / amigos
4. mujer joven / maestra

5. señora alta / mujer
6. chico atlético / estudiante
7. chico desorganizado / persona
8. hombres simpáticos / amigos

**To review**
• noun-adjective agreement p. 72

## 3 | Describe yourself and others

Read this entry in Alejandra's diary. Complete the entry with the correct form of the word in parentheses.

> lunes
>
> Todos mis amigos son muy __1.__ (simpático). Miguel es un chico __2.__ (inteligente) y muy __3.__ (guapo). Beatriz es __4.__ (bonito) y __5.__ (estudioso). A Miguel y a Beatriz les gusta practicar deportes porque son __6.__ (atlético). Carmen y yo no somos __7.__ (atlético). Nosotras somos __8.__ (artístico). Todos nosotros somos unos estudiantes __9.__ (serio) y muy __10.__ (bueno).

**To review**
• **ser** to describe what someone is like p. 63
• noun-adjective agreement p. 72

## 4 | Describe yourself and others

Ramón and Ramona are complete opposites. Write sentences describing them, based on the descriptions.

**modelo:** Ramón es malo.
Ramona es buena.

1. Ramón es viejo.
2. Ramona es seria.
3. Ramón es organizado.
4. Ramona es pequeña.
5. Ramón es perezoso.
6. Ramona es baja.

**To review**
. Comparación cultural pp. 58, 65, 75
. Lectura cultural pp. 80–81

## 5 | United States

### Comparación cultural

Answer these culture questions.

1. What can people do at San Antonio's Paseo del Río?
2. Give an example of a Tex-Mex dish and a Mexican dish.
3. When do people generally use **cascarones** and what do they do with them?
4. What can people do in San Antonio's El Mercado and Miami's Calle Ocho?

*Más práctica* | Cuaderno *pp. 35–46* | Cuaderno para hispanohablantes *pp. 37–46*

**Get Help Online**
ClassZone.com

Estados Unidos

México

Colombia

AUDIO

# Me gusta...

## Lectura y escritura

WebQuest
ClassZone.com

**1 Leer** Read how José Manuel, Martina, and Mónica describe themselves and state their favorite activities.

**2 Escribir** Using the three descriptions as models, write a short paragraph about yourself.

**STRATEGY   Escribir**
**Use a personal chart**
Make a chart showing information about yourself. This will help you write your description.

| Categoría | Detalles |
|---|---|
| país de origen | |
| descripción física | |
| personalidad | |
| actividades favoritas | |
| comidas favoritas | |

**Step 1** Complete the chart by adding details about where you are from, a physical description, personality, and favorite activities and foods.

**Step 2** Write your paragraph, including all the information from your chart. Check your writing by yourself or with help from a friend. Make final corrections.

### Compara con tu mundo
Use the paragraph you wrote to compare your personal description to a description by *one* of the three students. What similarities do you find? What differences?

Cuaderno *pp. 47–49*   Cuaderno para hispanohablantes *pp. 47–49*

### Colombia — *José Manuel*

Me llamo José Manuel. Soy de Bogotá. Soy cómico y un poco desorganizado pero también soy estudioso. Después de hacer la tarea me gusta jugar al fútbol con mis amigos en el parque El Tunal. También me gusta mirar el fútbol en la televisión.

### Estados Unidos — *Martina*

¡Hola! Me llamo Martina y soy de Miami. Soy inteligente, alta y atlética. Los domingos, me gusta montar en bicicleta. También me gusta preparar jugo de mango o de melón con mi amiga, María. Nos gusta beber mucho jugo porque en Miami hace calor.

### México — *Mónica*

¿Qué tal? Me llamo Mónica y soy de México, D.F. Tengo pelo castaño y soy seria. Mis amigas Maite y Alejandra también tienen pelo castaño y son muy simpáticas. Maite y yo somos artísticas. Nos gusta tocar la guitarra. También nos gusta dibujar.

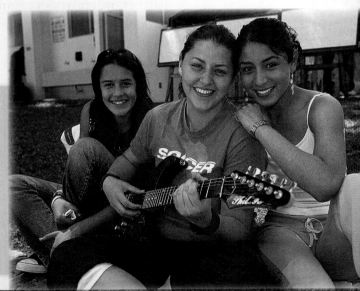

# Repaso inclusivo
♻ Options for Review

## 1 | Listen, understand, and compare

Escuchar

Listen to two teen radio reporters talk about typical after-school activities in Miami and San Antonio. Then answer the questions.

1. ¿Cómo son los estudiantes de Miami?
2. ¿Qué les gusta hacer a los estudiantes de Miami?
3. ¿Cómo son los estudiantes de San Antonio?
4. ¿Qué tiempo hace en San Antonio?
5. ¿Qué les gusta hacer a los estudiantes de San Antonio?

Are you and your friends like the students in Miami and/or San Antonio? Do you like to do the same kinds of activities?

## 2 | Oral presentation

Hablar

Your principal is making a video about your school and you are going to be a featured student. In a segment that lasts at least 30 seconds, introduce yourself, say where you are from, describe yourself, and talk about what you like to do after school.

## 3 | Role-play conversation

Hablar

Role-play a conversation with a new student at your school. The new student, played by your partner, will introduce himself or herself and ask you what you are like and what you and your friends like to do. Answer the new student's questions and ask questions of your own to get to know him or her. Your conversation should be at least two minutes long.

¿Cómo eres?

Soy inteligente y atlética.

# 4 | Create a yearbook entry

**Escribir**

Bring in a photo of yourself and create a caption that could be used in a yearbook. Give your name, where you are from, what you are like, who you like to spend time with, and what activities you like to do. Copy this chart on a piece of paper and use it to organize your information.

| ¿Cómo te llamas? | |
|---|---|
| ¿De dónde eres? | |
| ¿Cómo eres? | |
| ¿Qué te gusta hacer? | |

# 5 | Create a collage

**Hablar**

Work with a partner to create individual collages. Use magazine clippings, photos, or your own drawings. Use the collage to introduce yourself to your partner, say where you are from, and show some of the things you like to do. When you finish, exchange your collages and use them to introduce each other to the class.

# 6 | Write a profile

**Leer Escribir**

You are collecting information for this school's Web site. Read the questionnaire and write a profile of this student. Include his name, where he is from, and what he likes and doesn't like to do.

**Escuela Secundaria Cuauhtémoc**
Cuestionario estudiantil

Nombre: Esteban Leñeros

País de origen: México

**ACTIVIDADES**

¿Qué te gusta hacer? practicar deportes, estudiar, comer enchiladas, escuchar música

¿Qué no te gusta hacer? andar en patineta, comer helado, dibujar

# México

## ¡Vamos a la escuela!

## Lección 1
### Tema: **Somos estudiantes**

## Lección 2
### Tema: **En la escuela**

«¡*Hola!*
**Somos Pablo y Claudia.
Somos de México.**»

Estados Unidos

• Ciudad Juárez

• Chihuahua

BAJA
CALIFORNIA

Golfo de
México

*Golfo de California*

• Monterrey

México

Bahía de
Campeche

Chichén Itzá

Zempoala

*Océano
Pacífico*

• San Miguel de Allende

PENÍNSULA
DE YUCATÁN

Guadalajara •

México, D.F. ★

• Puebla

Oaxaca •

**Guatemala**

**El Salvador**

**Población:** 109.955.400

**Área:** 761.606 millas cuadradas

**Capital:** México, D.F. (Ciudad de México)

**Moneda:** el peso mexicano

**Idiomas:** español, maya y otras lenguas
indígenas; el país con más hispanohablantes
del mundo

**Comida típica:** tortillas, tacos, enchiladas

**Gente famosa:** Carlos Fuentes (escritor), Salma Hayek
(actriz), Mario Molina (químico), Thalía (cantante)

*Chocolate*

*Jóvenes en el Jardín Principal
de San Miguel de Allende*

◄ **Un rato con familia y amigos** In San Miguel de Allende, people of all ages go to the **Jardín Principal,** a tree-lined park in the center of town, to stroll, listen to live music, and spend time with family and friends. *When you want to spend time outside, where do you go?*

**Las ruinas de Chichén Itzá** The ruins of the ancient Mayan city of Chichén Itzá include structures built for worship, sports, and studying astronomy. The pyramid of **Kukulcán** was used as a temple. *What are some important buildings in your area used for?* ►

*La estatua de Chac-Mool y la pirámide de Kukulcán*

◄ **Una universidad con mucha historia y arte** La Universidad **Nacional Autónoma de México (UNAM)** is one of the oldest universities in the Americas, and the largest public university in Mexico, with over 270,000 students. The library's mosaic mural depicts moments in the cultural history of Mexico. *What are some well-known universities in your area?*

*La biblioteca de la UNAM
con el mural mosaico*

# México

## Lección **1**

*Tema:*

# Somos estudiantes

**¡AVANZA!**

## In this lesson you will learn to
- talk about daily schedules
- ask and tell time
- say what you have and have to do
- say what you do and how often you do things

### using
- the verb **tener** and **tener que**
- expressions of frequency
- present tense of **-ar** verbs

### ♺ *¿Recuerdas?*
- after-school activities
- days of the week

## Comparación cultural

### In this lesson you will learn about
- what students wear to school
- Mexican mural painter Diego Rivera
- courses in a school in Mexico

### Compara con tu mundo
These Mexican students are walking to school through a **zócalo,** or a town square. These are very common in Mexico and other Spanish-speaking countries, where they are also called **plazas.** *Does your city or town have a main square? If not, is there a central meeting place?*

### *¿Qué ves?*
*Mira la foto*
¿Hace sol?
¿Es domingo o lunes?
¿Cómo es el estudiante? ¿Y la estudiante?

**La fuente de San Miguel en el Zócalo**
*Puebla, México*

# Presentación de VOCABULARIO

**Goal:** Learn about Pablo's school and class schedule. Then practice what you have learned to talk about daily schedules. *Actividades 1–2*

**VIDEO DVD**

**AUDIO**

**A** ¡Hola! Me llamo Pablo. Mi amiga es Claudia. Somos estudiantes **en** Puebla, México. Me gusta **llegar** a clase **temprano**. Claudia, **¿qué hora es?**

7:00 matemáticas
8:10 ciencias
9:15 usar la computadora
10:15 inglés
11:50 arte
12:30 historia
1:30 español
3:30 jugar al fútbol

**el horario**

### Numbers from 11 to 100

| | | |
|---|---|---|
| **11** once | **20** veinte | **30** treinta |
| **12** doce | **21** veintiuno | **31** treinta y uno |
| **13** trece | **22** veintidós | |
| **14** catorce | **23** veintitrés | **40** cuarenta |
| **15** quince | **24** veinticuatro | **50** cincuenta |
| **16** dieciséis | **25** veinticinco | **60** sesenta |
| **17** diecisiete | **26** veintiséis | **70** setenta |
| **18** dieciocho | **27** veintisiete | **80** ochenta |
| **19** diecinueve | **28** veintiocho | **90** noventa |
| | **29** veintinueve | **100** cien |

### Más vocabulario

**de vez en cuando** *once in a while*
**muchas veces** *often, many times*
**nunca** *never*
**todos los días** *every day*
**casi** *almost*
**difícil** *difficult*
**fácil** *easy*
**hay...** *there is, there are . . .*
**la hora** *hour; time*
**el minuto** *minute*
**¿Cuántos(as)...?** *How many . . . ?*
*Expansión de vocabulario* p. R3

**B** ¿**A qué hora son** mis clases? Tengo **muchas** clases.

las matemáticas

La clase de **matemáticas** es **a las siete** de la mañana.

las ciencias

La clase de **ciencias** es **a las ocho y diez** de la mañana.

el inglés

La clase de **inglés** es **a las diez y cuarto** de la mañana.

el arte

La clase de **arte** es **a las doce menos diez** de la mañana.

la historia

La clase de **historia** es **a las doce y media** de la tarde.

el español

La clase de **español** es **a la una y media** de la tarde.

Continuará...

Lección 1
noventa y cinco **95**

**C** **Son las** ocho y diez y tengo la clase de ciencias. A Claudia **siempre** le gusta **contestar** las preguntas del maestro. Ella es muy inteligente. Yo **tengo que** estudiar **mucho** y **tomar apuntes** en clase.

contestar

enseñar

tomar apuntes

**D** Tengo que **sacar una buena nota** en la clase de inglés. A Claudia y a mí nos gusta estudiar a las ocho **de la noche.** Es un poco **tarde** pero **necesito** estudiar. ¡No me gusta **sacar una mala nota**!

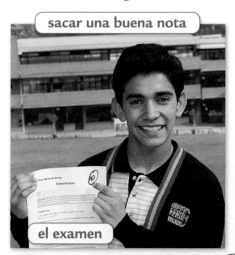

sacar una buena nota

el examen

usar la computadora

¡A responder! Escuchar

On separate pieces of paper, write the words **la mañana** and **la tarde.** Listen to Pablo describe his schedule. Hold up the piece of paper that indicates when he has each class.

*@HomeTutor* VideoPlus
**Interactive Flashcards**
ClassZone.com

# Práctica de VOCABULARIO

## 1 | Las clases de Claudia

Hablar
Escribir

Identify Claudia's classes according to the time.

modelo: a la una y diez
A la una y diez Claudia tiene la clase de español.

1:10

 8:40

 9:15

 10:45 _1_

 12:00 _3_

7:30 _2_

2:30

1. a las once menos cuarto _tene la clase_
2. a las siete y media _la clase de ciencia_
3. a las doce _tiene la clase de historia_
4. a las nueve menos veinte _tiene la clase de arte_
5. a las nueve y cuarto _tiene la clase de mathmaticas_
6. a las dos y media _tienes la back clase de musica_

_1#_

### Nota gramatical

For the numbers **21, 31,** and so on, use **veintiún, treinta y un,** and so on before a masculine noun and **veintiuna, treinta y una,** and so on before a feminine noun.

Hay **veintiún** maestros en la escuela.
*There are **twenty-one** teachers in the school.*

Hay **treinta y una** personas en mi clase.
*There are **thirty-one** people in my class.*

## 2 | ¿Cuántas personas?

Hablar

Ask a partner how many people there are in these classes.

modelo: chicos / historia
y arte (29)

**A** ¿Cuántos chicos hay en las clases de historia y arte?

**B** Hay veintinueve chicos en las clases de historia y arte.

1. chicas / matemáticas (16)
2. estudiantes / inglés y arte (58)
3. chicos / historia y ciencias (27)
4. estudiantes / historia y arte (62)
5. chicas / música y español (33)
6. estudiantes / arte (40)
7. chicas / todas las clases (71)
8. chicos / todas las clases (74)

*Más práctica*   Cuaderno *pp. 51–53*   Cuaderno para hispanohablantes *pp. 51–54*

**PARA Y PIENSA**

**Did you get it?**
1. Tell someone you like to draw in art class.
2. Say that there are 23 boys in math class.

**Get Help Online**
ClassZone.com

# VOCABULARIO *en contexto*

**Goal:** Listen to how Pablo and Claudia talk about at what time they will study. Then practice these words to ask and tell time. *Actividades 3–4*

## Telehistoria escena 1

**@HomeTutor** VideoPlus
**View, Read and Record**
ClassZone.com

### STRATEGIES

**Cuando lees**

**Focus on time** Read for expressions of time like **hoy** or **a las ocho.** How many can you find in this scene? What do they mean?

**Cuando escuchas**

**Listen for questions** Listen to find all the questions in this scene. Who asks most of the questions? What does that person ask about?

VIDEO
DVD

AUDIO

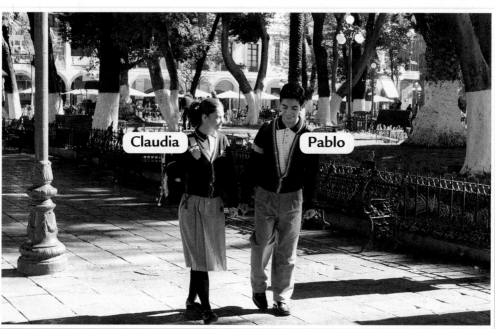

Claudia        Pablo

**Claudia:** Pablo, hay examen de ciencias mañana, ¿no?

**Pablo:** Sí... Me gusta la clase de ciencias, pero... sacar una buena nota, un 90 o un 100, ¡es difícil!

**Claudia:** Necesitas estudiar una o dos horas... ¿Te gusta estudiar con amigos?

**Pablo:** Sí... pero hoy no. ¡Hay fútbol! ¿Mañana?

**Claudia:** Sí. ¿En la escuela?

**Pablo:** Sí. ¿A las ocho de la mañana? ¿O más temprano?

**Claudia:** A las siete de la mañana. ¿Está bien?

**Pablo:** ¡Sí!

*The bell rings, and they part ways for class.*

**Pablo:** Hmmm... Hay chicas muy inteligentes en la escuela...

**Continuará...** p. 104

# 3 | Planes para estudiar *Comprensión del episodio*

True or false? If the statement is false, say what is true.

**1.** Hay un examen en la clase de español mañana.

**2.** A Pablo le gusta estudiar con amigos, pero hoy no.

**3.** A Pablo le gusta la clase de ciencias.

**4.** Hay fútbol hoy.

**5.** La clase de ciencias es fácil.

## Nota gramatical

- Use **Es la una** to say that it is one o'clock; use **Son las...** for any other time.

    **Son las** cinco.    *It is 5:00.*

- Use **y** + **minutes** for the number of minutes after the hour (up to 30).

    Son las dos **y diez.**    *It is 2:10.*

- Use **menos** + **minutes** for the number of minutes before the hour.

    Es la una **menos veinte.**    *It is 12:40.*

- Use **y** or **menos cuarto** for a quarter of an hour and **y media** for half an hour.

- To say at what time something happens, use **a la(s)...**

    La clase de arte es **a la** una y la clase de inglés es **a las** dos.

# 4 | El horario de clases

Escribir

Write the times of Marisol's classes.

**modelo:** La clase de historia es a las siete de la mañana.

| MARISOL AGUILAR | |
|---|---|
| **HORA** | **LUNES** |
| 7:00 | HISTORIA |
| 8:15 | MATEMÁTICAS |
| 9:30 | INGLÉS |
| 10:45 | ARTE |
| | |
| 1:05 | CIENCIAS |
| 2:10 | ESPAÑOL |

PARA Y PIENSA

**Did you get it?** Complete each sentence with the appropriate time.

**1.** El jueves Claudia tiene que llegar a la escuela _____ . (10:15)

**2.** Son _____ . (8:20)

**3.** A Pablo le gusta hacer la tarea _____ de la noche. (7:00)

**Get Help Online**
ClassZone.com

# Presentación de GRAMÁTICA

**¡AVANZA!**

**Goal:** Learn how to form the verb **tener.** Then use this verb to say what people have and have to do and how often. *Actividades 5–9*

♻ *¿Recuerdas?* After-school activities p. 32

**English Grammar Connection: Conjugating** is changing the forms of a verb to indicate who is doing the action. For example, the English verb *to have* is conjugated as *I have, you have, he/she/it has, we have, they have.*

Claudia **has** a computer.            Claudia **tiene** una computadora.

⬆                                                      ⬆

**conjugated verb**                         **conjugated verb**

## The Verb tener

**Animated** Grammar
ClassZone.com

Use the verb **tener** to talk about what you have.
How do you conjugate this verb?

*Here's how:*

| tener  *to have* | | | |
|---|---|---|---|
| yo | **tengo** | nosotros(as) | **tenemos** |
| tú | **tienes** | vosotros(as) | **tenéis** |
| usted, él, ella | **tiene** | ustedes, ellos(as) | **tienen** |

**Tenemos** clase el lunes.            ¿**Tienes** una bicicleta?
*We have* class on Monday.            *Do you have* a bike?

**Tener + que + infinitive** is used to talk about what someone has to do.

**Tengo que estudiar.**                  Miguel **tiene que leer** un libro.
*I have to* study.                            *Miguel has to read a book.*

---

*Más práctica*

🚀 **Conjuguemos.com**

Cuaderno *pp. 54–56*
Cuaderno para hispanohablantes *pp. 55–57*

**@HomeTutor**
Leveled Practice
ClassZone.com

# Práctica de GRAMÁTICA

## 5 | Los amigos de Raquel

**Leer**
**Escribir**

Use the appropriate forms of the verb **tener** to complete Raquel's description of her closest friends.

Yo __1.__ muchos amigos diferentes. Mi mejor amigo, Rafael, es un estudiante muy serio. Él __2.__ seis clases muy difíciles, y __3.__ que estudiar muchas horas todos los días. Mis amigas Clara y Linda son altas y __4.__ pelo castaño. ¡Son muy atléticas! Los lunes, martes y miércoles ellas __5.__ que practicar fútbol. Los viernes, mis amigos y yo __6.__ que trabajar. ¿Qué tipo de amigos __7.__ tú?

## 6 | Las clases

**Escribir**

Write what classes these people have, using forms of **tener.**

**1.** yo

**2.** nosotros

**3.** Claudia y Pablo

**4.** tú

**5.** Claudia

**6.** ustedes

---

**Pronunciación** **El sonido ch**

In Spanish, the **ch** sounds like the *ch* of the English word *chip*.

Listen and repeat.

| | |
|---|---|
| cha | mucha |
| che | noche |
| chi | chico |
| cho | dieciocho |
| chu | churro |

Muchas chicas escuchan música de Pancho Sánchez.

## 7 | ¿Qué tienes?

**Hablar**
Find out what items your partner has in his or her room by forming questions with the verb **tener.** Take turns asking and answering.

modelo: una computadora

**A** ¿Tienes **una computadora**?

**B** Sí, tengo **una computadora**. (No, no tengo **computadora**.)

**1.** un DVD

**5.** un teléfono

**2.** una patineta

**6.** una guitarra

**3.** un refresco

**7.** un libro de matemáticas

**4.** una bicicleta

**8.** una galleta

## 8 | ¿Qué tienen que hacer?

**Escuchar**
**Escribir**
Listen to Pablo's description of what he and his friends have to do. Then write sentences indicating what time it is and who has to do these activities.

**1.** estudiar

**4.** tocar la guitarra

**2.** usar la computadora

**5.** trabajar

**3.** hacer la tarea

**6.** leer un libro

### Comparación cultural

#### Uniformes escolares

*How does the way students dress reflect a culture?* In **Mexico,** it is common for students to wear uniforms in both public and private schools. The type and color of the uniforms can vary depending on the individual school. Most students in the **Dominican Republic** also wear uniforms. Public schools have the same uniforms, while private school uniforms may vary.

**Compara con tu mundo** *Why do some schools require uniforms? Are they common in your community? If you were a principal, would you have uniforms at your school?*

*Estudiantes en México y la República Dominicana*

The expressions of frequency **siempre** and **nunca** are usually placed before the verb.

| | |
|---|---|
| Antonio **siempre** toma apuntes. | Antonio **always** takes notes. |
| Rafael **nunca** llega a clase tarde. | Rafael **never** arrives late to class. |

**Mucho** is usually placed after the verb.

Raquel estudia **mucho**.    Raquel studies **a lot**.

**De vez en cuando, muchas veces,** and **todos los días** are usually placed at the beginning or the end of the sentence.

**Todos los días** Jaime trabaja.    Jaime works **every day**.

Jaime trabaja **todos los días**.

---

**9** | **Las obligaciones**  **¿Recuerdas?** After-school activities p. 32

**Hablar**

Ask other students whether they have to do these activities. They will respond using an expression of frequency.

**A** ¿Tienen que tomar apuntes ustedes?

**B** Sí, tengo que tomar apuntes muchas veces.

**C** Sí, tengo que tomar apuntes de vez en cuando.

**1.**

**2.**

**3.**

**4.**

**5.**

**6.**

*Más práctica*    Cuaderno *pp. 54–56*    Cuaderno para hispanohablantes *pp. 55–57*

**PARA Y PIENSA**

**Did you get it?** Answer each question with the word(s) in parentheses.
1. ¿Tiene que preparar la comida Juan? (nunca)
2. ¿Cuándo tenemos la clase de inglés? (todos los días)
3. ¿Tienes que usar la computadora? (siempre)

 **Get Help Online** ClassZone.com

# GRAMÁTICA *en contexto*

**Goal:** Notice how Pablo and Claudia use the verb phrase **tener que** to talk about what they do at school. Then use **tener** and **tener que** to say what you and others have and have to do. *Actividades 10–12*

♻ *¿Recuerdas?* Days of the week p. 18

## Telehistoria escena 2

@**HomeTutor** VideoPlus
**View, Read and Record**
ClassZone.com

### STRATEGIES

**Cuando lees**
**Find the "tag questions"** This scene contains the "tag question" **¿no?** Where are the tag questions in a sentence? How do they differ from questions like **¿Quién es?**

**Cuando escuchas**
**Weigh the motive** Listen for Pablo's reasons for not studying for the test. What are his reasons? Do they sound credible to you? Have you ever used them?

VIDEO
DVD

AUDIO

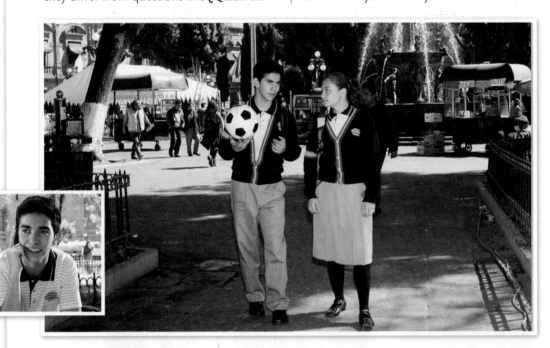

*Pablo's cell phone rings.*

**Pablo:** Hola... ¿Quién es? ¡Claudia! ¿Qué tal?... Sí, sí, a las siete. ¡Tenemos que estudiar mucho!

*The next morning, Claudia and Pablo walk to class.*

**Claudia:** Pablo, tienes que estudiar más, ¿no?

**Pablo:** Sí. Tenemos mucha tarea y los exámenes son muy difíciles.

**Claudia:** Pero te gusta sacar buenas notas, ¿no?

**Pablo:** Sí. Tenemos que estudiar más.

**Continuará...** p. 110

### También se dice

**México** Pablo uses the word **tarea** to talk about homework. In other Spanish-speaking countries you might hear:
· **muchos países** los **deberes**

## 10 | Un examen importante *Comprensión del episodio*

**Escuchar**
**Leer**

Choose the correct answers to the questions.

1. ¿Qué tienen que hacer Pablo
   y Claudia?
   **a.** Tienen que descansar mucho.
   **b.** Tienen que estudiar.
   **c.** Tienen que enseñar.

2. ¿A qué hora tienen que estudiar?
   **a.** a las siete
   **b.** a las siete y media
   **c.** a las ocho

3. ¿Qué tienen Pablo y Claudia?
   **a.** muchos libros
   **b.** un poco de tarea
   **c.** mucha tarea

4. ¿Qué le gusta hacer a Pablo?
   **a.** Le gusta estudiar.
   **b.** Le gusta llegar tarde.
   **c.** Le gusta sacar buenas notas.

## 11 | Las responsabilidades  *¿Recuerdas?* Days of the week p. 18

**Escribir**

You have a lot to do this week. Write an e-mail explaining five things that
you have to do this week.

**modelo:**

Hola, Jeff.
Tengo mucho que hacer. El lunes tengo que practicar
la guitarra. El martes tengo que hacer la tarea...

## 12 | ¿Y tú?

**Hablar**
**Escribir**

Answer the questions in complete sentences.

1. ¿Qué clases tienes? ¿Son fáciles
   o difíciles?

2. ¿A qué hora tienes la clase
   de español?

3. ¿Tienes que tomar apuntes?
   ¿En qué clases?

4. ¿Qué tienes que hacer
   todos los días?

5. ¿Qué tienes que hacer
   todos los sábados y domingos?

6. ¿Qué nunca tienes que hacer?

7. ¿Tienes que trabajar?
   ¿A qué hora?

8. ¿A qué hora necesitas llegar
   a la escuela?

**PARA Y PIENSA**

**Did you get it?** ¿**Tener** or **tener que**? Complete each sentence based on
the Telehistoria with the correct form of the verb or expression.

1. Pablo y Claudia _____ mucha tarea.
2. Pablo _____ estudiar mucho.
3. Ellos _____ un examen en la clase de ciencias.

**Get Help Online**
ClassZone.com

Lección 1
ciento cinco **105**

# Presentación de GRAMÁTICA

**¡AVANZA!** **Goal:** Learn the forms of **-ar** verbs. Then practice using the verbs to say what people do. *Actividades 13–19*

**English Grammar Connection:** A **verb tense** is the form of the verb that shows *when* an action is happening. The **present tense** shows that an action is happening *now*. The Spanish present-tense verb form **estudiamos** can be expressed in English in three different ways: *we study, we are studying,* or *we do study.*

We **study** Spanish.                    **Estudiamos** español.

⬆ **present-tense verb**                    ⬆ **present-tense verb**

## Present Tense of -ar Verbs

**Animated** Grammar
**ClassZone.com**

Many infinitives in Spanish end in **-ar.** How do you form the present tense of these verbs?

**Here's how:** In Spanish, the present tense is formed by changing the ending of the verb.

To form the present tense of a regular verb that ends in **-ar**, drop the **-ar** and add the appropriate **ending.**

**hablar** ◀ o, as, a, amos, áis, or an

| **hablar** *to talk, to speak* | | |
|---|---|---|
| yo | **hablo** | nosotros(as) | **hablamos** |
| tú | **hablas** | vosotros(as) | **habláis** |
| usted, él, ella | **habla** | ustedes, ellos(as) | **hablan** |

**Hablo** inglés.                    ¿**Hablan** español?

*I speak* English.                    *Do they speak* Spanish?
*I am speaking* English.              *Are they speaking* Spanish?
*I do speak* English.

*Más práctica*                     **Conjuguemos.com**

Cuaderno *pp. 57–59*
Cuaderno para hispanohablantes *pp. 58–61*

**@HomeTutor**
**Leveled Practice**
ClassZone.com

# Práctica de GRAMÁTICA

## 13 | ¿Tarde o temprano?

**Escribir**

Claudia is throwing a surprise party for Pablo and wants all the guests to arrive at seven o'clock sharp. Use the cues to state at what time people arrive at the party. Then tell whether they arrive early or late.

> **modelo:** Luis y Carmen / 8:00
> Luis y Carmen llegan a las ocho. Llegan tarde.

**1.** nosotros / 5:30

**2.** Marta / 7:15

**3.** yo / 6:45

**4.** Marcos y Benito / 6:00

**5.** la señora Jiménez / 7:40

**6.** ellas / 9:25

**7.** tú / 6:05

**8.** María y Enrique / 8:10

**9.** Sara y yo / 6:50

**10.** Pablo / 7:20

## 14 | Somos buenos estudiantes

**Hablar Escribir**

Pablo, Claudia, and their friends are good students. Explain whether they always or never do the following.

> **modelo:** Claudia / llegar a clase temprano
> Claudia **siempre** llega a clase temprano.

**1.** yo / escuchar en clase

**2.** Pablo / tomar apuntes

**3.** nosotros / sacar malas notas

**4.** Claudia y Pablo / estudiar

**5.** tú / contestar preguntas

**6.** Diego y yo / llegar a clase tarde

**7.** Lorena / mirar la televisión

**8.** ustedes / sacar buenas notas

## 15 | El fin de semana

**Leer Escribir**

Sandra likes to spend time with her friends. Complete the paragraph with the correct form of the appropriate verb.

escuchar   tocar   alquilar   estudiar

pasar   montar   dibujar   practicar

Nosotros **1.** en bicicleta después de las clases. Amy y Rosa **2.** deportes y yo **3.** la guitarra. A mi amigo Eduardo no le gusta descansar. Él **4.** inglés o **5.** para la clase de arte. Es muy artístico. Si llueve, nosotros **6.** música en un café o **7.** un DVD. ¿Dónde **8.** tú un rato con los amigos?

## 16 | ¿En la escuela?

**Hablar**

Ask another student whether he or she does these activities at school.
Use expressions of frequency.

**modelo:** dibujar

**A** ¿Dibujas en la escuela?

**B** No, nunca dibujo en la escuela.

1. estudiar
2. escuchar música
3. comprar refrescos
4. practicar deportes
5. tocar la guitarra
6. pasar un rato con los amigos

## 17 | De septiembre a mayo

**Hablar**
**Escribir**

Señorita Solar and her students have changed a great deal over the course
of the school year. Look at the two drawings below and note the differences
between the beginning and the end of the school year.

**modelo:** En septiembre, Susana escucha música.
En mayo, ella toma apuntes.

## 18 | ¿Qué estudias?

**Hablar**

### Comparación cultural

#### Los murales en México

*How does society affect public artwork?* The Mexican government commissioned Diego Rivera to paint murals about **Mexico's** history. *Alfabetización* reflects the idea of free public education. Between 1920 and 1924, more than 1,000 schools were established in rural areas to teach children to read and study subjects such as history and math.

#### Compara con tu mundo

*What would you paint in a mural representing your community? What objects or people would you include? What would your mural's message be?*

*Detalle de* Alfabetización *(1926), Diego Rivera*

Talk with a partner about your schedule and what you study.

**A** ¿Estudias ciencias?

**B** Sí, tengo la clase de ciencias a las once.

## 19 | Un sábado típico

**Escribir Hablar**

Describe what you do on Saturdays and how often you do it. Use verbs from the list. Then compare your activities with other students'.

| alquilar | estudiar | descansar | comprar |
|---|---|---|---|

| escuchar | usar | trabajar | ¿ ? |
|---|---|---|---|

**modelo:** Siempre hablo por teléfono los sábados. Muchas veces paso un rato con las amigas. Nosotras alquilamos un DVD...

*Más práctica*   Cuaderno *pp. 57–59*   Cuaderno para hispanohablantes *pp. 58–61*

**PARA Y PIENSA**

**Did you get it?** Complete each sentence with the correct form of the verb in parentheses.

1. Nosotros _____ la computadora mucho. (usar)
2. Yo _____ la comida de vez en cuando. (preparar)
3. Los chicos _____ en la clase de arte. (dibujar)
4. ¿ _____ tú sacar una buena nota? (necesitar)

 **Get Help Online** ClassZone.com

# Todo junto

**Goal: *Show what you know*** Pay attention to how Pablo and Claudia use **tener** and **-ar** verbs to talk about their test and what they do after school. Then use these verbs to say what you and others do during and after school. ***Actividades 20–24***

## Telehistoria completa

**@HomeTutor** VideoPlus
**View, Read and Record**
ClassZone.com

### STRATEGIES

**Cuando lees**

**Look for the unexpected** As you read, look for two surprises involving Pablo. What are they? Why are they unexpected? What did you expect to happen?

**Cuando escuchas**

**Listen for cognates** Listen for cognates like **examen** (exam, test). What cognates do you hear? What English word(s) do they sound like? What do they mean?

**Escena 1** *Resumen*

Pablo y Claudia necesitan estudiar porque tienen un examen de ciencias.

**Escena 2** *Resumen*

Pablo y Claudia hablan por teléfono. Tienen que estudiar más.

VIDEO
DVD

AUDIO

### Escena 3

Roberto

**Pablo:** ¡Claudia! En el examen de ciencias, tengo... ¡un 90!

**Claudia:** ¡Y yo, un 100!

**Pablo:** ¿Estudiamos, tú y yo, todos los días?

**Claudia:** Sí... pero tú necesitas tomar buenos apuntes, ¿no? *(Pablo grins.)* ¿A qué hora practican fútbol?

**Pablo:** Muchas veces practicamos a las cinco. Mañana practicamos temprano, a las tres y media. ¿Y tú? ¿Qué necesitas hacer mañana?

**Claudia:** ¿Mañana? Estudiar y hacer la tarea de ciencias.

*Claudia says goodbye and leaves. As his friend Roberto walks up, Pablo distractedly pulls Alicia's T-shirt out of his bag and puts it on.*

**Roberto:** ¡Ay, Pablo, qué interesante!

*Pablo, embarrassed, takes the shirt off quickly.*

## 20 | ¿Quién es? *Comprensión de los episodios*

Escuchar
Leer

Do these sentences refer to Claudia, Pablo, or Claudia and Pablo? Write the name or names and the correct form of the verb in parentheses.

**Pablo**   **Claudia y Pablo**   **Claudia**

**1.** _____ (tener) que practicar fútbol.

**2.** _____ (llegar) a la escuela a las siete de la mañana.

**3.** _____ (hablar) por teléfono.

**4.** _____ (necesitar) estudiar una o dos horas.

**5.** _____ (tener) un examen de ciencias.

**6.** _____ (sacar) una buena nota.

**7.** _____ (estudiar) para la clase de ciencias mañana.

**8.** _____ (practicar) a las tres y media mañana.

## 21 | ¿Qué hacen? *Comprensión de los episodios*

Escuchar
Leer

Complete the sentences with information from the episodes.

**1.** Pablo y Claudia tienen que...

**2.** A las siete Pablo y Claudia...

**3.** Mañana Claudia...

**4.** Pablo necesita tomar...

**5.** Claudia y Pablo sacan...

## 22 | ¿Qué tienes que hacer?

Hablar

> **STRATEGY Hablar**
> **Create a dialogue of your own** Use the model question and substitute different school subjects. Use the model answer, but change verbs, or use multiple verbs in a single sentence. Bring in humor if you can.

Talk with a partner about what you do and what you have to do in your classes.

**A** ¿Qué tienes que hacer en la clase de matemáticas?

**B** Tengo que tomar apuntes. Siempre escucho en clase...

Lección 1
ciento once **111**

## 23 | Integración

Leer
Escuchar
Hablar

Tomorrow is a teachers' meeting, so the class schedule is different. Read Manuel's schedule and listen to the principal's message. Tell at what time Manuel needs to arrive at each of his classes.

**Fuente 1  Horario de clases**

| Rojas, Manuel | | Colegio Benito Juárez |
|---|---|---|
| **HORA** | **CLASE** | **MAESTRO** |
| 7:10 | ciencias | Sra. Burgos |
| 8:30 | arte | Sr. Rivera |
| 9:50 | inglés | Sr. Ortiz |
| 11:10 | historia | Sra. Sánchez |
| 1:20 | español | Sr. Acevedo |
| 2:40 | matemáticas | Sra. Gala |

**Fuente 2  Mensaje del director**

**Listen and take notes**
- ¿Cuántos minutos después de la hora normal son las clases de la mañana? ¿Las clases de la tarde?

**modelo:** Manuel necesita llegar a la clase de... a las...

## 24 | Tu horario

Escribir

Describe your school schedule. What classes do you have? At what times? What do you have to do every day? What do you do once in a while? What activities do you never do in class?

**modelo:** Tengo muchas clases en mi horario. Tengo la clase de español todos los días a las nueve menos cuarto. Llego a clase temprano...

| Writing Criteria | Excellent | Good | Needs Work |
|---|---|---|---|
| **Content** | Your description includes a lot of information. | Your description includes some information. | Your description includes little information. |
| **Communication** | Most of your description is organized and easy to follow. | Parts of your description are organized and easy to follow. | Your description is disorganized and hard to follow. |
| **Accuracy** | Your description has few mistakes in grammar and vocabulary. | Your description has some mistakes in grammar and vocabulary. | Your description has many mistakes in grammar and vocabulary. |

*Más práctica*   Cuaderno *pp. 60–61*   Cuaderno para hispanohablantes *pp. 62–63*

**PARA Y PIENSA**

**Did you get it?** Write the correct form of **tomar, estudiar,** or **practicar.**

1. Claudia siempre _____ buenos apuntes.
2. Pablo tiene que _____ fútbol a las cinco.
3. Pablo y Claudia _____ todos los días.

**Get Help Online**
ClassZone.com

# Juegos y diversiones

Review numbers by playing a game.

# Silencio

## The Setup

The object of this game is to demonstrate understanding without speaking. For each round of play, your teacher will give each player an index card with a number written out in Spanish.

Your teacher will divide the class into several teams with one or two members of each team competing at a given time.

## Playing the Game

Each round will have a different number line for highest and lowest. You will be asked to silently line up in order according to what is on your index card and where your card fits in the number line. Your teacher will use a timer, so you need to line up quickly or you will be disqualified and not have a chance to gain points.

## The Winner!

Each student who lines up correctly will gain a point. The team with the most points at the end wins.

### Materials

- index cards with Spanish words for various numbers
- timer
- cards for number line

Lección 1
ciento trece
**113**

# Lectura

AUDIO

# Una escuela internacional en México

The following pages are from the student handbook for Colegio Internacional.

**STRATEGY Leer**

**Use what you know** As you read the graduation requirements of Colegio Internacional, use what you know. Find words that sound and look somewhat similar to those in English — cognates like **ciencias** or **matemáticas.** Then use the context and what you already know to guess what **desarrollo humano** and **optativas** mean.

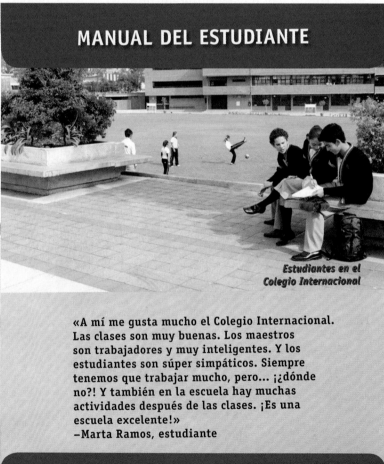

**MANUAL DEL ESTUDIANTE**

Estudiantes en el
Colegio Internacional

«A mí me gusta mucho el Colegio Internacional. Las clases son muy buenas. Los maestros son trabajadores y muy inteligentes. Y los estudiantes son súper simpáticos. Siempre tenemos que trabajar mucho, pero... ¡¿dónde no?! Y también en la escuela hay muchas actividades después de las clases. ¡Es una escuela excelente!»
—Marta Ramos, estudiante

**COLEGIO INTERNACIONAL**

**114** Unidad 2 México
ciento catorce

## Requisitos para graduarse de bachillerato

A continuación[1], los requisitos para graduarse con los dos certificados: el certificado mexicano y el certificado estadounidense.

| Clase | Número de unidades |
|---|---|
| Inglés | 4 unidades |
| Español | 4 unidades |
| Matemáticas | 4 unidades |
| Ciencias | 4 unidades |
| Ciencias Sociales de México | 1 unidad |
| Historia de México II | 1 unidad |
| Geografía de México | 1 unidad |
| Derecho[2] | 1 unidad |
| Ciencias Sociales | 3 unidades |
| Computación | 0,5 unidades |
| Educación Física | 0,5 unidades |
| Desarrollo Humano[3] | 1 unidad |
| Optativas[4] | 2 unidades |
| **Total** | **27 unidades** |

### COLEGIO INTERNACIONAL

---

[1] **A...** following are    [2] Law
[3] Human Development    [4] Electives

PARA Y PIENSA

## ¿Comprendiste?
**1.** ¿Cuántas clases necesitas para los dos programas?
**2.** ¿Cuántas unidades de matemáticas tienes que tomar?

## ¿Y tú?
¿Qué clases del Colegio Internacional hay en tu escuela? ¿Cómo son?

## El pueblo de Zempoala

In 1577, the Spanish crown sent a questionnaire to Mexico to get information about its territories in the New World. The responses that were sent back included local maps drawn by indigenous mapmakers.

The map below depicts the town (**pueblo**) of Zempoala, located in the modern Mexican state of Hidalgo. Research Zempoala to learn more about the town and this map. Then choose three specific map symbols not listed in the legend (**leyenda**) and explain what you think they mean.

**El mapa de Zempoala**

MÉXICO

Zempoala, Hidalgo

México, D.F.

*Símbolo del nombre Zempoala*

**leyenda**

*un pueblo o un barrio*

*el gobernador de un pueblo*

### Proyecto 1 *El arte*

Draw a map of your town or city similar to the one of Zempoala. Give information about people, buildings, roads, and vegetation. Use symbols like the ones in the map above and label them in Spanish.

### Proyecto 2 *Las ciencias sociales*

In 1968, Mexico established a televised system of secondary schools called **Telesecundaria.** Today, educational video programs are broadcast via satellite to more than 15,000 schools. Write two paragraphs about the use of technology in education. How is it used in your school? Can you think of other ways it can be used in education?

### Proyecto 3 *La salud*

The map of Zempoala shows a number of cacti. The cactus has been an important source of food and medicine for people in Mexico for many years. Make a list of different types of cacti found in Mexico and create a chart showing how people have used them for health and beauty purposes.

*Un nopal con flores*

# En resumen
## Vocabulario y gramática

## Vocabulario

### Tell Time and Discuss Daily Schedules

| | | | |
|---|---|---|---|
| ¿A qué hora es...? | At what time is...? | la hora | hour; time |
| ¿Qué hora es? | What time is it? | el horario | schedule |
| A la(s)... | At... o'clock. | menos | to, before (telling time) |
| Es la... / Son las... | It is... o'clock. | | |
| de la mañana | in the morning (with a time) | el minuto | minute |
| | | ...y cuarto | quarter past |
| de la tarde | in the afternoon (with a time) | ...y (diez) | (ten) past |
| | | ...y media | half past |
| de la noche | at night (with a time) | | |

### Describe Frequency

| | |
|---|---|
| de vez en cuando | once in a while |
| muchas veces | often, many times |
| mucho | a lot |
| nunca | never |
| siempre | always |
| todos los días | every day |

### Describe Classes

**School Subjects**

| | |
|---|---|
| el arte | art |
| las ciencias | science |
| el español | Spanish |
| la historia | history |
| el inglés | English |
| las matemáticas | math |

**Classroom Activities**

| | |
|---|---|
| contestar | to answer |
| enseñar | to teach |
| llegar | to arrive |
| necesitar | to need |
| sacar una buena / mala nota | to get a good / bad grade |
| tomar apuntes | to take notes |
| usar la computadora | to use the computer |

### Other Words and Phrases

| | |
|---|---|
| casi | almost |
| ¿Cuántos(as)...? | How many...? |
| difícil | difficult |
| en | in |
| el examen (pl. los exámenes) | exam, test |
| fácil | easy |
| hay... | there is, there are... |
| muchos(as) | many |
| tarde | late |
| temprano | early |
| tener que | to have to |

**Numbers from 11 to 100** *p. 94*

## Gramática

**Notas gramaticales:** Numbers *p. 97,* Telling time *p. 99,* Expressions of frequency *p. 103*

### The Verb tener

Use the verb **tener** to talk about what you have.

| tener *to have* | | | |
|---|---|---|---|
| yo | **tengo** | nosotros(as) | **tenemos** |
| tú | **tienes** | vosotros(as) | **tenéis** |
| usted, él, ella | **tiene** | ustedes, ellos(as) | **tienen** |

**Tener + que + infinitive** is used to talk about what someone has to do.

### Present Tense of -ar Verbs

To form the present tense of a regular verb that ends in **-ar**, drop the **-ar** and add the appropriate **ending**.

| hablar *to talk, to speak* | | | |
|---|---|---|---|
| yo | **hablo** | nosotros(as) | **hablamos** |
| tú | **hablas** | vosotros(as) | **habláis** |
| usted, él, ella | **habla** | ustedes, ellos(as) | **hablan** |

# Repaso de la lección

¡LLEGADA!

**Now you can**
- talk about daily schedules
- ask and tell time
- say what you have and have to do
- say what you do and how often you do things

**Using**
- the verb **tener** and **tener que**
- expressions of frequency
- present tense of **-ar** verbs

---

**To review**
- the verb **tener** and **tener que** p. 100
- expressions of frequency p. 103
- present tense of **-ar** verbs p. 106

AUDIO

## 1 | Listen and understand

Listen to Martín and Lupe talk about their classes. Then match the questions and answers.

1. ¿Qué hora es?
2. ¿A qué hora es la clase de historia?
3. ¿En qué clase tiene que sacar una buena nota Martín?
4. ¿En qué clases contestan muchas preguntas?
5. ¿Cómo es la maestra de ciencias?
6. ¿En qué clase usan la computadora?

a. joven
b. en la clase de ciencias
c. Son las diez y cuarto.
d. Es a las diez y media.
e. en las clases de historia y ciencias
f. en la clase de historia

---

**To review**
- the verb **tener** and **tener que** p. 100

## 2 | Say what you have and have to do

Tell what classes Beto and his friends have at these times and what they have to do.

**8:00**  modelo: Adela: arte / dibujar
Adela tiene la clase de arte a las ocho.
Tiene que dibujar.

1. **9:15** yo: historia / tomar muchos apuntes

2. **10:30** ustedes: matemáticas / estudiar los problemas

3. **11:45** tú: español / hablar español

4. **1:20** David y yo: inglés / contestar muchas preguntas

5. **2:15** Lilia: ciencias / usar la computadora

6. **3:30** Eva y Víctor: música / tocar la guitarra

To review
• present tense of
-ar verbs p. 106

## 3 | Talk about daily schedules

Read the information about Pati León. Then complete the information with the correct form of the verbs in parentheses.

Mi horario es muy bueno. Yo __1.__ (trabajar) mucho los lunes, martes y miércoles. Los jueves Gustavo y yo __2.__ (andar) en patineta. Los viernes Gustavo __3.__ (descansar), pero yo __4.__ (montar) en bicicleta con Eloísa y Héctor. Ellos __5.__ (practicar) deportes casi todos los días. Los viernes nosotros __6.__ (comprar) una pizza y __7.__ (mirar) la televisión. ¿Y los sábados y domingos? Muchas veces mis amigos y yo __8.__ (pasear). ¿Y tú? ¿También __9.__ (pasar) un rato con los amigos los sábados y domingos?

To review
• expressions of
  frequency p. 103
• present tense of
  -ar verbs p. 106

## 4 | Say what you do and how often you do things

Write sentences telling how often these people do the following activities.

| 0 días | 1 – 2 días | 3 – 4 días | 5 – 6 días | 7 días |
|---|---|---|---|---|
| nunca | de vez en cuando | muchas veces | casi siempre | todos los días |

**modelo:** nosotros / mirar un DVD (2 días)
Miramos un DVD de vez en cuando.

1. Roberta / contestar preguntas (0 días)
2. tú / hablar español (5 días)
3. Nicolás / practicar deportes (6 días)
4. yo / escuchar música (3 días)
5. Carlos y Pilar / estudiar historia (2 días)
6. nosotros / tocar la guitarra (4 días)
7. los maestros / usar la computadora (7 días)

## 5 | Mexico and the Dominican Republic

### Comparación cultural

Answer these culture questions.

1. What is Chichén Itzá and what can you find there?
2. What are **zócalos**?
3. What do many students in Mexico and the Dominican Republic wear to school?
4. What does the mural *Alfabetización* represent?

*Más práctica* Cuaderno *pp. 62–73* Cuaderno para hispanohablantes *pp. 64–73*

**Get Help Online**
ClassZone.com

# México

## Lección 2

**Tema:**

## En la escuela

**¡AVANZA!** **In this lesson you will learn to**

- describe classes and classroom objects
- say where things are located
- say where you are going
- talk about how you feel

*using*

- the verb **estar**
- the conjugated verb before the subject to ask a question
- the verb **ir**

♲ *¿Recuerdas?*

- class subjects
- telling time

## Comparación cultural

### In this lesson you will learn about
- museums of anthropology and artist Frida Kahlo
- schools in Mexico, the Dominican Republic, and Paraguay
- Huichol yarn painting and Taino rock art

### Compara con tu mundo
School years vary from country to country. Mexican students go to school from the end of August until June, with short breaks in December and April. *How is this different or similar to your school year?*

### ¿Qué ves?

*Mira la foto*

¿Hay una escuela en la foto?

¿Pablo dibuja o escucha música?

¿Qué practican las chicas?

**El patio de una escuela secundaria**
*México*

# Presentación de VOCABULARIO

**¡AVANZA!**

**Goal:** Learn about Pablo and Claudia's school and how they spend their day. Then practice what you have learned to talk about your school day. **Actividades 1–3**

VIDEO
DVD

AUDIO

**A** La clase de historia no es **aburrida** porque la maestra es **interesante.** La clase es **divertida** pero es difícil. **Cuando** una clase no es fácil, tengo que trabajar mucho. Necesito sacar buenas notas.

el reloj

el pizarrón

la ventana

el mapa

la tiza

el borrador

la silla

el escritorio

**B** En la escuela siempre tengo mi **mochila.**

el cuaderno

la pluma

el papel

el lápiz

la calculadora

la mochila

**En México se dice...**

In Mexico the word for *chalk* is **el gis.**

**C** Mi escuela es grande. Hay **una cafetería**, **un gimnasio** y **una biblioteca**.

la cafetería

el gimnasio

la biblioteca

los baños

el pasillo

la oficina del director

---

### Más vocabulario

¿(A)dónde? *(To) Where?*  ocupado(a) *busy*

¿Cuándo? *When?*  el problema *problem*

deprimido(a) *depressed*  la puerta *door*

emocionado(a) *excited*

*Expansión de vocabulario* p. R3

Continuará...

# Presentación de VOCABULARIO

*(continuación)*

**D** Me gusta pasar un rato con Claudia en la biblioteca. Claudia usa la computadora pero yo tengo que estudiar.

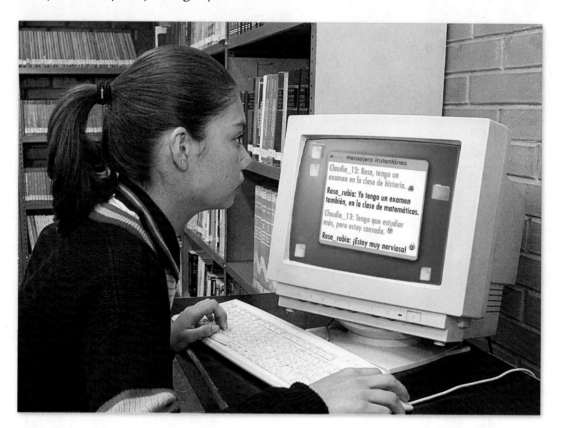

mensajero instantáneo

Claudia_13: Rosa, tengo un examen en la clase de historia.

Rosa_rubia: Yo tengo un examen también, en la clase de matemáticas.

Claudia_13: Tengo que estudiar más, pero estoy cansada.

Rosa_rubia: ¡Estoy muy nerviosa!

cansado(a)

nervioso(a)

contento(a)

enojado(a)

triste

tranquilo(a)

**¡A responder!** Escuchar

Listen to the list of adjectives and draw a face representing each one.

# Práctica de VOCABULARIO

## 1 | Para la escuela

Hablar
Escribir

What do they have at Tienda Martínez? Name the items.

PARA LA ESCUELA...

250 pesos

3 pesos

5 por 30 pesos

2 por 80 pesos

300 pesos

5 por 10 pesos

Tenemos todo para tus clases en
TIENDA MARTÍNEZ
Avenida Hermanos Soriano 80, Puebla, México

## 2 | ¿Qué lugar es?

Leer
Escribir

Claudia is talking about various places in the school. Complete the sentences with the appropriate place words.

| biblioteca | gimnasio | oficina del director |

| cafetería | baños | clase |

En el gimnasio hay dos __1.__, uno para chicas y uno para chicos. Tenemos que correr y practicar deportes en el __2.__. Hay muchos libros en la __3.__. Nos gusta comer pizza y pasar un rato con los amigos en la __4.__. Hablamos con el director en la __5.__. Hay escritorios y pizarrones en la __6.__.

## 3 | ¿Cuántos hay en la clase?

Hablar

Talk with another student about objects in the classroom.

| puerta | ventana | mapa | pizarrón |

| tiza | escritorio | reloj | ¿ ? |

modelo: mapa

A ¿Cuántos mapas hay en la clase?

B Hay tres mapas en la clase.

*Más práctica*   Cuaderno *pp. 74–76*   Cuaderno para hispanohablantes *pp. 74–77*

**PARA Y PIENSA**

**Did you get it?**
1. Name three rooms in your school.
2. Name three objects you could find in your classroom.

Get Help Online
ClassZone.com

# VOCABULARIO en contexto

**¡AVANZA!**

**Goal:** Identify the words Pablo and Claudia use to talk about what they do after school. Then use the words you have learned to describe classes and classroom objects. *Actividades 4–5*

 *¿Recuerdas?* Class subjects p. 95

## Telehistoria escena 1

@**HomeTutor** VideoPlus
View, Read and Record
ClassZone.com

**STRATEGIES**

**Cuando lees**
**Look for exclamations** Many sentences below are exclamations. Exclamations reveal emphasis, warning, or emotions. How many exclamation-type sentences can you find? Why is each one used?

**Cuando escuchas**
**Listen for emotions** What different emotions do Claudia and Pablo show? How do they express them? How would you feel in their place?

VIDEO
DVD

AUDIO

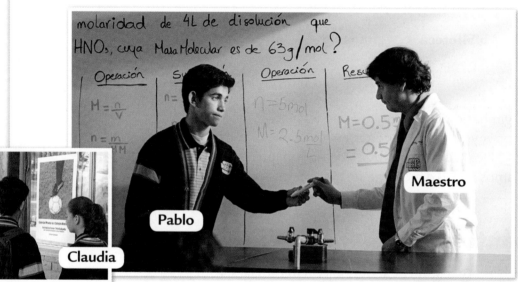

Claudia

Pablo

Maestro

*A poster announces Trini Salgado's guest appearance in the school gym.*

**Maestro:** Trini Salgado, ¿eh? ¿Y vas tú al gimnasio?

**Pablo:** ¡Sí!

**Maestro:** ¡Muy divertido! *(later on in science class...)* ¿Quién contesta la pregunta? ¿Pablo? Bueno, ¡al pizarrón!

*Pablo tries, but gets the problem wrong. Claudia goes to the board and corrects it. The bell rings and they leave class together.*

**Claudia:** Pablo, ¿vamos a la biblioteca? Estudiamos, hacemos la tarea y llegamos bien al gimnasio... ¡Trini Salgado, Pablo!

**Pablo:** ¡Sí! Necesito estudiar, ¡y tú enseñas muy bien! ¿Y tu mochila? *(He points to her backpack, which she has left in the classroom.)*

**Claudia:** ¡Gracias, Pablo!

**Continuará...** p. 132

### También se dice

**México** The teacher uses the word **pizarrón** to call Pablo to the board. In other Spanish-speaking countries you might hear:
• **muchos países**
  **la pizarra**

## 4 | En clase  *Comprensión del episodio*

Escuchar
Leer

Describe what happens in the episode by matching phrases from each column.

**1.** Pablo no contesta la pregunta

**2.** Después de Pablo, Claudia contesta

**3.** Pablo y Claudia necesitan ir

**4.** Pablo necesita

**5.** Claudia no tiene

**6.** Claudia enseña

**a.** la pregunta en el pizarrón.

**b.** la mochila.

**c.** estudiar con Claudia.

**d.** a la biblioteca y al gimnasio.

**e.** porque el problema es difícil.

**f.** muy bien.

## 5 | ¿Cómo son las clases?  ♻ *¿Recuerdas?* Class subjects p. 95

Hablar

Describe your classes to another student.

**A** ¿Cómo es la clase de español?

**B** Es divertida y fácil.

**1.**

**2.**

**3.**

**4.**

**5.**

**6.**

**PARA Y PIENSA**

**Did you get it?** Tell where Pablo and Claudia are going by writing **la biblioteca** or **el gimnasio**.

1. Pablo y Claudia tienen que estudiar.
2. Pablo necesita practicar fútbol.
3. Ellos necesitan un libro.

 **Get Help Online**
ClassZone.com

# Presentación de GRAMÁTICA

**¡AVANZA!** **Goal:** Learn to use the verb **estar** to talk about location and condition. Then practice using **estar** to say and ask where things are located and how people feel. *Actividades 6–12*

**English Grammar Connection:** There are two ways to say the English verb *to be* in Spanish: **ser** and **estar.** You already learned **ser** (see p. 38).

## The Verb estar

Use **estar** to indicate location and say how people feel.

**Here's how:**

| estar *to be* | | | |
|---|---|---|---|
| yo | **estoy** | nosotros(as) | **estamos** |
| tú | **estás** | vosotros(as) | **estáis** |
| usted, él, ella | **está** | ustedes, ellos(as) | **están** |

Pedro **está** en la cafetería.     *Pedro **is** in the cafeteria.*

Use **estar** with the following words of location.

| | | | |
|---|---|---|---|
| **al lado (de)** | **debajo (de)** | **dentro (de)** | **encima (de)** |
| **cerca (de)** | **delante (de)** | **detrás (de)** | **lejos (de)** |

Use the word **de** after the location word when a specific location is mentioned. When **de** is followed by the word **el,** they combine to form the contraction **del.**

La biblioteca **está al lado** de la cafetería.     La tiza **está encima del** borrador.
*The library **is next to the** cafeteria.*     *The chalk **is on top of the** eraser.*

**Estar** is also used with **adjectives** to say how someone feels at a given moment.

El maestro **está tranquilo.**     Las chicas **están cansadas.**
*The teacher **is** calm.*     *The girls **are** tired.*

♻ **¿Recuerdas?** Adjectives agree in gender and number with the nouns they describe (see p. 72).

---

*Más práctica*     **Conjuguemos.com**
Cuaderno *pp. 77–79*
Cuaderno para hispanohablantes *pp. 78–80*

**@HomeTutor**
**Leveled Practice**
**ClassZone.com**

# Práctica de GRAMÁTICA

## 6 | ¿Dónde están?

Hablar
Escribir

Tell where the people are, according to Pablo.

**modelo:** el señor Díaz
El señor Díaz está en la oficina.

**1.** ustedes

**2.** yo

**3.** Miguel y Alejo

**4.** Sergio

**5.** Claudia y yo

**6.** Cristina y Sarita

## 7 | El horario

Hablar
Escribir

Indicate the most logical place at school for each person to be.

**modelo:** Víctor llega a la escuela.
Está en el pasillo.

**1.** Carlos y Juan dibujan.

**2.** Maya habla español.

**3.** Yo toco la guitarra.

**4.** Nosotros compramos la comida.

**5.** Luz practica deportes.

**6.** Tú necesitas muchos libros.

**7.** Ustedes usan la calculadora.

**8.** El maestro habla con el director.

## Nota gramatical

You already know that you can use rising intonation to ask a yes/no question. You can also switch the position of the **verb** and the **subject** to form a question.

**María tiene** una patineta.          ¿**Tiene María** una patineta?
*María has a skateboard.*              *Does María have a skateboard?*

## 8 | Las emociones

**Hablar**

Talk with another student about how these people are feeling.

modelo: el maestro / nervioso
        el maestro

Ⓐ ¿Está nervioso el maestro?

Ⓑ No, está tranquilo.

**Estudiante Ⓐ**

1. Pablo / tranquilo
2. Claudia / triste
3. los maestros / cansado
4. los amigos / enojado
5. las amigas / emocionado
6. tú / ocupado

Pablo 😌
Claudia 🙁
los maestros 😫
los amigos 😠
las amigas 🙁
yo ¿ ?

## 9 | Las salas del museo

**Hablar**

**Comparación cultural**

*Piedra del Sol*

### El Museo de Antropología

*What do ancient artifacts teach us about a culture?* The National Museum of Anthropology in Mexico City contains artifacts from **Mexico's** many indigenous cultures. A main attraction is the *Piedra del Sol,* or Sun Stone, an Aztec calendar that weighs almost 25 tons. In **Paraguay,** the Andrés Barbero Museum of Ethnography in Asunción contains tools, musical instruments, and artwork from its indigenous cultures.

**Compara con tu mundo** *What items might people find 1,000 years from now that give clues about life in the 21st century? What would you put in a time capsule?*

Use the map to tell a partner where the rooms are located in the museum.

**El Museo Nacional de Antropología**

1. Sala Mexica (Azteca)
2. el patio central
3. la oficina
4. Sala Norte de México
5. Sala Maya
6. Sala Oaxaca
7. Sala Tolteca
8. Sala Teotihuacán
9. Sala Preclásico
10. Sala de Introducción
11. el auditorio

*Un plano de El Museo Nacional de Antropología en la Ciudad de México*

Ⓐ ¿Dónde está la Sala Tolteca?

Ⓑ La Sala Tolteca está al lado de la Sala Teotihuacán.

## 10 | ¿Lejos de la escuela?

**Escribir**

Rewrite the statements below to say that the opposite is true.

1. Nosotros estamos lejos de la escuela.
2. El cuaderno está detrás de la silla.
3. El libro está debajo del escritorio.
4. Los lápices están delante de la mochila.
5. Yo estoy cerca de la biblioteca.
6. La pluma está encima del papel.

## 11 | ¿Cómo estás?

**Hablar Escribir**

Describe how you feel in the following situations.

**modelo:** hablar español
Estoy nerviosa cuando hablo español.

1. pasar un rato con los amigos
2. tener que hacer la tarea
3. sacar una mala nota
4. llegar tarde a clase
5. sacar una buena nota
6. escuchar música
7. mirar la televisión
8. tener un examen
9. practicar deportes
10. estudiar mucho

## 12 | ¿Qué es?

**Hablar**

Give clues about an object in the drawing to another student. He or she has to guess the object.

**A** Está encima del cuaderno. Está al lado del libro.

**B** Es la calculadora.

*Más práctica*  Cuaderno *pp. 77–79*  Cuaderno para hispanohablantes *pp. 78–80*

**PARA Y PIENSA**

**Did you get it?** 1. Tell someone that you are near the windows.
2. Ask Pablo if he is nervous.

*Get Help Online*
ClassZone.com

# GRAMÁTICA en contexto

**Goal:** Listen to how Pablo and Claudia use **estar** to talk about how Pablo feels. Then practice using **estar** to talk about emotions and locations. *Actividades 13–15*

## Telehistoria escena 2

@HomeTutor VideoPlus
View, Read and Record
ClassZone.com

### STRATEGIES

**Cuando lees**
**Read for motives behind actions**
This scene contains a physical action related to Pablo's complaints. What is the action, and what are his complaints? Are his complaints justified?

**Cuando escuchas**
**Listen for feelings** What feelings are mentioned in this scene? How does Pablo explain how he feels? Have you ever felt this way?

VIDEO
DVD

AUDIO

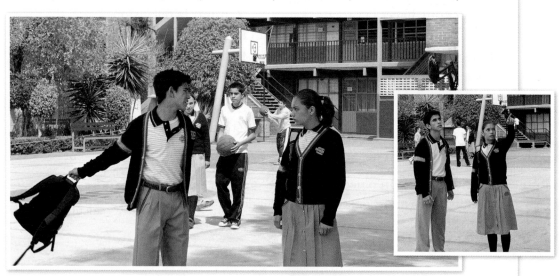

**Claudia:** Eh, Pablo, ¿qué pasa? ¿Estás deprimido? ¿Estás enojado?

**Pablo:** No, no estoy enojado... Estoy nervioso... Tengo que estar en el gimnasio a las cinco pero tengo que hacer la tarea.

*Pablo leaves the library. Later Claudia joins him outside.*

**Pablo:** Ay, Claudia, nunca descanso... Me gusta pasar un rato con los amigos... Y ¡esta mochila!

**Claudia:** ¿Qué pasa?

*Pablo starts swinging his backpack back and forth.*

**Pablo:** Aquí tengo libros, cuadernos, plumas, calculadoras... ¡estoy cansado!

*Suddenly Pablo lets go of his backpack.*

**Pablo:** ¡Ay! ¿Dónde está mi mochila?

**Claudia:** ¡Pablo, tu mochila!

*She points to his backpack, which is caught in a basketball hoop.*

**Continuará...** p. 138

### También se dice

**México** To say he has pens in his backpack, Pablo uses the word **plumas.** In other Spanish-speaking countries you might hear:
· **muchos países** el bolígrafo, el boli

## 13 | El problema de Pablo *Comprensión del episodio*

Escuchar
Leer

Read the sentences and decide whether they are true or false. Correct the false statements.

1. Claudia y Pablo están en la oficina.
2. Pablo está nervioso porque tiene que jugar al fútbol.
3. Claudia tiene que estar en el gimnasio a las cinco.
4. Pablo está enojado.
5. A Claudia y a Pablo les gusta pasar un rato con los amigos.
6. Pablo está deprimido porque tiene libros, cuadernos, plumas y calculadoras en la mochila.

## 14 | ¿Cuándo?

Hablar

Ask another student when he or she feels these emotions.

**A** ¿Cuándo estás triste?

**B** Estoy triste cuando saco una mala nota.

**Estudiante A**

1.    2.

3.    4.

5.    6.

**Estudiante B**

sacar una buena / mala nota
escuchar música
practicar deportes
trabajar
estudiar
¿ ?

## 15 | ¡A jugar! ¿Dónde estoy?

Hablar

Give clues for other students to guess where you are in the school.

**A** Compro papas fritas y jugo. Paso un rato con los amigos. Estoy tranquilo.

**B** ¿Estás en la cafetería?

**PARA Y PIENSA**

**Did you get it?** Give three sentences about Pablo and Claudia using the verb **estar.** Use one of the following words in each sentence: **la biblioteca, nervioso(a), el gimnasio.**

**Get Help Online**
ClassZone.com

# Presentación de GRAMÁTICA

**¡AVANZA!**

**Goal:** Learn how to form the verb **ir** in order to say where you and others are going. Then practice using **ir** to say where you go during and after school. *Actividades 16–21*

**English Grammar Connection:** Remember that **conjugating** is changing the forms of a verb to indicate who is doing the action (see p. 100). In English, *to go* is conjugated as *I go, you go, he/she/it goes, we go, they go.*

Pablo **goes** to the cafeteria at twelve.     Pablo **va** a la cafetería a las doce.

↑                                            ↑

**conjugated verb**                          **conjugated verb**

## The Verb ir

**Animated Grammar**
ClassZone.com

Use **ir** to talk about where someone is going.
How do you form the present tense of this verb?

*Here's how:*

| ir  *to go* | | | |
|------|------|------|------|
| yo | **voy** | nosotros(as) | **vamos** |
| tú | **vas** | vosotros(as) | **vais** |
| usted, él, ella | **va** | ustedes, ellos(as) | **van** |

Use **ir** with the word **a** to say that someone is going to a specific place. When **a** is followed by the word **el,** they combine to form the contraction **al.**

**Voy a la** biblioteca.        Los estudiantes **van al** gimnasio.
*I'm going to the library.*       *The students **are going to the** gym.*

To ask where someone is going, use ¿**adónde**...?

¿**Adónde vas**?
*Where **are you going**?*

*Más práctica*        **Conjuguemos.com**
Cuaderno *pp. 80–82*
Cuaderno para hispanohablantes *pp. 81–84*

**@HomeTutor**
**Leveled Practice**
ClassZone.com

# *Práctica de* GRAMÁTICA

## 16 ¿Un estudiante serio?

**Leer
Escribir**

Claudia and Pablo are talking at school. Complete their conversation with forms of **ir.**

**Claudia:** ¡Tengo mucha tarea en la clase de inglés! Yo __1.__ a la biblioteca... ¿ __2.__ tú y yo?

**Pablo:** No, yo no __3.__ a la biblioteca hoy.

**Claudia:** ¿No __4.__ tú a la biblioteca? ¡Tienes que hacer la tarea!

**Pablo:** Sí, pero necesito comprar pizza y un refresco. Mis amigos y yo __5.__ a la cafetería. Después yo __6.__ al gimnasio y ellos __7.__ a la clase de matemáticas.

**Claudia:** ¿ __8.__ Carlos al gimnasio?

**Pablo:** No, él __9.__ a la biblioteca.

**Claudia:** ¡Ay, Pablo! Tú también necesitas ir. ¿ __10.__ tú y Carlos mañana?

**Pablo:** Sí, todos nosotros __11.__ mañana.

## 17 ¿Por qué vas allí?

**Escribir**

Match the statements with the places the people would go. Then write a sentence saying that they are going to these places.

1. Claudia tiene una calculadora.
2. Yo necesito libros.
3. A ti te gusta practicar deportes.
4. Nosotros tenemos lápices para dibujar.
5. A Pablo le gusta comer pizza.
6. Los amigos llegan tarde a la escuela.

  **a.** la clase de arte
  **b.** la oficina del director
  **c.** la clase de matemáticas
  **d.** el gimnasio
  **e.** la biblioteca
  **f.** la cafetería

AUDIO

### Pronunciación   La letra d

In Spanish, the letter **d** has two sounds. At the beginning of a sentence, after a pause, or after the letters **l** or **n,** the **d** sounds like the English *d* in *door.* In all other cases, the **d** sounds like the *th* of the word *the.*

Listen and repeat, paying close attention to the two sounds of **d.**

| | | |
|---|---|---|
| comida | divertido | ¿Dónde está David? |
| adiós | falda | Daniel está al lado de la puerta. |
| lado | grande | ¿Adónde vas con mi cuaderno? |

Soy Diego. Dibujo en mi cuaderno.

## 18 | ¿Adónde van?

**Escuchar
Escribir**

Where are Pablo and other people going? Listen to the description and write sentences saying where these people are going.

| la oficina de la directora | el gimnasio | la biblioteca |

| la clase de inglés | la clase de matemáticas | la cafetería |

**1.** Pablo

**2.** Claudia

**3.** Martín y Sara

**4.** la maestra de inglés

**5.** María y Claudia

**6.** el señor Treviño

## 19 | En el pasillo

**Hablar
Escribir**

The bell has just rung to change classes. Tell where the students and the teachers are going, based on the clues in the drawing.

**modelo:** Las amigas van a la cafetería.

## 20 | ¿Cuándo vas a...?

**Hablar**

Ask a partner when he or she goes to these places.

**modelo:** la oficina

**A** ¿Cuándo vas a la oficina?

**B** Voy a la oficina cuando tengo problemas.

**Estudiante A**

**1.** el gimnasio
**2.** la oficina
**3.** la escuela
**4.** la biblioteca
**5.** la cafetería
**6.** la clase de...

**Estudiante B**

tengo (que)
necesito
hay
¿ ?

## 21 | ¿Y tú?

**Hablar**
**Escribir**

Answer the questions in complete sentences.

**1.** ¿A qué hora vas a la escuela?
**2.** ¿Cuándo van tú y tus amigos(as) a la cafetería?
**3.** ¿Adónde vas después de la clase de español?
**4.** ¿Vas mucho a la oficina del (de la) director(a)?
**5.** ¿Adónde vas cuando tienes que estudiar?
**6.** ¿Qué hay dentro de tu mochila?

## Comparación cultural

### El autorretrato

*What does a self-portrait reveal about an artist?*
Mexican artist Frida Kahlo painted many self-portraits, including *Autorretrato con collar*. She was influenced by the indigenous cultures of **Mexico** in both her style of painting and style of clothing. She often wore traditional native clothing, as depicted in the photograph. What similarities and differences do you see between the two images?

**Compara con tu mundo** *What would you include in a portrait of yourself and why? What would your clothing be like?*

Autorretrato con collar *(1933), Frida Kahlo*

*Una fotografía de Frida Kahlo (1941), Nickolas Muray*

*Más práctica*  Cuaderno *pp. 80–82*  Cuaderno para hispanohablantes *pp. 81–84*

**PARA Y PIENSA**

**Did you get it?** Tell where the following people are going.

**1.** Teresa / la cafetería
**2.** los estudiantes / la oficina del director
**3.** nosotros / el gimnasio
**4.** yo / la clase de matemáticas

**Get Help Online**
ClassZone.com

# Todo junto

**Goal:** *Show what you know* Notice how Pablo and Claudia use **ir** to talk about where they are going, and **estar** to say where things are. Then use **ir** and **estar** to talk about your own schedule. *Actividades 22–26*

 *¿Recuerdas?* Telling time p. 99

## Telehistoria completa

**@HomeTutor** VideoPlus
**View, Read and Record**
ClassZone.com

### STRATEGIES

**Cuando lees**

**Read for locations** This scene mentions specific places people are going. What are those places? Alicia's T-shirt is now located in a specific place. Where is it?

**Cuando escuchas**

**Notice the problems** In this scene, Pablo's problems go from bad to worse. What are the problems? How does he react?

**Escena 1** *Resumen*
Pablo no contesta la pregunta en la clase de ciencias porque el problema es difícil. Claudia contesta la pregunta.

**Escena 2** *Resumen*
Pablo no está contento porque tiene mucho que hacer y no tiene la mochila con la camiseta de Alicia.

VIDEO
DVD

AUDIO

### Escena 3

Roberto — Pablo — Claudia

*Roberto approaches, holding a poster.*

**Roberto:** ¿Qué pasa?

**Claudia:** Vamos al gimnasio. Bueno, Pablo va al gimnasio, yo voy a la cafetería...

**Pablo:** ¡Necesito ir al gimnasio a las cinco, y son las cinco menos cuarto!

**Claudia:** ¡Y necesita la mochila! Dentro está la camiseta de Alicia.

**Pablo:** A las cinco Trini Salgado va al gimnasio, y yo...

**Roberto:** No, no. ¡A las cuatro!

**Pablo:** No... ¡A las cinco!

**Roberto:** Mira... a las cuatro.

*He shows his autographed poster to Pablo. It says four o'clock.*

**Pablo:** *(dejectedly)* No...

## 22 | ¡A organizar! *Comprensión de los episodios*

Escuchar
Leer

Put the sentences in order to describe the episodes.

1. La camiseta está en la mochila y Pablo no tiene la mochila.
2. Pablo y Claudia hablan con Roberto.
3. Claudia y Pablo van a la biblioteca y estudian.
4. Pablo está nervioso; tiene que ir al gimnasio a las cinco.
5. Pablo va a la clase de ciencias y no contesta la pregunta.

## 23 | ¡A describir! *Comprensión de los episodios*

Escuchar
Leer

Describe what is happening in the photos. Include where the people in the photos are and how they feel.

**modelo:** Pablo está en la clase de ciencias. Va al pizarrón porque tiene que contestar una pregunta. Está nervioso.

**1.**   **2.**   **3.**

## 24 | ¿Adónde vamos? ♻ *¿Recuerdas?* Telling time p. 99

Hablar

**STRATEGY Hablar**
**Make it lively** Keep the discussion interesting! Add as many details about your classes as possible. Don't just talk about your classes; include other places in your school.

Talk with other students about schedules: where they go and at what times.

**A** ¿A qué hora van ustedes a la cafetería?

**B** Voy a la cafetería a las doce y media.

**C** Voy a la cafetería a la una.

## 25 | Integración

Raquel and Mario need to study in the library. Read Raquel's daily planner and listen to Mario's message. Then tell when Raquel and Mario will go to the library to study. Explain why they won't go at the other times mentioned.

**Fuente 1  Agenda personal**

**28** de octubre

7:30  clase de matemáticas
8:40  estudiar
9:50  clase de ciencias
11:00  inglés: presentación oral
12:30  descansar
1:40  cafetería con Amanda
2:45  examen de historia
4:00  estudiar en la biblioteca

**Fuente 2  Un mensaje por teléfono**

**Listen and take notes**
· Escribe qué hace Mario y a qué hora.

**modelo:** Ellos van a la biblioteca a las... No estudian a las siete y media porque...

## 26 | El periódico escolar

You have to write an article for the school newspaper about your typical school day. Explain what classes you go to, what they are like, and what you use in each class.

**modelo:** Yo siempre estoy muy ocupado. A las siete y media voy a la clase de matemáticas. La clase es muy divertida. Usamos calculadoras, pero no es fácil. A las ocho y cuarto...

| Writing Criteria | Excellent | Good | Needs Work |
|---|---|---|---|
| **Content** | Your article includes a lot of information. | Your article includes some information. | Your article includes little information. |
| **Communication** | Most of your article is organized and easy to follow. | Parts of your article are organized and easy to follow. | Your article is disorganized and hard to follow. |
| **Accuracy** | Your article has few mistakes in grammar and vocabulary. | Your article has some mistakes in grammar and vocabulary. | Your article has many mistakes in grammar and vocabulary. |

*Más práctica*   Cuaderno *pp. 83–84*   Cuaderno para hispanohablantes *pp. 85–86*

PARA Y PIENSA

**Did you get it?**  Complete each sentence with the correct forms of **estar** and **ir + a.**

**Get Help Online**
ClassZone.com

1. A la una Pablo _____ en la clase de arte, pero a las dos _____ la cafetería.
2. ¿Dónde _____ Roberto y Claudia? Ellos _____ la cafetería.
3. Claudia _____ nerviosa porque _____ la oficina de la directora.

# Juegos y diversiones

Review **estar,** classroom objects, and location words by playing a game.

## ¿Cierto o falso?

### The Setup

Your teacher will divide the class into two teams. Each student will make up a sentence using classroom objects and location words.

### Playing the Game

Players from each team go up to the front of the class with their sentences in hand.

The player from Team A reads the sentence to the player from Team B. The player from Team B has to say whether the sentence is true (**cierto**) or false (**falso**). Then they change roles.

### Scoring

Players receive one point for correct answers. Points are taken away for incorrectly formed sentences.

A player can earn an extra point by correcting a false sentence to say something true about the location of the object. A player can also earn an extra point by adding more information to a true sentence.

### The Winner!

The team with the most points at the end is the winner.

El libro está debajo del escritorio.

Falso. El libro está encima del escritorio.

# Lectura cultural

**Goal:** Read the excerpts from the essays of two students from Mexico and the Dominican Republic. Then compare the descriptions of their favorite classes and talk about your favorite class.

## Comparación cultural

AUDIO

# Mi clase favorita

### STRATEGY Leer

**Use the title** The title *Mi clase favorita* helps you anticipate the contents of the reading. Write down the things that you would expect to find, then search for them.

| Expected contents | Actual contents |
|---|---|
| El (La) maestro(a)... | |
| La clase... | |
| Más información: | |

Below are compositions by two finalists who entered the essay contest called "Mi clase favorita."

Tomás Gutiérrez Moreno
Colegio de la Providencia
Guadalajara, México

Mi nombre es Tomás Gutiérrez Moreno. Soy de Guadalajara, México. Estudio en el Colegio de la Providencia.

La historia es muy interesante; es mi clase favorita. Me gusta mucho estudiar el pasado[1] de México. Soy estudioso y siempre saco buenas notas en la clase.

En la universidad deseo[2] estudiar historia. Deseo ser maestro y enseñar historia mexicana en Guadalajara.

---

[1] past  [2] I wish to

*Mural en la Biblioteca Central de la Universidad Nacional Autónoma de México en la Ciudad de México*

**México**

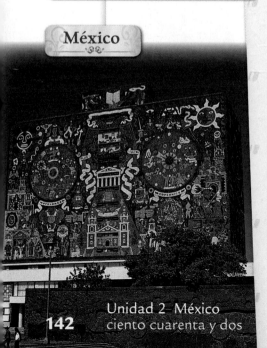

María González
Colegio San Esteban
San Pedro de Macorís, República Dominicana

Me llamo María  González. Soy de la República Dominicana.  Estudio en el Colegio San Esteban.

Tengo dos clases favoritas: el inglés y el español. Deseo estudiar idiomas[3] en Santo Domingo, la capital, y después, trabajar en mi país.

El turismo es muy importante para[4] la economía de la República Dominicana. Deseo trabajar en un hotel, en las famosas playas[5] de Punta Cana o de Puerto Plata.

---

[3] languages    [4] for    [5] beaches

*Mural en la Universidad Nacional en Santo Domingo, República Dominicana*

República Dominicana

**PARA Y PIENSA**

## ¿Comprendiste?
**1.** ¿Dónde estudia Tomás?
**2.** ¿Cómo es Tomás?
**3.** ¿De dónde es María?
**4.** ¿Qué le gusta estudiar más a María?

## ¿Y tú?
¿Cuál es tu clase favorita? ¿Cómo es?

# Proyectos culturales

## Arte de México y la República Dominicana

*How does art reflect a culture's view of the natural world?* Many cultures use art to capture the beauty and wonder of their natural surroundings. Two indigenous groups whose art can still be appreciated are the Huichol of **Mexico** and the Taino of the Greater Antilles (including what is now known as the **Dominican Republic**).

### Proyecto 1 *Yarn Painting*

**México** Some Huichol still live in the isolated mountains of western Mexico. They make yarn paintings of birds, flowers, and other natural shapes. Make your own Huichol-style yarn painting.

**Materials for yarn painting**
Cardboard
2–3 colors yarn
Glue

**Instructions**
1. On a piece of cardboard, draw a pencil outline of the design you'd like to make.
2. Place one strand of yarn along the outline's length. Glue the yarn to the cardboard.
3. Fill in the design by laying yarn just inside the outline you made, coiling the yarn around until the figure is filled.
4. Section off the background and fill it in the same way.

### Proyecto 2 *Rock Drawing*

**República Dominicana** The Taino lived in the islands of the Caribbean until the 16th century. Their rock art can still be seen in the caverns of the Dominican Republic. Try making your own rock art.

**Materials for rock drawing**
Rock
Pencil
*Optional:* Markers, pens, or chalk

**Instructions**
1. Begin by finding a smooth, oval rock about the size of your hand with an adequate surface for drawing.
2. Use a pencil to sketch the animal or design you'd like to make.
3. Then use a black felt tip pen to make it permanent. Add color by using colored felt tip pens or colored chalk.

## En tu comunidad

Visit an arts and crafts store or a museum in your community. Look for any items that have been influenced by Spanish-speaking cultures.

# En resumen
## Vocabulario y gramática

## Vocabulario

### Describe Classroom Objects

| | | | |
|---|---|---|---|
| el borrador | eraser | el pizarrón (pl. los pizarrones) | board, chalkboard |
| la calculadora | calculator | | |
| el cuaderno | notebook | la pluma | pen |
| el escritorio | desk | la puerta | door |
| el lápiz (pl. los lápices) | pencil | el reloj | clock; watch |
| | | la silla | chair |
| el mapa | map | la tiza | chalk |
| la mochila | backpack | la ventana | window |
| el papel | paper | | |

### Say Where Things Are Located

| | | | |
|---|---|---|---|
| al lado (de) | next to | dentro (de) | inside (of) |
| cerca (de) | near (to) | detrás (de) | behind |
| debajo (de) | underneath, under | encima (de) | on top (of) |
| delante (de) | in front (of) | lejos (de) | far (from) |

### Talk About How You Feel

| | | | |
|---|---|---|---|
| cansado(a) | tired | nervioso(a) | nervous |
| contento(a) | content, happy | ocupado(a) | busy |
| deprimido(a) | depressed | tranquilo(a) | calm |
| emocionado(a) | excited | triste | sad |
| enojado(a) | angry | | |

### Describe Classes

| | |
|---|---|
| aburrido(a) | boring |
| divertido(a) | fun |
| interesante | interesting |

### Places in School

| | |
|---|---|
| el baño | bathroom |
| la biblioteca | library |
| la cafetería | cafeteria |
| el gimnasio | gymnasium |
| la oficina del (de la) director(a) | principal's office |
| el pasillo | hall |

### Other Words and Phrases

| | |
|---|---|
| ¿(A)dónde? | (To) Where? |
| ¿Cuándo? | When? |
| cuando | when |
| el problema | problem |

## Gramática

**Nota gramatical:** Conjugated verb before the subject to ask a question  *p. 130*

### The Verb estar

Use **estar** to indicate location and say how people feel.

| estar  to be | | | |
|---|---|---|---|
| yo | **estoy** | nosotros(as) | **estamos** |
| tú | **estás** | vosotros(as) | **estáis** |
| usted, él, ella | **está** | ustedes, ellos(as) | **están** |

### The Verb ir

Use **ir** to talk about where someone is going.

| ir  to go | | | |
|---|---|---|---|
| yo | **voy** | nosotros(as) | **vamos** |
| tú | **vas** | vosotros(as) | **vais** |
| usted, él, ella | **va** | ustedes, ellos(as) | **van** |

# Repaso de la lección

¡LLEGADA!

¡AvanzaRap!
DVD
Sing and Learn

@HomeTutor
ClassZone.com

**Now you can**
- describe classes and classroom objects
- say where things are located
- say where you are going
- talk about how you feel

**Using**
- the verb **estar**
- the conjugated verb before the subject to ask a question
- the verb **ir**

---

**To review**
- the verb **estar** p. 128
- the conjugated verb before the subject to ask a question p. 130
- the verb **ir** p. 134

## 1 | Listen and understand

AUDIO

Copy this chart on a piece of paper. Listen to the phone messages and complete the chart. Write sentences using the information.

| La hora | ¿Dónde está Ana? | ¿Adónde va Ana? |
|---------|------------------|-----------------|
| modelo: 8:00 | delante de la clase de arte | clase de español |
| 10:15 | | |
| 12:30 | | |
| 2:45 | | |
| 4:10 | | |

modelo:  A las ocho Ana está delante de la clase de arte.
Ella va de la clase de arte a la clase de español.

---

**To review**
- the verb **estar** p. 128
- the conjugated verb before the subject to ask a question p. 130

## 2 | Talk about how you feel

Write questions to find out how these people are feeling.

modelo:  Bárbara
¿Está emocionada Bárbara?

**1.**  Jorge y Pilar

**4.**  usted

**2.**  las maestras

**5.**  tú

**3.**  la directora

**6.**  ustedes

---

To review
• the verb **ir** p. 134

## 3 | Say where you are going

Read Mario's e-mail message and complete it with the correct form of **ir**.

> Hola, Luis. Yo __1.__ a la clase de ciencias en quince minutos. Es una clase interesante, pero es difícil. A las doce y media mis amigos y yo __2.__ a la cafetería. Después Inés __3.__ al gimnasio y Jerónimo __4.__ a la oficina del director. A las cinco ellos __5.__ a la biblioteca para estudiar. ¿Adónde __6.__ tú después de las clases?

To review
• the verb **estar** p. 128

## 4 | Say where things are located

Write sentences telling where Señora Romero's students have put the erasers.

**modelo:** pizarrón (cerca / lejos)
Un borrador está cerca del pizarrón.

1. reloj (al lado / debajo)
2. silla (debajo / encima)
3. mochila (dentro / debajo)
4. ventana (delante / detrás)
5. escritorio (encima / delante)
6. maestra (lejos / detrás)

To review
• Comparación cultural pp. 120, 130, 137
• Lectura cultural pp. 142–143

## 5 | Mexico and the Dominican Republic

### Comparación cultural

Answer these culture questions.

1. When do Mexican students attend school?
2. How did indigenous cultures influence Frida Kahlo?
3. What can you find in Mexico City's National Museum of Anthropology?
4. Why is tourism important in the Dominican Republic?

Get Help Online
ClassZone.com

*Más práctica* Cuaderno *pp. 85–96* Cuaderno para hispanohablantes *pp. 87–96*

México

Paraguay

República Dominicana

AUDIO

# Horarios y clases

## Lectura y escritura

WebQuest
ClassZone.com

**1 Leer** School subjects and daily schedules vary around the world. Read how Rafael, Andrea, and Juan Carlos spend a typical day at school.

**2 Escribir** Using the three descriptions as models, write a short paragraph about your daily schedule.

> **STRATEGY Escribir**
>
> **Create a schedule** Draw two large clocks, one for a.m. and the other for p.m. Write your school schedule on these clocks.
>
>
>
> clase   a.m.   p.m.   actividad

**Step 1** Complete the two clocks by listing your classes and after-school activities. Use arrows to point to the correct times.

**Step 2** Write your paragraph. Make sure to include all the classes, activities, and times. Check your writing by yourself or with help from a friend. Make final corrections.

### Compara con tu mundo

Use the paragraph you wrote to compare your school schedule to the schedule of *one* of the three students. What are the similarities in the schedules? What are the differences?

Cuaderno *pp. 97–99*   Cuaderno para hispanohablantes *pp. 97–99*

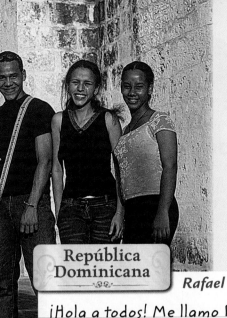

## República Dominicana

### Rafael

¡Hola a todos! Me llamo Rafael y estudio en una escuela en Santo Domingo. Tengo clases todos los días de las ocho de la mañana a la una de la tarde. A las diez tenemos un descanso de quince minutos. Luego, voy a la clase de historia. Es interesante y yo tomo muchos apuntes. En la tarde muchas veces paso un rato con los amigos.

## Paraguay

### Andrea

¿Qué tal? Me llamo Andrea y estudio en Asunción, Paraguay. Mis clases son en la tarde, de la una a las cinco. En la escuela los estudiantes tienen muchas clases. Todos los días, tengo clases de español, ciencias, historia y matemáticas. También tengo clase de guaraní[1]. Después de las clases, voy al gimnasio y practico deportes. De vez en cuando uso la computadora en la biblioteca.

[1] an indigenous language spoken in Paraguay

## México

### Juan Carlos

¡Hola! Soy Juan Carlos. Soy estudiante en México, D.F. En la escuela necesito trabajar mucho porque tengo nueve clases. Las clases son de las siete de la mañana a las dos de la tarde. ¡Tengo que llegar muy temprano! Mi clase favorita es la clase de matemáticas. Es interesante y divertida. Después de las clases mis amigos y yo estudiamos en la biblioteca.

# Repaso inclusivo
♻ Options for Review

¡AvanzaRap!
DVD
Sing and Learn

## 1 | Listen, understand, and compare

Escuchar

Javier interviewed teachers and administrators at his school for Teacher Appreciation Day. Listen to his report and answer the questions.

1. ¿Qué enseña el señor Minondo?
2. ¿Qué deporte practica el señor Minondo?
3. ¿Quién es la señora Cruz?
4. ¿Qué le gusta hacer a la señora Cruz?
5. ¿Cómo son los maestros?

Are your teachers and administrators like those at Javier's school? What kind of activities do your teachers like to do after classes?

## 2 | Give a school orientation

Hablar

You are giving a talk at an orientation meeting for students who are new to your school. Greet the new students, introduce yourself, and give them some background information about yourself: what classes you have, what you like to do after school, etc. Then tell them where the gym, cafeteria, and other locations around the school are. Finish by describing some of the classes that are available and what they have to do in each class. Your talk should be at least two minutes long.

## 3 | Talk with a school counselor

Hablar

Role-play a conversation with a school counselor. The counselor wants to know what your classes are like and what you like to do after classes. Answer your partner's questions, tell him or her what you do in each class, and ask a few questions of your own about the school. Your conversation should be at least two minutes long.

¿Cómo son tus clases?

Son difíciles. Estudio mucho.

# 4 | Write a brochure

**Escribir**

Create a brochure about your school that would be helpful to a new student from a Spanish-speaking country. Include some of the following: places in the school, classes offered, school supplies needed, teachers, and extracurricular activities. Copy this chart on a piece of paper and use it to organize your information. Your brochure should have illustrations and at least six sentences.

| Lugares | Clases | Materiales | Maestros | Actividades |
|---------|--------|------------|----------|-------------|
|         |        |            |          |             |
|         |        |            |          |             |

# 5 | Hold a press conference

**Hablar**
**Escribir**

Hold a mock press conference. You and your classmates are reporters and have to ask your teacher questions about his or her school schedule and favorite activities. Use the answers to write a short profile of your teacher that could appear in a Spanish edition of the school newspaper. The profile should have at least five sentences.

# 6 | Write a postcard

**Leer**
**Escribir**

You received the following postcard from your new pen pal in Mexico. Write back, answering all of your pen pal's questions and asking a few of your own. Your letter should have at least eight sentences.

PUEBLA

Hola. Me llamo Manuel Salazar. Soy de Puebla, México. Soy estudioso y atlético. Soy un estudiante organizado. Siempre saco buenas notas. ¿Cómo eres tú? ¿Cómo son tus clases? Tengo clases difíciles pero los maestros son muy simpáticos. Estudio mucho y también paso un rato con los amigos. Me gusta jugar al fútbol y andar en patineta. ¿Qué te gusta hacer con los amigos?

Tu amigo,

Manuel

MÉXICO
© Tarjetas Puebla, S.A.

# Puerto Rico

## Comer en familia

Océano
Atlántico

## Lección 1
*Tema:* **Mi comida favorita**

## Lección 2
*Tema:* **En mi familia**

Puerto Rico

Golfo de México

Cuba

«**¡Hola!**
**Somos Marisol y Rodrigo.**
**Somos de Puerto Rico.**»

**México**

**Guatemala**

**El Salvador**

**Honduras**

**Nicaragua**

**Costa Rica**

**Panamá**

**República Dominicana**

*Mar Caribe*

**Venezuela**

**Colombia**

Océano Atlántico

Golfo de
México

**Arecibo**

**San
Juan**

**Culebra**

**Mayagüez**

**Puerto
Rico**

EL YUNQUE

**Humacao**

**Vieques**

**Ponce**

**Guayama**

Mar Caribe

**Población:** 3.958.128

**Área:** 3.515 millas cuadradas

**Capital:** San Juan

**Moneda:** el dólar
estadounidense

**Idiomas:** español, inglés (los
dos son oficiales)

**Comida típica:** pasteles, arroz
con gandules, pernil

**Gente famosa:** Julia de Burgos (poetisa), Roberto
Clemente (beisbolista), Rosario Ferré (escritora),
Luis Muñoz Marín (político)

*Pasteles*

*Una familia come en la playa*

◀ **Comidas al aire libre** Many Puerto Ricans enjoy informal gatherings at a beach or park, where families can spend the day together, barbecue, and listen to music. **Pinchos** (skewers of chicken or pork) are popular at barbecues and snack stands. *Where do people like to eat outdoors where you live?*

**Casas de colores vivos** San Juan is famous for its well-preserved colonial quarter, called **Viejo San Juan.** Its narrow streets are lined with brightly-colored houses with balconies. *What are some historic areas close to where you live?* ▶

*Casas coloniales en Viejo San Juan*

*La Cascada de la Coca en El Yunque*

◀ **Un parque nacional** El Yunque is the only tropical rain forest in the care of the U.S. Forest Service. The park has many waterfalls, such as the Cascada de la Coca, and is home to the **coquí,** a tiny tree frog named for its distinctive song. *What are some features of other parks in the United States?*

# Puerto Rico

## Lección

## 1

*Tema:*

# *Mi comida favorita*

**¡AVANZA!**

## In this lesson you will learn to
- talk about foods and beverages
- ask questions
- say which foods you like and don't like

### using
- interrogative words
- **gustar** with nouns
- present tense of **-er** and **-ir** verbs
- the verb **hacer**

### ♻ *¿Recuerdas?*
- **gustar** with an infinitive
- snack foods
- the verb **estar**
- telling time

## Comparación cultural

### In this lesson you will learn about
- traditional cooking
- historic landmarks in Puerto Rico
- grocery shopping in Puerto Rico

### Compara con tu mundo
These teenagers are buying ice cream from a street vendor. Another popular cold treat in Puerto Rico is **la piragua,** a kind of shaved ice with fruit syrup. *What do you like to eat or drink during hot weather?*

### *¿Qué ves?*

*Mira la foto*

¿Están contentos los chicos?

¿Están delante o detrás del señor?

¿Qué les gusta comer a los chicos?

**La Plaza de Colón
en el Viejo San Juan**
*San Juan, Puerto Rico*

# Presentación de VOCABULARIO

**Goal:** Learn about what Rodrigo and Marisol eat for breakfast, lunch, and dinner. Then practice what you have learned to talk about foods and beverages. **Actividades 1–2**

 *¿Recuerdas?* **gustar** with an infinitive p. 44

VIDEO
DVD

AUDIO

**A** ¡Hola! Me llamo Rodrigo y ella es Ana. Son las ocho de la mañana. **Es importante** comer **un desayuno nutritivo** todos los días.

el desayuno

los huevos

el pan

**B** Cuando **tengo hambre**, me gusta comer **huevos** y **pan**. Cuando **tengo sed**, bebo **jugo de naranja**. Me gusta mucho porque es **rico**. Nunca bebo **café** porque es **horrible**.

el cereal

el yogur

de fresa

En **Puerto Rico** se dice...

In Puerto Rico the word for *orange juice* is **el jugo de china.**

las bebidas

el jugo de naranja

el café

la leche

**C** Es la una y **ahora** Marisol y yo comemos **el almuerzo**. En la cafetería **venden** muchas **comidas**: sándwiches, hamburguesas y sopa. También venden **bebidas**: leche, jugos y refrescos.

el almuerzo

el sándwich de jamón y queso

la hamburguesa

la sopa

## Más vocabulario

| | |
|---|---|
| **¿Cómo?** *How?* | **¿Quién(es)?** *Who?* |
| **¿Cuál(es)?** *Which?* | **compartir** *to share* |
| **¿Por qué?** *Why?* | **otro(a)** *other* |
| **¿Qué?** *What?* | *Expansión de vocabulario* p. R4 |

Continuará...

**D** Marisol y yo compramos fruta **para** mi papá: **manzanas, bananas** y **uvas.**
**La cena** es a las siete y **tengo ganas de** comer. Siempre como mucho
cuando mi mamá prepara la comida.

la manzana

las uvas

la banana

En **Puerto Rico** se dice...
The word for *banana* is
**el guineo.**

la cena

¡A responder!   Escuchar

Write **desayuno** and **almuerzo** on separate pieces of paper. Listen to
the list of foods. Hold up the correct piece or pieces of paper to indicate
when you eat each food.

**@HomeTutor** VideoPlus
**Interactive Flashcards**
ClassZone.com

# Práctica de VOCABULARIO

## 1 | ¡A jugar! Busca, busca

Escribir

Find and write the names of the eight foods hidden in the cafeteria scene.

## 2 | ¿Qué te gusta más? ♻ *¿Recuerdas?* **gustar** with an infinitive p. 44

Hablar

Talk with a partner about which foods and drinks you like more.

**A** ¿Te gusta más comer papas fritas o pizza?

**B** Me gusta más comer pizza.

1.  2.  3.

4.  5.  6.

*Más práctica*   Cuaderno *pp. 101–103*   Cuaderno para hispanohablantes *pp. 101–104*

**PARA Y PIENSA**

**Did you get it?**
1. Name three breakfast foods.   2. Name three lunch foods.

Get Help Online
ClassZone.com

# VOCABULARIO *en contexto*

¡AVANZA!

**Goal:** Identify the words Rodrigo and Marisol use to ask questions. Then practice these words to ask questions and give answers. *Actividades 3–4*

*¿Recuerdas?* Snack foods p. 33

## Telehistoria escena 1

**@HomeTutor** VideoPlus
**View, Read and Record**
ClassZone.com

### STRATEGIES

**Cuando lees**

**List the question words** As you read, list the words that indicate questions, such as **Qué** in **¿Qué amiga?** Save the list so that you can add more question words as you encounter them.

**Cuando escuchas**

**Think about motives** In this scene, Marisol asks questions repeatedly. Think of possible reasons why she does this. Which reason seems the most probable to you?

VIDEO
DVD

AUDIO

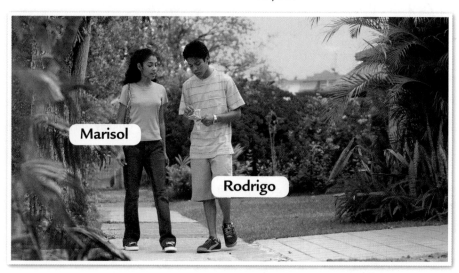

Marisol

Rodrigo

*Rodrigo and Marisol walk to the grocery store. Rodrigo is counting his money.*

**Marisol:** ¿A la escuela? ¿Por qué vas a la escuela hoy? Es sábado.

**Rodrigo:** Trini Salgado llega hoy y necesito un autógrafo en una camiseta. Es importante.

**Marisol:** ¿En una camiseta? ¿Qué camiseta?

**Rodrigo:** Tengo una amiga...

**Marisol:** *(teasing him)* ¿Una amiga? ¿Qué amiga? ¿Cómo se llama?

**Rodrigo:** Se llama Alicia.

**Marisol:** ¿De dónde es?

**Rodrigo:** Es de Miami. *(He loses count and starts over, sighing.)*

**Marisol:** ¿Cuándo tienes que estar en la escuela?

**Rodrigo:** A las cuatro de la tarde. *(Rodrigo loses count.)* ¡Y por favor! ¡No más preguntas! *(He starts to count again.)*

**Marisol:** Quince, veinte, cuarenta...     **Continuará...** p. 166

### También se dice

**Puerto Rico** Rodrigo uses the word **la camiseta** when he mentions Alicia's T-shirt. In other Spanish-speaking countries you might hear:
• **Argentina** **la remera**
• **Perú** **el polo**
• **Venezuela** **la franela**
• **México** **la playera**

## 3 | Muchas preguntas *Comprensión del episodio*

Escuchar
Leer

Complete each question with the appropriate interrogative word and choose the correct answer according to the episode.

cómo     dónde     quién

por qué     qué

1. ¿ _____ necesita Rodrigo?
2. ¿ _____ se llama la amiga de Rodrigo?
3. ¿De _____ es Alicia?
4. ¿ _____ va a la escuela Rodrigo?
5. ¿ _____ es Trini Salgado?

a. Es de Miami.
b. porque Trini Salgado está allí
c. un autógrafo
d. Alicia
e. una atleta famosa

## 4 | ¿Cómo es? ♻ *¿Recuerdas?* Snack foods p. 33

Hablar

Work with a partner to describe the following foods and drinks in your school's cafeteria.

Ⓐ ¿Cómo es la leche?

Ⓑ La leche es buena.

**Estudiante Ⓐ**

1.   2.   3.   4.

5.   6.   7.   8.

**Estudiante Ⓑ**

nutritivo(a)
bueno(a)
malo(a)
horrible
rico(a)

---

**PARA Y PIENSA**

**Did you get it?** Choose the correct interrogative word.
1. ¿(Qué / Quiénes) son las amigas de Rodrigo?
2. ¿(Cuándo / Cuál) llega Trini Salgado?
3. ¿(Quién / Por qué) necesita Rodrigo el autógrafo?

**Get Help Online**
ClassZone.com

# Presentación de GRAMÁTICA

**Goal:** Learn how to use **gustar** with nouns. Then practice using this verb to express what foods you like and don't like. *Actividades 5–11*

**English Grammar Connection:** In English, the phrase *I like* doesn't change. In Spanish, there are two ways to say it, depending on whether what you like is singular or plural. This is because the Spanish phrase **me gusta** literally means that something *is pleasing to me.*

## Gustar with Nouns

**Animated** Grammar
ClassZone.com

 **¿Recuerdas?** You have already learned to use **gustar** with infinitives to say what people like to do (see p. 44).

To talk about the things that people like, use **gustar** + **noun.**

*Here's how:*

If what is liked is singular, use the **singular** form **gusta.**

| Singular |
|---|
| me gusta **la sopa** |
| te gusta **la sopa** |
| le gusta **la sopa** |
| nos gusta **la sopa** |
| os gusta **la sopa** |
| les gusta **la sopa** |

*matches singular noun*
**Me gusta el cereal.**
*I like cereal.*

If what is liked is plural, use the **plural** form **gustan.**

| Plural |
|---|
| me gustan **los jugos** |
| te gustan **los jugos** |
| le gustan **los jugos** |
| nos gustan **los jugos** |
| os gustan **los jugos** |
| les gustan **los jugos** |

*matches plural noun*
**Me gustan las uvas.**
*I like grapes.*

Notice that the singular and plural forms of **gustar** match what is liked, not the person who likes it.

*Más práctica*
   Cuaderno *pp. 104–106*
   Cuaderno para hispanohablantes *pp. 105–107*

**@HomeTutor**
Leveled Practice
ClassZone.com

# Práctica de GRAMÁTICA

## 5 | ¿Qué les gusta?

**Hablar**
**Escribir**

Tell whether the following people like or don't like the following foods and drinks.

> **modelo:** a Luis / el yogur
> A Luis **le gusta** el yogur.

**1.** a los maestros / el café

**2.** a nosotros / las papas fritas 🙂

**3.** a Adela / las manzanas 🙁

**4.** a mí / las hamburguesas 🙁

**5.** a mis amigos / los sándwiches 🙂

**6.** a ti / las uvas 🙂

**7.** a Jaime y a Rafael / la leche 🙁

**8.** a usted / el cereal

**9.** a ellos / las bananas 🙁

**10.** a ustedes / el jugo 🙂

## 6 | En el supermercado

**Leer**
**Escribir**

Indicate what these people like and don't like at the supermarket, according to the description.

> **modelo:** El yogur es horrible. (a Rodrigo)
> A Rodrigo no le gusta el yogur.

**1.** Las uvas son ricas. (a ti)

**2.** La sopa es buena. (a Marisol)

**3.** El cereal es malo. (a nosotros)

**4.** Los huevos son horribles. (a mí)

**5.** El café es muy bueno. (a usted)

**6.** Los jugos son nutritivos. (a ellos)

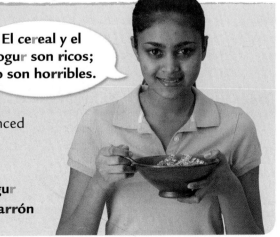

**Pronunciación** **Las letras r y rr**

**AUDIO**

In Spanish, the letter r in the middle or the end of a word is pronounced by a single tap of the tongue against the gum above the upper front teeth. The letter r at the beginning of a word or **rr** within a word is pronounced by several rapid taps called a trill.

El cereal y el yogur son ricos; no son horribles.

Listen and repeat.

| para | cereal | beber | yogur |
| rico | rubio | horrible | pizarrón |

# 7 | Las comidas favoritas

**Hablar** **Comparación cultural**

## La cocina criolla

*How do historical influences affect the food that people eat?* Traditional cooking in **Puerto Rico,** known as *la cocina criolla,* combines Spanish, African, and indigenous influences. *Tostones* (fried plantains) are a common side dish. Popular snack foods are *alcapurrias* (fried plantains stuffed with meat) and *bacalaítos* (codfish fritters). In **El Salvador,** traditional cuisine blends indigenous and Spanish influences. A typical food is the *pupusa,* a corn tortilla filled with beans, pork, and cheese. *Pupusas* are often served with *curtido,* a spicy coleslaw. *Semita,* a sweet bread layered with pineapple marmalade, is also popular.

*Tostones*

**Compara con tu mundo** *Which of these dishes would you most like to try and why? What is the most interesting dish that you have ever tried?*

*Pupusas*

Use the information to talk with a partner about food preferences in Puerto Rico and El Salvador.

**A** ¿A quiénes les gustan los tostones?

**B** A los chicos de Puetro Rico les gustan.

# 8 | Opiniones

**Hablar** Work in a group of three to talk about the foods and drinks you like and don't like.

**la pizza**   **las uvas**   **la leche**

**las manzanas**   **el jugo de naranja**   **¿ ?**

**A** ¿A ustedes les gusta la pizza?

**B** A mí no me gusta la pizza. No me gusta el queso.

**C** Sí, a mí me gusta la pizza con jamón.

## 9 | El menú

**Leer**
**Hablar**

Ask a partner questions about which foods on the menu he or she likes more and why.

**A** ¿Te gusta más el desayuno uno o el desayuno dos?

**B** Me gusta más el desayuno dos porque me gusta el cereal y no me gustan los huevos.

### Restaurante Borinquen

**Desayunos (de 8:00 a 11:00)**

1. Huevos fritos o revoltillo con jamón ..........$4.00
2. Cereal frío y fruta....................................$4.00
3. Frutas frescas
   (uvas, guineos, manzanas), yogur..............$3.50

Bebidas incluidas: jugo de china, café o leche

**Almuerzos (de 12:00 a 3:00)**

1. Hamburguesa americana, papas fritas.........$5.50
2. Sándwich de jamón y queso, con fruta........$6.50
3. Pizza con jamón y queso............................$5.50
4. Asopao de vegetales
   (sopa tradicional de Puerto Rico)................$4.00

Bebidas incluidas: jugos, refrescos o café
Postres incluidos: helado, flan o pastel del día

## 10 | ¿Y tú?

**Hablar**
**Escribir**

Answer the questions in complete sentences.

1. ¿Qué comida te gusta cuando tienes mucha hambre?
2. ¿Qué bebida te gusta cuando tienes mucha sed?
3. ¿Cuál es una comida nutritiva?
4. ¿Qué comidas nutritivas te gustan y no te gustan?
5. ¿Qué comidas en la cafetería de la escuela te gustan?
6. ¿Qué comidas en la cafetería de la escuela no te gustan?

## 11 | Le gusta...

**Escribir**

Think of someone you know who leads an especially healthy lifestyle. Write a short description of that person's favorite activities and the foods he or she likes and doesn't like.

**modelo:** Mi amigo Javier es muy atlético. Le gusta practicar deportes. Le gustan las frutas, pero no le gusta la pizza porque no es nutritiva...

*Más práctica*   Cuaderno *pp. 104–106*   Cuaderno para hispanohablantes *pp. 105–107*

**PARA Y PIENSA**

**Did you get it?**
1. Tell a friend you like eggs for breakfast.
2. Say that José likes pizza with ham.
3. Ask a friend why he or she doesn't like fruit.

**Get Help Online**
ClassZone.com

ciento sesenta y cinco   **165**

# GRAMÁTICA *en contexto*

**Goal:** Listen to how Marisol and Rodrigo use **gustar** to talk about what they like to eat. Then use **gustar** to talk about likes and dislikes. *Actividades 12–14*

## Telehistoria escena 2

*@HomeTutor* VideoPlus
**View, Read and Record**
ClassZone.com

### STRATEGIES

**Cuando lees**

**Organize with a chart** To keep thoughts organized, make a chart listing Rodrigo's and Marisol's likes and dislikes about breakfast foods. Are your preferences more like Rodrigo's or more like Marisol's?

**Cuando escuchas**

**Use mental pictures to remember words** Listen for names of foods. For each name you hear, picture the food mentally. Remember these words by repeatedly linking them to the mental pictures.

VIDEO
DVD

AUDIO

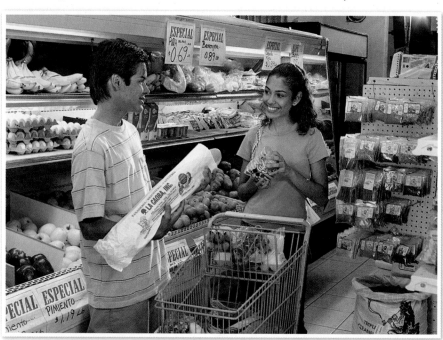

**Marisol:** ¿Qué te gusta comer en el desayuno?

**Rodrigo:** Me gustan el cereal, el yogur, las frutas... Y a ti, Marisol, ¿qué te gusta comer en el desayuno?

**Marisol:** No me gusta el yogur y no me gustan los huevos.

**Rodrigo:** ¿Te gustan las frutas? ¿Las uvas, las manzanas?

**Marisol:** No me gusta comer mucho en el desayuno.

**Rodrigo:** ¡Tienes que comer bien en el desayuno! ¿Te gusta el pan? ¿O la leche?

**Marisol:** Me gustan las galletas. Tengo hambre.

**Rodrigo:** Sí. ¡Porque no te gusta comer mucho en el desayuno!

**Continuará...** p. 172

## 12 | ¿Un desayuno grande? *Comprensión del episodio*

Answer the questions about the episode.

**1.** ¿Qué le gusta comer a Rodrigo en el desayuno?

**2.** ¿A quién no le gustan los desayunos grandes?

**3.** ¿Qué le gusta comer a Marisol?

**4.** ¿Por qué tiene hambre Marisol?

## 13 | En el desayuno y el almuerzo

Escribir

Write a description of what foods and drinks you like and don't like for breakfast and lunch.

**modelo:** En el desayuno me gusta el pan. Para beber, me gusta el jugo de naranja. También me gustan las bananas. Es importante comer fruta. No me gustan los huevos. Son horribles. En el almuerzo...

## 14 | Una entrevista

Hablar
Escribir

Ask another student what he or she likes and doesn't like for lunch. Write the responses. Then compare your likes and dislikes, using a Venn diagram.

**modelo:** A Nicolás le gustan los sándwiches de queso en el almuerzo. También le gusta la fruta. No le gusta la pizza...

**A mí**      **A Nicolás**

Me gustan las hamburguesas.    Nos gusta la fruta.    No le gusta la pizza.

**PARA Y PIENSA**

**Did you get it?** Complete each sentence based on the Telehistoria with the correct form of **gustar**.

**1.** A Marisol no le _____ la comida nutritiva.

**2.** A Rodrigo le _____ el cereal.

**3.** A Marisol le _____ las galletas.

**Get Help Online**
ClassZone.com

# Presentación de GRAMÁTICA

**Goal:** Learn how to form **-er** and **-ir** verbs. Then use these verbs and **hacer** to talk about school activities and what you and others eat and drink. *Actividades 15–20*

 *¿Recuerdas?* The verb **estar** p. 128

English Grammar Connection: Remember that the **present tense** shows an action happening now (see p. 106).

## Present Tense of -er and -ir Verbs

Animated Grammar
ClassZone.com

Regular verbs that end in **-er** or **-ir** work a little differently than regular **-ar** verbs. How do you form the present tense of regular **-er** and **-ir** verbs?

*Here's how:*

The endings for **-er** and **-ir** verbs are the same except in the **nosotros(as)** and **vosotros(as)** forms. The letter change in these two forms matches the ending of the infinitive.

| vender *to sell* | | | |
|---|---|---|---|
| yo | **vendo** | nosotros(as) | **vendemos** |
| tú | **vendes** | vosotros(as) | **vendéis** |
| usted, él, ella | **vende** | ustedes, ellos(as) | **venden** |

-**er** verbs = -**emos**, -**éis**

Mario **vende** comida en la cafetería.
*Mario **sells** food in the cafeteria.*

| compartir *to share* | | | |
|---|---|---|---|
| yo | **comparto** | nosotros(as) | **compartimos** |
| tú | **compartes** | vosotros(as) | **compartís** |
| usted, él, ella | **comparte** | ustedes, ellos(as) | **comparten** |

-**ir** verbs = -**imos**, -**ís**

**Compartimos** las uvas.
*We are sharing the grapes.*

*Más práctica*
Cuaderno *pp. 107–109* 🚀 **Conjuguemos.com**
Cuaderno para hispanohablantes *pp. 108–111*

*@HomeTutor*
**Leveled Practice**
**ClassZone.com**

# Práctica de GRAMÁTICA

## 15 | ¿Comer o beber?

**Hablar
Escribir**

Tell what these people eat or drink.

> **modelo:** Rodrigo (cereal)
> Rodrigo come cereal.

1. Rodrigo y Marisol (uvas)
2. tú (refrescos)
3. ustedes (pan)
4. Marisol y yo (sopa)
5. Ana (hamburguesas)
6. usted (sándwiches)
7. yo (jugo de naranja)
8. los maestros (café)

## 16 | ¿En la cafetería o en clase? ♻ *¿Recuerdas?* The verb **estar** p. 128

**Hablar
Escribir**

Tell what these people are doing and where they are right now.

> **modelo:** Marisol / vender fruta
> Marisol vende fruta. Ahora está **en la cafetería.**

1. yo / beber leche
2. ellas / leer un libro
3. tú / comer yogur
4. Rodrigo / aprender el español
5. ustedes / escribir en el pizarrón
6. tú y yo / compartir una pizza

## 17 | Actividades en el almuerzo

**Escuchar
Escribir**

Listen to the descriptions of Marisol and her friends, and take notes. Then write sentences saying who does what, using elements from each puzzle piece.

1. Marisol
2. la cafetería
3. Rodrigo y Mateo
4. Carmen
5. Raúl y David
6. Laura y Diana

The verb **hacer** is irregular in the present tense only in the **yo** form: **hago.**
In the other forms, it follows the pattern for **-er** verbs. (See p. R12 for the complete conjugation.)

| | |
|---|---|
| **Hago** un sándwich. | Carmen **hace** la tarea. |
| *I am making a sandwich.* | *Carmen is doing her homework.* |

## 18 | ¿Con quién?

Hablar

Ask a partner with whom he or she does the following activities.

modelo: comer pizza

**A** ¿Con quién comes pizza?

**B** Como pizza con Alicia.

1. correr
2. compartir el almuerzo
3. hacer la tarea
4. comer ¿ ?
5. escribir correos electrónicos
6. beber ¿ ?

## Comparación cultural

### La Plaza de Colón

*How do some cities reflect their historical colonial past?* In Old San Juan you will find cobblestone streets, Spanish colonial buildings, and many plazas as part of **Puerto Rico's** Spanish heritage. The Plaza de Colón is popular with both tourists and locals. A statue of Christopher Columbus in the center of the square includes plaques commemorating the explorer's achievements.

**Compara con tu mundo** *What is a well-known landmark in your area? What does it represent? Why is it important?*

La Plaza de Colón

## 19 | En el café Buenavida

Hablar
Escribir

Look at the picture below and tell what the people are doing.

## 20 | Una encuesta

Hablar

Survey your classmates about the following activities.

**modelo:** leer: en la biblioteca, en la cafetería, en la clase de inglés

**A** ¿Lees en la biblioteca, en la cafetería o en la clase de inglés?

**B** Leo en la clase de inglés.

**C** Leo en la biblioteca y en la cafetería.

1. beber: leche, refrescos, jugo
2. hacer la tarea: en la clase, en la biblioteca, en la cafetería
3. escribir: en un cuaderno, en el pizarrón, en la computadora
4. comer: sándwiches, pizza, hamburguesas
5. aprender: historia, matemáticas, ciencias
6. compartir: pizza, uvas, papas fritas

*Más práctica*    Cuaderno *pp. 107–109*    Cuaderno para hispanohablantes *pp. 108–111*

**PARA Y PIENSA**

**Did you get it?** Complete each sentence with the correct form of the verb in parentheses.

1. ¿Qué _____ ellas? (hacer) Ellas _____ el desayuno. (comer)
2. ¿Qué _____ tú? (hacer) Yo _____ un libro. (leer)
3. ¿Qué _____ Rafael? (hacer) Rafael _____ un refresco. (beber)

**Get Help Online**
ClassZone.com

# Todo junto

¡AVANZA!

**Goal:** *Show what you know* Pay attention to the **-er** and **-ir** verbs Rodrigo and Marisol use to talk about eating healthy food. Then practice these verbs and **gustar** to talk about lunchtime in the cafeteria. *Actividades 21–25*

♻ ¿*Recuerdas?* Telling time p. 99

## Telehistoria completa

**@HomeTutor** VideoPlus
**View, Read and Record**
ClassZone.com

### STRATEGIES

**Cuando lees**

**Find the twist** There is sometimes a "twist," or something unexpected, toward the end of a story or scene. Find the twist in this scene. What is it? Why is it unexpected?

**Cuando escuchas**

**Listen for attitude changes** To understand the scene fully, notice people's attitudes. At the beginning of the scene, what are Marisol's and Rodrigo's contrasting attitudes? Whose attitude changes during the scene? Why?

**Escena 1** *Resumen*

Rodrigo necesita el autógrafo de Trini Salgado para Alicia. Tiene que estar en la escuela a las cuatro de la tarde.

**Escena 2** *Resumen*

Rodrigo compra comida. Le gusta la comida nutritiva. Marisol tiene hambre porque no le gusta comer mucho en el desayuno.

### Escena 3

VIDEO
DVD

AUDIO

**Marisol:** ¿Venden papas fritas?

**Rodrigo:** Tienes que comer comidas buenas.

**Marisol:** Sí, sí. Yo como comida nutritiva de vez en cuando.

**Rodrigo:** ¿Sí? ¿Qué comes?

**Marisol:** Me gusta la sopa.

**Rodrigo:** La sopa es muy buena.

**Marisol:** Necesito una bebida.

*Marisol walks away. Rodrigo sneaks a taste of her ice cream.*

**Rodrigo:** El helado es muy rico.

*Marisol stops to order an ice cream.*

**Rodrigo:** ¿Helado? ¿En el almuerzo?

**Marisol:** Sí, tengo ganas de comer helado. ¿Compartimos?

**Rodrigo:** El helado no es nutritivo.

**Marisol:** ¡Pero es muy rico!

**Rodrigo:** ¿Qué comes en la cena? ¿Una hamburguesa con papas fritas?

## 21 ¡A completar! *Comprensión de los episodios*

Escuchar
Leer

Complete the following sentences, based on the episodes.

1. Rodrigo necesita...
2. La amiga de Miami se llama...
3. En el desayuno Rodrigo come...
4. Marisol tiene hambre porque...
5. Marisol tiene ganas de...
6. Cuando Marisol compra una bebida, Rodrigo...

## 22 Organiza la información *Comprensión de los episodios*

Escuchar
Leer

Write an article about Marisol or Rodrigo. Copy this map on a piece of paper and use it to organize the information.

## 23 ¿Qué hacen en la cafetería? ♻ *¿Recuerdas?* Telling time p. 99

Hablar

> **STRATEGY  Hablar**
>
> **Think and practice in advance** First write down words or phrases you want to say. Then practice pronouncing them aloud. Say them in sentences several times and you will be ready for your conversation!

Work in a group of three to talk about what you do in the cafeteria. Include what time you go and what they sell there. Also explain what you eat and drink and why.

**A** ¿A qué hora van ustedes a la cafetería? ¿Qué hacen?

**B** Como en la cafetería a la una. Los lunes como pizza y bebo jugo porque no me gusta la leche.

**C** Yo compro una manzana y leo un libro...

## 24 | Integración

Leer
Escuchar
Hablar

Read the newspaper ad for Supermercado Grande. Then listen to the radio ad for Supermercado Econo. Say what foods you like and where they sell them.

**Fuente 1 Anuncio**

Supermercado Grande

Uvas
$149 lb.
Reg. $1.95 lb.

Galletas
dos por $100
Reg. $1.50

Manzanas
75¢ lb.
Reg. 99¢ lb.

$499 Reg. $6.99

Pizza de queso

**Fuente 2 Anuncio de radio**

**Listen and take notes**
• ¿Qué comidas venden en el Supermercado Econo?
• ¿Qué venden en la cafetería?

**modelo:** A mí me gustan las uvas. Venden uvas en el Supermercado Grande...

## 25 | La cafetería de la escuela

Escribir

Write a letter to your principal about the school cafeteria. What is good and bad there? Why? Do you have any questions about it?

**modelo:** Sr. Hogan:

¿Cómo está usted? Me gusta la escuela pero no me gusta mucho la cafetería. No es muy grande y hay muchos estudiantes. ¿Por qué no venden...

| Writing Criteria | Excellent | Good | Needs Work |
|---|---|---|---|
| **Content** | Your letter includes a lot of information. | Your letter includes some information. | Your letter includes little information. |
| **Communication** | Most of your letter is organized and easy to follow. | Parts of your letter are organized and easy to follow. | Your letter is disorganized and hard to follow. |
| **Accuracy** | Your letter has few mistakes in grammar and vocabulary. | Your letter has some mistakes in grammar and vocabulary. | Your letter has many mistakes in grammar and vocabulary. |

*Más práctica*   Cuaderno *pp. 110–111*   Cuaderno para hispanohablantes *pp. 112–113*

**PARA Y PIENSA**

**Did you get it?** Complete the first sentence with a form of **gustar,** and the second sentence with the correct form of **compartir** or **beber.**
1. A Rodrigo le _____ la fruta. Él _____ jugo de naranja.
2. A Rodrigo y a Ana les _____ los sándwiches. Siempre _____ un sándwich.

**Get Help Online**
ClassZone.com

# Juegos y diversiones

Review food vocabulary by playing a game of Fly Swatter.

# MATAMOSCAS

### The Setup

Your teacher will tape a number of picture cards on the board and divide the class into two teams.

### Playing the Game

The first player from each team will go up to the board. Your teacher will give each player a fly swatter and then say a vocabulary word represented by one of the pictures. The player who "swats" the correct picture first gets a point.

Play continues with new players from each team.

### The Winner!

The team with the most points at the end wins.

**Materials**
- picture cards representing vocabulary words
- two fly swatters
- tape

# Lectura

**¡AVANZA!**   **Goal:** Read a section from a supermarket ad and then a shopping list. Compare this information with the foods and beverages you eat and drink.

**AUDIO**

# ¡A comprar y a comer!

The following is a supermarket ad from Supermercados La Famosa and a shopping list.

**STRATEGY  Leer**
**Don't translate; use pictures!**
Sketch and label pictures of the foods and beverages on the shopping list. Below each picture, write the brand or type of item you can buy at Supermercados La Famosa.

SUPERMERCADOS LA FAMOSA

TENEMOS BUENOS PRECIOS Y PRODUCTOS SUPERIORES

Hamburguesas El bohío, 1.5 lbs.
$4.29

$1.79
Queso americano de sándwich Vitarroz 12 oz. [1]

Jamón de sándwich Astor
$5.79/LB.

Uvas de California
$2.59/LB.

Yogur de mango La Yogurt
$1.09

$1.29
Queso crema La Cremosa 8 oz.

Leche condensada La Fe 14 oz.
.99¢

---

[1] onzas    [2] libra

**Huevos del país**
$2.19

**Jamón ovalado Hak**
5 lbs.
$9.99

**Manzanas rojas**
$1.99/LB.

**Jugo de china Valemil**
64 oz.
$2.69

**Jugo de piña Tropical, de concentrado**
12 oz.
.99¢

**Pan de sándwich Club**
24 oz.
$1.69

**Café El Morro**
16 oz.
$6.00

**Pan Criollo** [4]
1 lb.
$1.29

Precios válidos el viernes, el sábado y el domingo.

*Lista de compras*

café
huevos
leche condensada
jugo de china
pan
yogur
cereal
jamón de sándwich
queso de sándwich
uvas
manzanas

---

[3] En Puerto Rico usan dólares estadounidenses

[4] bread similar to French bread

**PARA Y PIENSA**

## ¿Comprendiste?

**1.** ¿Qué hay en la lista que no está en la circular?

**2.** ¿Qué venden en Supermercados La Famosa que no está en la lista?

**3.** ¿Qué frutas hay en la lista?

### ¿Y tú?

¿Qué comida en Supermercados La Famosa comes tú? ¿Qué bebes?

# Conexiones    *Las ciencias*

## Los huracanes

The Caribbean island of Puerto Rico is located in an area prone to hurricanes (**huracanes**). The word *hurricane* comes from the Taino word *hurákan*, which was used by the pre-Columbian inhabitants of the island to describe these storms (**tormentas**). Hurricanes draw energy from the surface of warm tropical waters and from moisture in the air. The extreme winds of 74 miles per hour or more can create storm surges—domes of water up to 20 feet high and 100 miles wide—and can spawn tornadoes, torrential rain, and floods. Research and write about the most severe weather condition where you live. Create a diagram or drawing to illustrate your report.

**La ruta del huracán Georges**

el 27 de septiembre
el 25 de septiembre
el 22 de septiembre
Puerto Rico
el 20 de septiembre
el 18 de septiembre
el 17 de septiembre

**Las etapas del huracán Georges**

| | |
|---|---|
| 17/09/98 | Tormenta tropical |
| 18/09/98 | Huracán – categoría 2 |
| 20/09/98 | Huracán – categoría 4 |
| 22/09/98 | Huracán – categoría 3 |
| 25/09/98 | Huracán – categoría 1 |
| 27/09/98 | Huracán – categoría 2 |

### Proyecto 1  *Las matemáticas*

Hurricane Georges passed over Puerto Rico at a speed of about 24 kilometers per hour (**kilómetros por hora**). Find the distance from Humacao to Mayagüez in kilometers and calculate the time it took for the storm to move from one city to the other.

### Proyecto 2  *La historia*

Research another major hurricane that has hit Puerto Rico in the past two decades. Draw a map showing the trajectory of the hurricane. Then write a paragraph describing the storm.

### Proyecto 3  *La geografía*

Compare this map to the one on page xxxiii to name three other countries that were hit by Hurricane Georges. Make a chart in Spanish showing the three countries, the dates of the storm, and the category of the hurricane at the time it hit.

*La playa Ocean Park, Puerto Rico, durante el huracán Georges*

## Vocabulario

### Talk About Foods and Beverages

**Meals**

| | |
|---|---|
| el almuerzo | lunch |
| la bebida | beverage, drink |
| la cena | dinner |
| compartir | to share |
| la comida | food; meal |
| el desayuno | breakfast |
| vender | to sell |

**For Breakfast**

| | |
|---|---|
| el café | coffee |
| el cereal | cereal |
| el huevo | egg |
| el jugo de naranja | orange juice |
| la leche | milk |
| el pan | bread |
| el yogur | yogurt |

**For Lunch**

| | |
|---|---|
| la hamburguesa | hamburger |
| el sándwich de jamón y queso | ham and cheese sandwich |
| la sopa | soup |

**Fruit**

| | |
|---|---|
| la banana | banana |
| la manzana | apple |
| las uvas | grapes |

**Describe Feelings**

| | |
|---|---|
| tener ganas de... | to feel like . . . |
| tener hambre | to be hungry |
| tener sed | to be thirsty |

**Ask Questions**

| | |
|---|---|
| ¿Cómo? | How? |
| ¿Cuál(es)? | Which?; What? |
| ¿Por qué? | Why? |
| ¿Qué? | What? |
| ¿Quién(es)? | Who? |

**Other Words and Phrases**

| | |
|---|---|
| ahora | now |
| Es importante. | It's important. |
| horrible | horrible |
| nutritivo(a) | nutritious |
| otro(a) | other |
| para | for; in order to |
| rico(a) | tasty, delicious |

## Gramática

**Notas gramaticales:** Interrogative words *p. 161,* The verb **hacer** *p. 170*

### Gustar with Nouns

To talk about the things that people like, use
**gustar + noun.**

| Singular |
|---|
| me gusta **la sopa** |
| te gusta **la sopa** |
| le gusta **la sopa** |
| nos gusta **la sopa** |
| os gusta **la sopa** |
| les gusta **la sopa** |

| Plural |
|---|
| me gustan **los jugos** |
| te gustan **los jugos** |
| le gustan **los jugos** |
| nos gustan **los jugos** |
| os gustan **los jugos** |
| les gustan **los jugos** |

### Present Tense of -er and -ir Verbs

| vender *to sell* | |
|---|---|
| vendo | vendemos |
| vendes | vendéis |
| vende | venden |

| compartir *to share* | |
|---|---|
| comparto | compartimos |
| compartes | compartís |
| comparte | comparten |

# Repaso de la lección

¡LLEGADA!

**Now you can**
- talk about foods and beverages
- ask questions
- say which foods you like and don't like

**Using**
- interrogative words
- **gustar** with nouns
- present tense of **-er** and **-ir** verbs
- the verb **hacer**

**To review**
- **gustar** with nouns p. 162
- present tense of **-er** and **-ir** verbs p. 168

## 1 | Listen and understand

AUDIO

Lola never eats traditional meals. Listen to the radio interview. Write **el desayuno, el almuerzo,** or **la cena,** according to when she eats or drinks each item.

1. huevos
2. café
3. leche
4. hamburguesas
5. banana
6. refresco
7. pan
8. cereal

**To review**
- present tense of **-er** and **-ir** verbs p. 168
- the verb **hacer** p. 170

## 2 | Talk about foods and beverages

Write what these people are doing in the cafeteria.

modelo: Daniel / comer
Daniel come pan.

1. Irene / beber
2. ustedes / compartir
3. yo / hacer
4. nosotros / vender

5. yo / comer
6. tú / hacer
7. los estudiantes / beber
8. Trinidad y yo / compartir

**To review**
• interrogative words p. 161

## 3 | Ask questions

Gilberto is a new student. It's lunchtime, and he is in the cafeteria with Julia. Complete the conversation with interrogative words.

**modelo:** ¿<u>Cuál</u> es el sándwich del día?
Es el sándwich de jamón y queso.

**Gilberto:** ¿ __1.__ está el yogur?

**Julia:** Está al lado de las frutas.

**Gilberto:** ¿ __2.__ no venden pizza?

**Julia:** Porque hoy no es viernes.

**Gilberto:** ¿ __3.__ venden los martes?

**Julia:** Venden hamburguesas.

**Gilberto:** ¿ __4.__ es la sopa?

**Julia:** Es muy rica.

**Gilberto:** ¿ __5.__ prepara la comida?

**Julia:** La señora Aguirre.

**Gilberto:** ¿ __6.__ personas trabajan en la cafetería?

**Julia:** Nueve o diez.

**Gilberto:** ¿ __7.__ compramos la bebida?

**Julia:** Ahora, con la comida.

**Gilberto:** ¿ __8.__ vamos después del almuerzo?

**Julia:** A la clase de inglés.

**To review**
• **gustar** with nouns p. 162

## 4 | Say which foods you like and don't like

These people are in the supermarket and are talking about foods and drinks. Write sentences about what they like and don't like, according to what they say.

**modelo:** la señora Medina: «El yogur es bueno.»
A la señora Medina le gusta el yogur.

1. ustedes: «No, el yogur es horrible.»
2. Adán y Susana: «Necesitamos manzanas. Son nutritivas.»
3. el señor Chávez: «El café es bueno.»
4. nosotros: «No, el café es malo.»
5. yo: «Tengo ganas de comer uvas.»
6. tú: «Las hamburguesas son ricas.»

**To review**
• El Yunque p. 153
• Comparación cultural pp. 154, 164, 170

## 5 | Puerto Rico and El Salvador

### Comparación cultural

Answer these culture questions.

1. What is El Yunque and what can you find there?
2. What is a popular cold treat in Puerto Rico?
3. What can you find in Plaza de Colón?
4. Describe some popular foods from Puerto Rico and El Salvador.

**Get Help Online**
ClassZone.com

*Más práctica* Cuaderno *pp. 112–123* Cuaderno para hispanohablantes *pp. 114–123*

# Puerto Rico

# 2

**¡AVANZA!**

**Tema:**

# En mi familia

## In this lesson you will learn to
- talk about family
- ask and tell ages
- express possession
- give dates
- make comparisons

## using
- **de** to show possession
- possessive adjectives
- comparatives

## ♻ ¿Recuerdas?
- the verb **tener**, describing others
- numbers from 11 to 100
- after-school activities

## Comparación cultural

### In this lesson you will learn about
- government elections
- portraits and instruments from Puerto Rico and Peru
- **quinceañeras** in Puerto Rico and Peru
- meals in Puerto Rico, El Salvador, and Peru

### Compara con tu mundo

In many Spanish-speaking countries, families share time together at the table long after a meal is over. This custom is called **la sobremesa.** *Does your family have any traditions involving mealtimes? What are they?*

### ¿Qué ves?

*Mira la foto*
¿Tiene sed Rodrigo?

¿Qué beben los señores, café o refrescos?

¿Cómo es la chica?

## Una familia come en casa
*San Juan, Puerto Rico*

# Presentación de VOCABULARIO

**Goal:** Learn about Rodrigo's family. Then practice what you have learned to talk about families and express possession. *Actividades 1–2*

VIDEO
DVD

AUDIO

**A** Soy Rodrigo. **Vivo** en Puerto Rico con **mis padres.** Ellos tienen dos **hijos.** Yo soy **su hijo** y **mi hermana** Ana es su **hija.** Te presento a las otras personas en **nuestra familia.**

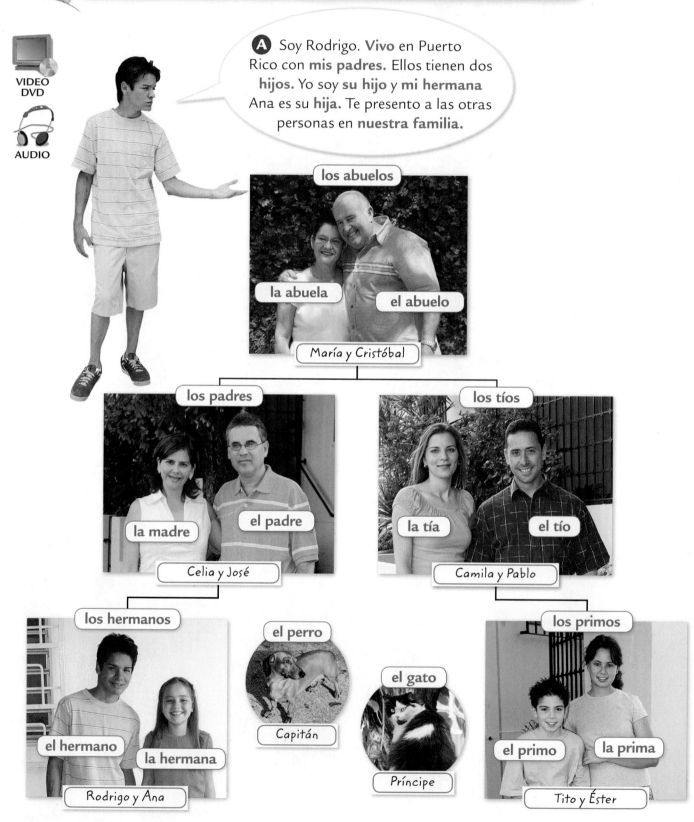

los abuelos

la abuela

el abuelo

María y Cristóbal

los padres

la madre

el padre

Celia y José

los tíos

la tía

el tío

Camila y Pablo

los hermanos

el hermano

la hermana

Rodrigo y Ana

el perro

Capitán

el gato

Príncipe

los primos

el primo

la prima

Tito y Éster

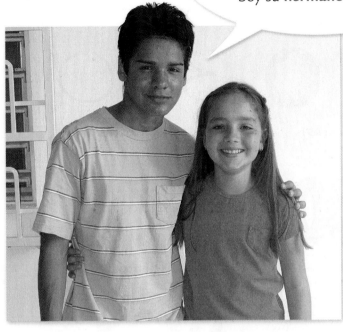

**B** **¿Cuántos años tienes tú?** Yo **tengo** quince **años**. Ana, mi hermana **menor,** tiene nueve años. Soy su **hermano mayor.**

**C** **¿Cuál es la fecha?** Hoy **es el primero de abril.** Es mi **cumpleaños.** ¿Cuándo es **tu** cumpleaños?

los meses

enero
febrero
marzo
abril
mayo
junio
julio
agosto
septiembre
octubre
noviembre
diciembre

abril

¡Feliz cumpleaños!

Continuará...

# Presentación de VOCABULARIO

(continuación)

Los números de 101 a 1.000.000

**101**
ciento uno(a)

**102**
ciento dos

**200**
doscientos(as)

**300**
trescientos(as)

**400**
cuatrocientos(as)

**500**
quinientos(as)

**600**
seiscientos(as)

**700**
setecientos(as)

**800**
ochocientos(as)

**900**
novecientos(as)

**1,000**
mil

**1,000,000**
un millón (de)

## Más vocabulario

| | |
|---|---|
| **la madrastra** *stepmother* | **la fecha de nacimiento** *birth date* |
| **el padrastro** *stepfather* | **ya** *already* |

*Expansión de vocabulario* p. R4

**¡A responder!**  Escuchar

Listen to the sentences about Rodrigo's family. If the sentence is true, raise your left hand. If it is false, raise your right hand.

**@HomeTutor** VideoPlus
**Interactive Flashcards**
ClassZone.com

# Práctica de VOCABULARIO

## 1 | La familia de Rodrigo

Hablar
Escribir

Tell how each person is related to Rodrigo. Use the family tree on page 184 to help you.

modelo: José es el padre.

1. 2. 3.

4. 5. 6. 7.

### Nota gramatical

In Spanish, **'s** is never used. To show possession, use **de** and the **noun** that refers to the owner/possessor.

el gato **de Marisa**     *Marisa's cat*          los primos **de Juan**     *Juan's cousins*

## 2 | La familia de Marisol

Leer

Match the columns to describe the relationship between various members of Marisol's family.

1. El padre de mi madre es...
2. Las hermanas de mi padre son...
3. La hija de mi padre es...
4. Los hijos de mis padres son...
5. Las hijas de mi tía son...
6. La hermana de mi tía es...

a. mi hermana.
b. mi madre.
c. mis tías.
d. mi abuelo.
e. mis primas.
f. mis hermanos.

*Más práctica*     Cuaderno *pp. 124–126*     Cuaderno para hispanohablantes *pp. 124–127*

**PARA Y PIENSA**

**Did you get it?** Fill in the blank with the correct vocabulary word.

**Get Help Online**
ClassZone.com

1. El _____ de tus tíos es tu primo.
2. Los _____ de tus padres son tus abuelos.
3. Las _____ de tu madre son tus tías.

# VOCABULARIO *en contexto*

**Goal:** Identify the words Marisol and Rodrigo use to talk about birthdays and other family members. Then practice the words you have learned to ask and tell a person's age. *Actividades 3–4*

♻️ *¿Recuerdas?* The verb **tener** p. 100, numbers from 11 to 100 p. 94

## Telehistoria escena 1

@*HomeTutor* VideoPlus
**View, Read and Record**
ClassZone.com

### STRATEGIES

**Cuando lees**
**Analyze the scene** This scene starts out calmly and ends with a problem. What do the characters talk about at the beginning? What is the problem, and whose problem is it?

**Cuando escuchas**
**Remember, listen, and predict**
Before listening, remember why Rodrigo wanted Alicia's T-shirt. What happens to the T-shirt in this scene? After listening, predict what will happen next.

VIDEO
DVD

AUDIO

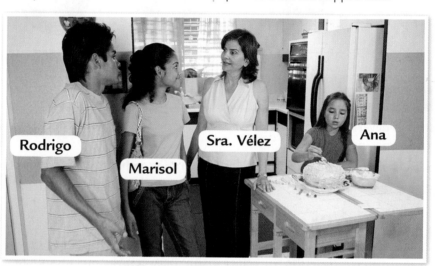

Rodrigo · Marisol · Sra. Vélez · Ana

*Rodrigo and Marisol arrive in Rodrigo's kitchen.*

**Marisol:** Señora Vélez, ¿es su cumpleaños?

**Sra. Vélez:** No, es el cumpleaños de Ana.

**Marisol:** ¡Feliz cumpleaños! ¿Cuántos años tienes?

**Ana:** Hoy tengo nueve años. Mañana, ¡diez!

**Marisol:** ¿Mañana? ¿El veintiocho de febrero?

**Rodrigo:** No. El primero de marzo.

**Marisol:** El cumpleaños de mi abuela es el primero de marzo.

**Ana:** Ah, ¿sí? ¿Cuántos años tiene?

**Marisol:** Tiene sesenta y ocho años.

**Rodrigo:** Mamá, ¿dónde está la camiseta? Trini Salgado está en la escuela a las cuatro.

**Continuará...** p. 194

### También se dice

**Puerto Rico** Marisol uses the word **abuela** to talk about her grandmother. In other Spanish-speaking countries you might hear:
• **Perú, Argentina** **la mamama**

## 3 | Un cumpleaños Comprensión del episodio

Tell if the sentences are true or false. Correct the false statements to make them true.

**1.** Es el cumpleaños de la señora Vélez.

**2.** Mañana es el veintiocho de febrero.

**3.** El cumpleaños de Ana es en el mes de febrero.

**4.** El cumpleaños de la abuela de Marisol es el primero de marzo.

---

**Nota gramatical**  **¿Recuerdas?** The verb **tener** p. 100

Use the verb **tener** to talk about how old a person is.

¿Cuántos años **tiene** tu amiga?     ¿Violeta? **Tiene** quince años.
*How old is your friend?*     *Violeta? She's fifteen years old.*

---

## 4 | ¿Cuántos años tienen?  ¿Recuerdas? Numbers from 11 to 100 p. 94

Talk with a partner about how old the members of Rodrigo's family are. If you need help, look at the family tree on page 184.

45 años

**A** ¿Cuántos años tiene la madre de Rodrigo?

**B** Tiene cuarenta y cinco años.

**1.** 10 años

**2.** 3 años

**3.** 66 años

**4.** 14 años

**5.** 38 años

**6.** 47 años

**7.** 39 años

**8.** 64 años

---

**PARA Y PIENSA**

**Did you get it?** Give each age, using **tener** and the word for each number in parentheses.

**1.** Marisol _____ _____ años. (14)

**2.** El gato de la familia Vélez _____ _____ años. (8)

**3.** Los padres de Marisol _____ _____ años. (52)

**Get Help Online**
ClassZone.com

# Presentación de GRAMÁTICA

**¡AVANZA!**

**Goal:** Learn to express possession. Then practice using possessive adjectives to talk about your family members and to give dates. *Actividades 5–9*

♺ *¿Recuerdas?* After-school activities p. 32, describing others p. 60

**English Grammar Connection: Possessive adjectives** tell you who owns something or describe a relationship between people or things. The forms of possessive adjectives do not change in English, but they do change in Spanish.

They are **my** cousins.          Ellos son **mis** primos.

## Possessive Adjectives

In Spanish, **possessive adjectives** agree in number with the nouns they describe.

*Here's how:*

### Singular Possessive Adjectives

| | |
|---|---|
| **mi** *my* | **nuestro(a)** *our* |
| **tu** *your (familiar)* | **vuestro(a)** *your (familiar)* |
| **su** *your (formal)* | **su** *your* |
| **su** *his, her, its* | **su** *their* |

### Plural Possessive Adjectives

| | |
|---|---|
| **mis** *my* | **nuestros(as)** *our* |
| **tus** *your (familiar)* | **vuestros(as)** *your (familiar)* |
| **sus** *your (formal)* | **sus** *your* |
| **sus** *his, her, its* | **sus** *their* |

Es **mi** tía.
*She is **my** aunt.*

Son **mis** tías.
*They are **my** aunts.*

**Nuestro(a)** and **vuestro(a)** must also agree in gender with the nouns they describe.

*agrees*
**Nuestra abuela** tiene 70 años.
***Our** grandmother is 70 years old.*

*agrees*
**Nuestros abuelos** viven en San Francisco.
***Our** grandparents live in San Francisco.*

*Más práctica*
Cuaderno *pp. 127–129*
Cuaderno para hispanohablantes *pp. 128–130*

**@HomeTutor**
**Leveled Practice**
ClassZone.com

# Práctica de GRAMÁTICA

## 5 | Las familias

**Leer**

Marisol is talking about families and their pets. Choose the correct possessive adjective to express what she says.

1. Nosotros tenemos tres primas. (Nuestros / **Nuestras**) primas son altas.
2. Ustedes tienen un abuelo. (**Su** / Nuestro) cumpleaños es el dos de abril.
3. Mi familia y yo tenemos una gata vieja. (**Nuestra** / Su) gata es Rubí.
4. Yo tengo dos hermanos mayores. (Mi / **Mis**) hermanos son estudiosos.
5. Mis abuelos tienen un perro. (**Su** / Mi) perro es perezoso.
6. ¡Feliz cumpleaños! Hoy tienes quince años. Es (**tu** / su) cumpleaños.

## 6 | ¿Qué hacen?  *¿Recuerdas?* After-school activities p. 32

**Leer**
**Escribir**

Use a possessive adjective and tell what activities these people do.

**modelo:** La hermana de Alicia es inteligente. (sacar buenas notas)
Su hermana saca buenas notas.

1. Los abuelos de nosotros no son muy serios. (escuchar música rock)
2. Los tíos de ustedes son trabajadores. (trabajar mucho)
3. La prima de Marisol no es perezosa. (hacer la tarea)
4. La madre de Rodrigo es atlética. (practicar deportes)
5. La hermana de nosotros es muy estudiosa. (leer muchos libros)
6. El padrastro de Luz es simpático. (pasar un rato con la familia)

---

**AUDIO**

### Pronunciación · La letra j

The **j** in Spanish sounds similar to the English *h* in the word *hello*.

Listen and repeat.

| jamón | mujer |
|-------|-------|
| dibujar | joven |
| junio | hija |

La mujer pelirroja es joven.
El cumpleaños del hijo es en julio.

Soy Javier, el hijo de la mujer pelirroja. Mi cumpleaños es en julio.

## 7 | Unos puertorriqueños famosos

Hablar

Work with a partner. Use the timeline to give the birth dates of these famous Puerto Ricans.

**A** ¿Cuál es la fecha de nacimiento de Carlos Beltrán?

**B** Su fecha de nacimiento es el veinticuatro de abril de mil novecientos setenta y siete.

**Francisco Oller** (artista) 17/5/1833

**José Enrique Pedreira** (compositor) 1/2/1904

**Sila Calderón** (política) 23/9/1942

**Olga Tañón** (cantante) 13/4/1967

**Lola Rodríguez de Tío** (poetisa) 14/9/1843

**Raúl Juliá** (actor) 9/3/1940

**Carlos Beltrán** (atleta) 24/4/1977

## 8 | ¿Cómo son? ♻ *¿Recuerdas?* Describing others p. 60

Hablar

Talk with another student about the people and pets in your family.

modelo: serio(a)

**A** ¿Hay una persona seria en tu familia?

**B** Sí, mi tío David es muy serio.

1. atlético(a)
2. cómico(a)
3. desorganizado(a)
4. inteligente
5. perezoso(a)
6. artístico(a)
7. simpático(a)
8. trabajador(a)
9. ¿ ?

**Escribir**

Write sentences with the names and birth dates of five of your family members and friends.

| madre/madrastra | abuelo(a) | hermano(a) |
| --- | --- | --- |

| padre/padrastro | amigo(a) | ¿ ? |
| --- | --- | --- |

**modelo:** Mi madre se llama Julia. Su fecha de nacimiento es el veintitrés de marzo de mil novecientos sesenta y dos...

## Comparación cultural

### Las elecciones en Puerto Rico

*What do elections reveal about a culture?*
**Puerto Rico** is a commonwealth of the United States. Puerto Ricans have U.S. citizenship and those living on the mainland can vote in presidential elections. On the island, Puerto Ricans vote for their governor and local legislature. Voter turnout is high, often over 80 percent. Puerto Rico has three main political parties: the *Partido Popular Democrático* favors the current political status, the *Partido Nuevo Progresista* wants Puerto Rico to become the 51st state, and the *Partido Independentista Puertorriqueño* supports independence from the U.S.

**Compara con tu mundo** *What issues would motivate you to vote when you are 18? Have you ever voted in any school elections?*

*Residencia y oficina del gobernador, Viejo San Juan*

*Más práctica*  Cuaderno *pp. 127–129*  Cuaderno para hispanohablantes *pp. 128–130*

**PARA Y PIENSA**

**Did you get it?** Fill in the correct possessive adjective and dates.

**Get Help Online**
ClassZone.com

1. El cumpleaños de _____ *(my)* madrastra es _____ . (6/9)
2. El cumpleaños de _____ *(our)* hermano es _____ . (25/1)
3. El cumpleaños de _____ *(his)* amigo es _____ . (17/4)

¡AVANZA!

**Goal:** Listen to the possessive adjectives Marisol and Rodrigo use to talk about the members of his family. Then use possessive adjectives to talk about your family and the birthdays of people you know. *Actividades 10–12*

## Telehistoria escena 2

@**HomeTutor** VideoPlus
**View, Read and Record**
ClassZone.com

### STRATEGIES

**Cuando lees**
**List and practice words** While reading, list the words for family members, such as **madre.** Then practice! Say these words aloud several times. Say them in sentences and create questions with them.

**Cuando escuchas**
**Track the people and actions** While listening, identify the people involved and the actions. What does each one say? Who helps solve the key problem? What new problem arises?

VIDEO
DVD

AUDIO

**Rodrigo:** ¿Dónde está la camiseta?

**Sra. Vélez:** ¡Ah, tus primos! *(She picks up the phone and dials.)*

**Rodrigo:** *(explaining to Marisol)* Ellos comen con nosotros todos los viernes. A nuestros primos les gusta jugar al fútbol.

**Sra. Vélez:** *(on the phone)* ¿Camila? Es Celia. Tengo una pregunta...

**Rodrigo:** Es mi tía Camila. La tía Camila es la madre de Éster y Tito. Mis primos tienen catorce y diez años.

**Marisol:** *(pointing to a family portrait)* ¿Es tu familia?

**Rodrigo:** Mi madre tiene dos hermanas: Inés y Mónica. Mi padre tiene un hermano, Sergio, y una hermana, Camila.

**Sra. Vélez:** Rodrigo, tu primo Tito tiene la camiseta de tu amiga Alicia.

**Rodrigo:** *(to Marisol)* Mi primo tiene perros muy grandes. ¡No me gustan los perros de Tito!

**Continuará...** p. 200

## 10 | Una familia grande *Comprensión del episodio*

Escuchar
Leer

Complete the sentences to describe the episode.

**1.** La madre de Rodrigo
- **a.** no tiene la camiseta.
- **b.** no tiene hermanas.

**2.** Los primos de Rodrigo
- **a.** comen en su casa todos los días.
- **b.** comen en su casa todos los viernes.

**3.** A los primos de Rodrigo
- **a.** les gusta jugar al fútbol.
- **b.** les gusta hablar por teléfono.

**4.** La tía Camila
- **a.** es la madre de Tito y Éster.
- **b.** es la hermana de Inés y Mónica.

**5.** El padre de Rodrigo
- **a.** tiene dos hermanas.
- **b.** tiene una hermana.

**6.** A Rodrigo
- **a.** no le gusta la camiseta.
- **b.** no le gustan los perros.

## 11 | ¿Cuál es tu fecha de nacimiento?

Hablar

Find out the birth dates of eight classmates and make a chart. Share the results with the class.

**A** ¿Cuál es tu fecha de nacimiento?

**B** Mi fecha de nacimiento es el quince de enero de...

| enero | febrero | marzo |
|---|---|---|
| Sandy 15/1/... | Lillian 24/2/... | |
| Doug 21/1/... | | |

## 12 | Tu familia

Escribir

Write a paragraph about your family. Include the answers to the following questions.

- ¿Es grande o pequeña tu familia?
- ¿Cuántos hermanos y hermanas tienes?
- ¿Cómo son las personas de tu familia?
- ¿Cuántos años tienen las personas de tu familia?

**modelo:** Mi familia es grande. Tengo tres hermanos y una hermana. Mi madre tiene treinta y siete años. Es...

**PARA Y PIENSA**

**Did you get it?** Using complete sentences, tell the birthdays of the following people.

**1.** Camila (12/6)   **2.** Éster (1/10)   **3.** Tito (28/3)   **4.** Celia (17/1)

**Get Help Online**
ClassZone.com

# Presentación de GRAMÁTICA

**¡AVANZA!**

**Goal:** Learn to make comparisons. Then use them to describe your family, your friends, and yourself. **Actividades 13–18**

**English Grammar Connection: Comparatives** are expressions used to compare two people or things. In English, comparative adjectives are formed by adding *-er* to the end of a word or by using *more, less,* and *as.*

Rodrigo is **taller** than his sister.        Rodrigo es **más alto** que su hermana.

## Comparatives

**Animated Grammar**
ClassZone.com

There are several phrases in Spanish used to make comparisons.

**Here's how:** Use the following phrases with an **adjective** to compare two things. The adjectives agree with the first noun.

*agrees*

| | |
|---|---|
| **más... que**<br>*more . . . than* | Mi abuel**a** es **más artística** que mi padre.<br>*My grandmother is **more** artistic **than** my father.* |
| **menos... que**<br>*less . . . than* | La clase de ciencias es **menos divertida** que la clase de inglés.<br>*Science class is **less** fun **than** English class.* |
| **tan... como**<br>*as . . . as* | Tus hermanas son **tan serias como** la maestra.<br>*Your sisters are **as** serious **as** the teacher.* |

When a comparison does not involve an adjective, use these phrases.

| | |
|---|---|
| **más que...**<br>*more than . . .* | Me gusta ir a la biblioteca **más que** al gimnasio.<br>*I like to go to the library **more than** to the gym.* |
| **menos que...**<br>*less than . . .* | Me gustan las hamburguesas **menos que** los tacos.<br>*I like hamburgers **less than** tacos.* |
| **tanto como...**<br>*as much as . . .* | ¿Te gusta hablar **tanto como** escuchar?<br>*Do you like to talk **as much as** listen?* |

There are a few irregular comparative words. They agree in number with the first noun.

| **mayor** | **menor** | **mejor** | **peor** |
|---|---|---|---|
| *older* | *younger* | *better* | *worse* |

*agrees*

Mis tío**s** son **mayores** que mi tía.
*My uncles are **older** than my aunt.*

*Más práctica*
Cuaderno *pp. 130–132*
Cuaderno para hispanohablantes *pp. 131–134*

**@HomeTutor**
**Leveled Practice**
ClassZone.com

# Práctica de GRAMÁTICA

## 13 | Sus familias

Escribir

Complete the sentences with **que** or **como** to describe the families of Rodrigo and Marisol.

**1.** Marisol es tan simpática _____ su madrastra.

**2.** Ana es menor _____ Rodrigo.

**3.** Marisol corre tanto _____ sus padres.

**4.** Rodrigo tiene menos hermanos _____ José.

**5.** El tío Pablo toca la guitarra mejor _____ la tía Camila.

**6.** Éster es mayor _____ Tito.

## 14 | Comparaciones

Hablar
Escribir

Look at the drawings and make comparisons using **más... que, menos... que, tan... como,** or **tanto como.**

**modelo:** Nicolás / grande / Sara
Nicolás es más grande que Sara.

**1.** Nora / alto(a) / Patricia

**2.** Marcos / serio(a) / José

**3.** Ana / perezoso(a) / Alí

**4.** Pablo / desorganizado(a) / Pedro

**5.** María / atlético(a) / David

**6.** a Elena / gustar / correr / escuchar música

## 15 | ¿Son diferentes?

Escribir

Marta and her friend Clara have some things in common and some differences. Make comparisons between the two girls.

**modelo:** Marta estudia todos los días. Clara estudia de vez en cuando.
Marta es más estudiosa que Clara.

1. Marta tiene doce años. Clara tiene trece años.
2. Marta es baja. Clara es alta.
3. Marta trabaja mucho. Clara trabaja mucho también.
4. Marta es muy desorganizada. Clara es un poco desorganizada.
5. Marta tiene dos hermanos. Clara tiene tres hermanos.
6. Marta es cómica. Clara es cómica también.

## 16 | Las diferencias

Escribir

Look at the drawing and write sentences with as many differences and similarities as you can find between the members of each pair.

**modelo:** La señora Suárez es más baja que Raquel Suárez.

## 17 | Capitán y Príncipe

Escuchar
Escribir

Ana is talking about her pets, Capitán and Príncipe. Listen to her description and indicate whether the following sentences are true or false.

1. La familia de Ana tiene más perros que gatos.
2. Príncipe es tan simpático como Capitán.
3. Capitán es más grande que Príncipe.
4. A Príncipe le gusta comer más que descansar.
5. Príncipe es menor que Capitán.
6. Capitán es más perezoso que Príncipe.

## 18 | Compara a las personas

Escribir

### Comparación cultural

#### Los retratos

*How do portraits represent the people in a country?* Rafael Tufiño was born in New York and moved to **Puerto Rico,** his parents' homeland, as a child. Much of his work reflects the people and culture of Puerto Rico. In addition to paintings like *Lavandera*, he painted many portraits of his mother, giving them the title *Goyita*. These portraits came to represent not just his mother, but Puerto Rican women overall. Fernando Sayán Polo, an artist from **Peru,** also reflects the people of his country through his artwork. His painting *Niña campesina sonriente* depicts a young wearing traditional Andean dress.

Lavandera *(1960),*
*Rafael Tufiño*

Niña campesina
sonriente *(2005),*
*Fernando Sayán Polo*

**Compara con tu mundo** *If you had to paint a portrait of someone famous, which person would you choose and why? How would you portray him or her? What colors or objects would you include?*

Write five sentences comparing the people in the paintings.

> **modelo:** La mujer es mayor que la chica.
> La chica es más...

---

*Más práctica*   Cuaderno *pp. 130–132*   Cuaderno para hispanohablantes *pp. 131–134*

**PARA Y PIENSA**

**Did you get it?** 1. Say that your brother is taller than your father.
2. Say that you like apples as much as bananas.
3. Say that math class is better than art class.

**Get Help Online**
ClassZone.com

# Todo junto

**Goal:** *Show what you know* Notice the comparative words Marisol and Rodrigo use to talk about why Rodrigo doesn't like Tito's dogs. Then use comparative words and possessive adjectives to describe your family and friends. *Actividades 19–23*

## Telehistoria completa

**@HomeTutor** VideoPlus
**View, Read and Record**
ClassZone.com

### STRATEGIES

**Cuando lees**
**Work with comparisons** This scene contains comparisons of animals and of people. How many comparisons do you see? Write down the "comparison words." Practice them in sentences.

**Cuando escuchas**
**Remember, listen, and predict** At the beginning of this scene, Marisol is calm. How does she change and why? Does this happen suddenly or slowly? How do you know?

**Escena 1** *Resumen*
Mañana es el cumpleaños de Ana, la hermana de Rodrigo. Rodrigo está nervioso porque no tiene la camiseta de Alicia.

**Escena 2** *Resumen*
Tito, el primo de Rodrigo, tiene la camiseta. A Rodrigo no le gustan los perros de Tito.

VIDEO
DVD

AUDIO

### Escena 3

Tito

*Rodrigo and Marisol are walking to Tito's house.*

**Marisol:** ¿No te gustan los perros? Son simpáticos.

**Rodrigo:** Me gustan más los gatos. Son más simpáticos que los perros.

**Marisol:** Los perros son menos perezosos que los gatos.

**Rodrigo:** Los perros de Tito son perezosos y muy grandes. ¡Son tan grandes como tú!

*They stop outside the gate and look around. Tito appears, wearing Alicia's T-shirt, which is filthy.*

**Tito:** ¡Hola, Rodrigo! Tu camiseta.

*Suddenly the dogs begin growling. Rodrigo and Marisol run away frightened.*

## 19 | ¿Rodrigo, Marisol o Tito? *Comprensión de los episodios*

**Escuchar**
**Leer**

Tell whether each sentence refers to Rodrigo, Marisol, or Tito.

1. Pasa un rato con su tía Celia.
2. Tiene perros muy grandes.
3. El cumpleaños de su abuela es el primero de marzo.
4. Necesita la camiseta de su amiga Alicia.
5. Come con la familia de Rodrigo todos los viernes.
6. Es menor que Rodrigo.
7. No le gustan los perros.
8. Tiene la camiseta de Alicia.

**Rodrigo**

**Tito**

**Marisol**

## 20 | ¿Comprendiste? *Comprensión de los episodios*

**Escuchar**
**Leer**

Answer the questions according to the episodes.

1. ¿Cuándo es el cumpleaños de Ana?
2. ¿A qué hora está Trini Salgado en la escuela?
3. ¿A quién le gustan más los gatos, a Rodrigo o a Marisol?
4. ¿Cuántos años tienen los primos de Rodrigo?
5. ¿Cuántas hermanas tiene la madre de Rodrigo?
6. ¿Quién tiene la camiseta de Alicia?

## 21 | La familia ideal

**Hablar**

> **STRATEGY Hablar**
>
> **Consider your beliefs** Before the conversation, consider your beliefs about families. What is an ideal family? Describe it on paper and then aloud. Do you know such a family?

Work in a group of three to express opinions about the ideal family. Include your answers to the following questions.

**Para organizarte**
- ¿Es grande o pequeña la familia? ¿Dónde vive?
- ¿Cuántas personas hay en la familia?
- ¿Cómo son las personas de la familia? ¿Qué hacen?
- ¿Cuántos años tienen las personas de la familia?

**A** Una familia pequeña es buena.

**B** Una familia grande es mejor que una familia pequeña porque es más interesante.

**C** No, una familia cómica es mejor...

doscientos uno **201**

## 22 | Integración

Read the flyer from a family looking for a new home for their dog. Then listen to the radio ad by an animal shelter. Match each dog to someone in your family and explain your choices.

**Fuente 1 Cartel**

Es tan inteligente como su madre y... ¡más activo!

Le gusta correr, nadar y jugar al fútbol. ¡Es más atlético que yo! ☺

Vamos a Nueva York en enero y Rayo no va con nosotros. ☹

Si necesitas un amigo, Rayo necesita una familia.

Llámanos: 555-8231

Rayo
Labrador marrón.
Tiene un año.

**Fuente 2 Anuncio de radio**

**Listen and take notes**
• ¿Cómo es Dino?
• ¿Qué le gusta hacer a Dino?

**modelo:** Rayo es un buen perro para mi primo Alberto. Rayo es menos tranquilo que Dino y a mi primo le gusta correr...

## 23 | Un amigo nuevo

Write a letter to an exchange student from Puerto Rico who is going to stay with your family. Use comparatives to describe the members of your family.

**modelo:** ¡Hola! Te presento a mi familia. Tengo dos hermanos. Yo soy mayor que mis hermanos. Mi hermano Lance es menor que...

| Writing Criteria | Excellent | Good | Needs Work |
|---|---|---|---|
| **Content** | Your letter includes a lot of information. | Your letter includes some information. | Your letter includes little information. |
| **Communication** | Most of your letter is organized and easy to follow. | Parts of your letter are organized and easy to follow. | Your letter is disorganized and hard to follow. |
| **Accuracy** | Your letter has few mistakes in grammar and vocabulary. | Your letter has some mistakes in grammar and vocabulary. | Your letter has many mistakes in grammar and vocabulary. |

*Más práctica*  Cuaderno *pp. 133–134*   Cuaderno para hispanohablantes *pp. 135–136*

**PARA Y PIENSA**

**Did you get it?** Create sentences based on the Telehistoria using possessive adjectives and comparatives.
1. los perros (de Tito) / tan grande / Marisol
2. el primo (de Rodrigo) / menor / él
3. los perros (de Tito) / más perezoso(a) / los gatos

**Get Help Online**
ClassZone.com

# Juegos y diversiones

Review possessive adjectives and possession using **de** by playing a game.

## ¿De quién es?

### The Setup

Your teacher will ask you to bring in two items that represent vocabulary words that you have learned. All the items will be put in a box.

**Materials**
- items collected from students
- box

### Playing the Game

You and your classmates will take turns picking an item out of the box and trying to guess who owns it by asking questions using possessive adjectives.

### The Winner!

The winner is the student who has guessed the owner of the most items.

Juan, ¿es tu pluma?

No, no es mi pluma. Es la pluma de Lorena.

# Lectura cultural

**Goal:** Read about the **quinceañera** celebrations in Peru and Puerto Rico. Then compare the parties and talk about the activities at the birthday parties you go to.

## Comparación cultural

AUDIO

# La quinceañera

**STRATEGY Leer**

**Compare and contrast** Draw a Venn diagram like this one. Use it to compare the **quinceañera** celebrations of Peru and Puerto Rico.

Perú          Puerto Rico

La fiesta[1] de quinceañera es muy popular en muchos países de Latinoamérica. Es similar al *Sweet Sixteen* de Estados Unidos. Muchas veces hay una ceremonia religiosa y una fiesta con banquete. En la fiesta hacen un brindis[2] en honor a la quinceañera y después todos bailan un vals[3].

La chica que celebra su cumpleaños también se llama la quinceañera. En Perú (y otros países) la quinceañera tiene catorce o quince damas de honor[4]: una por cada[5] año que tiene. No hay un menú especial de banquete, pero en Perú es común comer comida típica del país, bailar y escuchar música tradicional.

---

[1] party   [2] toast   [3] **bailan...** dance a waltz
[4] **damas...** maids of honor   [5] **por...** for each

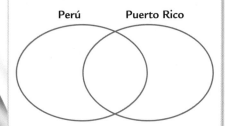

Perú

*Comidas tradicionales: lomo saltado, chupe, mondongo y guiso*

Una quinceañera en Puerto Rico
con familia y amigos

Puerto Rico

En Puerto Rico, la celebración se llama el quinceañero. Muchas veces las chicas tienen la gran fiesta en su cumpleaños número dieciséis (por influencia del *Sweet Sixteen*) y no en el cumpleaños de los quince años.

En el banquete de una quinceañera de Puerto Rico es normal comer comida típica del país, como arroz con pollo[6]. Todos bailan y escuchan música del Caribe: salsa, merengue, reggaetón y el hip-hop cubano.

---

[6] chicken and rice dish

**PARA Y PIENSA**

### ¿Comprendiste?
1. ¿Qué fiesta en Estados Unidos es similar a la fiesta de quinceañera?
2. ¿Cuántas damas de honor tiene una quinceañera en Perú?
3. ¿Cuándo tienen la fiesta las chicas de Puerto Rico?

### ¿Y tú?
¿Te gustan las fiestas de cumpleaños? ¿Qué haces en las fiestas?

# Proyectos culturales

## Instrumentos de Puerto Rico y Perú

*How do certain instruments and music become associated with a particular region?* Percussion instruments that produce strong beats and rhythms are the base of much of the music of **Puerto Rico.** In **Peru,** the **zampoña** is a wind instrument that adds a deep and distinctive sound to traditional Andean music.

### Proyecto 1 *Percussion*

**Puerto Rico** Make your own rhythm on a homemade percussion instrument.

**Materials for your own percussion instrument**
An object that can be used as a "found" percussion instrument, such as:
- coffee or juice can
- yogurt cup with pebbles, sand or seeds, secured inside with a lid on top
- wooden, plastic, or metal spoons
- pan lid and long-handled brush
- upside-down basket

**Instructions**
Practice making a rhythm pattern you can repeat on your "found" percussion instrument. Try creating different tones by striking the instrument in different places or with different objects.

### Proyecto 2 *Zampoña*

**Perú** Use these simple materials to create your own **zampoña.**

**Materials for zampoña**
4 or more plastic or glass bottles, all the same size
Water

**Instructions**
1. Bring to class four or more bottles (all the same size) and add water so that they all have different amounts, ranging from empty to two thirds full.
2. Put your mouth to the top of each bottle and blow as if playing the flute. Because each bottle contains a different amount of air and water, you should hear various pitches.
3. Add tape so that the bottles are connected in a row. Arrange the bottles according to their pitch, from low to high.

### En tu comunidad

Find out if any Andean music groups play in your community, perhaps at a cultural heritage fair or at a local university. Share your findings with the class.

# En resumen
## Vocabulario y gramática

**Animated** Grammar

**Interactive Flashcards**
ClassZone.com

## Vocabulario

| Talk About Family | | | |
|---|---|---|---|
| la abuela | grandmother | la madrastra | stepmother |
| el abuelo | grandfather | la madre | mother |
| los abuelos | grandparents | el padrastro | stepfather |
| la familia | family | el padre | father |
| la hermana | sister | los padres | parents |
| el hermano | brother | el (la) primo(a) | cousin |
| los hermanos | brothers, brother(s) and sister(s) | los primos | cousins |
| | | la tía | aunt |
| | | el tío | uncle |
| la hija | daughter | los tíos | uncles, uncle(s) and aunt(s) |
| el hijo | son | | |
| los hijos | son(s) and daughter(s), children | | |

| Give Dates | |
|---|---|
| ¿Cuál es la fecha? | What is the date? |
| Es el... de... | It's the . . . of . . . |
| el primero de... | the first of . . . |
| el cumpleaños | birthday |
| ¡Feliz cumpleaños! | Happy birthday! |
| la fecha de nacimiento | birth date |

| Pets | |
|---|---|
| el (la) gato(a) | cat |
| el (la) perro(a) | dog |

| Ask, Tell, and Compare Ages | | | |
|---|---|---|---|
| ¿Cuántos años tienes? | How old are you? | mayor | older |
| Tengo... años. | I am . . . years old. | menor | younger |

| Other Words and Phrases | |
|---|---|
| vivir | to live |
| ya | already |

**Numbers from 101 to 1,000,000** *p. 186*

**Months** *p. 185*

## Gramática

**Notas gramaticales: de** to express possession *p. 187*, **tener... años** *p. 189*, Giving dates *p. 192*

### Possessive Adjectives

In Spanish, **possessive adjectives** agree in number with the nouns they describe. **Nuestro(a)** and **vuestro(a)** must also agree in gender with the nouns they describe.

| Singular Possessive Adjectives | |
|---|---|
| **mi** *my* | **nuestro(a)** *our* |
| **tu** *your (familiar)* | **vuestro(a)** *your (familiar)* |
| **su** *your (formal)* | **su** *your* |
| **su** *his, her, its* | **su** *their* |

| Plural Possessive Adjectives | |
|---|---|
| **mis** *my* | **nuestros(as)** *our* |
| **tus** *your (familiar)* | **vuestros(as)** *your (familiar)* |
| **sus** *your (formal)* | **sus** *your* |
| **sus** *his, her, its* | **sus** *their* |

### Comparatives

Use the following phrases with an adjective to compare two things.
**más... que**
**menos... que**
**tan... como**

When a comparison does not involve an adjective, use these phrases.
**más que...**
**menos que...**
**tanto como...**

There are a few irregular comparative words.

| mayor | menor | mejor | peor |
|---|---|---|---|
| older | younger | better | worse |

# Repaso de la lección

¡LLEGADA!

¡AvanzaRap!
DVD
Sing and Learn

@HomeTutor
ClassZone.com

## Now you can
- talk about family
- ask and tell ages
- express possession
- give dates
- make comparisons

## Using
- **de** to express possession
- possessive adjectives
- comparatives

---

**To review**
- **de** to express possession p. 187
- possessive adjectives p. 190

## 1 | Listen and understand

**AUDIO**

Marcos has a family photo and is explaining who everyone is. Listen to Marcos and then indicate each person's relationship to him.

**modelo:** Pedro
Pedro es el hermano de Marcos.

1. Elena y Rosa
2. Julio
3. Norma
4. Alberto
5. Diego y Felipe
6. Carmen

---

**To review**
- possessive adjectives p. 190

## 2 | Talk about family

Write sentences describing what family members these people have, and what their ages are. Use possessive adjectives.

**modelo:** yo / hermano menor (5 años)
Yo tengo un hermano menor. Mi hermano tiene cinco años.

1. Bárbara / hermana mayor (19 años)
2. tú / dos primos (7 y 11 años)
3. nosotros / abuelo (67 años)
4. Manuel y Óscar / padre (34 años)
5. yo / perro (5 años)
6. ustedes / madre (36 años)
7. tú y yo / dos tíos (48 y 44 años)
8. usted / abuela (81 años)
9. ellas / dos gatos (2 años)
10. yo / tía (30 años)

---

**To review**
• comparatives
  p. 196

## 3 | Make comparisons

Josefina is describing her cat, Memo, and her dog, Sancho. Read the description and choose the appropriate words.

Memo, mi gato, y Sancho, mi perro, viven con mi familia. Memo tiene diez años y Sancho tiene cinco. Memo es **1.** (menor / mayor) que Sancho. Pero Sancho es **2.** (tan / más) grande que Memo y come más **3.** (como / que) él. Memo come **4.** (mejor / menor) comida que Sancho porque come buena comida para gatos. Sancho come comida **5.** (mayor / menos) nutritiva porque muchas veces come pizza y papas fritas. Memo y Sancho son muy perezosos. Memo es **6.** (tanto / tan) perezoso como Sancho. Descansan mucho. A Memo le gusta descansar **7.** (tanto / más) como a Sancho. Pero Memo y Sancho no son aburridos. También les gusta jugar un poco todos los días. Jugar con ellos es más divertido **8.** (como / que) mirar la televisión.

**To review**
• **de** to express
  possession p. 187

## 4 | Give dates

Write sentences giving these people's birthdays.

**modelo:** el señor Gómez: 13/4
El cumpleaños del señor Gómez es el trece de abril.

1. Berta: 23/12
2. Emilio y Emilia: 1/2
3. la señora Serrano: 14/1
4. Olga: 5/8
5. Germán: 15/10
6. el director: 11/6
7. la maestra: 30/9
8. Luis: 27/3
9. Víctor: 12/11

**To review**
• Comparación
  cultural pp. 182,
  193, 199
• Lectura cultural
  pp. 204–205

## 5 | Puerto Rico and Peru

### Comparación cultural

Answer these culture questions.

1. What do people do during **la sobremesa**?
2. Which political positions do people vote for in Puerto Rico?
3. Who does Rafael Tufiño portray in *Goyita*?
4. What are some **quinceañera** traditions? Describe at least three.

*Más práctica* Cuaderno *pp. 135–146* Cuaderno para hispanohablantes *pp. 137–146*

**Get Help Online**
ClassZone.com

Perú

Puerto Rico

El Salvador

AUDIO

# ¿Qué comemos?

## Lectura y escritura

WebQuest
ClassZone.com

1 **Leer** Meals vary for people around the world. Read how María Luisa, Silvia, and José enjoy a meal on Sundays.

2 **Escribir** Using the three descriptions as models, write a short paragraph about a typical Sunday meal.

**STRATEGY  Escribir**

**Make a mind map** To write about a real or imaginary Sunday meal, make a mind map like the one shown.

La comida del domingo

¿Dónde?  ¿Qué?  ¿Con quién?

**Step 1** Complete the mind map of your Sunday meal by adding details to the categories of place (where you eat), foods (what you eat), and people (with whom you eat).

**Step 2** Write your paragraph. Make sure to include all the information from your mind map. Check your writing by yourself or with help from a friend. Make final corrections.

## Compara con tu mundo

Use the paragraph you wrote to compare your Sunday meal to a meal described by *one* of the three students. In what ways is your meal similar? In what ways is it different?

Cuaderno *pp. 147–149*   Cuaderno para hispanohablantes *pp. 147–149*

### El Salvador

*María Luisa*

Hola, soy María Luisa. Yo soy de El Salvador. Los domingos, voy con mi hermana mayor y mi prima a Metrocentro[1]. Después de pasear unas horas, vamos a un café porque estamos cansadas y tenemos sed y hambre. En el café venden sándwiches, refrescos y jugos de papaya, mango, melón y otras frutas. A mí me gusta más la horchata[2]. Es una bebida muy rica.

[1] popular mall in San Salvador

[2] beverage made of rice, water, and milk

### Perú

*Silvia*

Yo soy Silvia y vivo en Lima, Perú. Todos los domingos comemos la cena con mis tíos. Mi tío Ricardo siempre prepara su comida favorita, el ceviche[3]. A mí me gusta más el ají de gallina[4] que hace mi abuela. ¡Es mejor que el ceviche de mi tío! Después de la cena, mis padres y mis tíos beben café y hablan. Mis primos y yo comemos helado y escuchamos música.

[3] fish marinated in lime juice      [4] spicy chicken and potato dish

### Puerto Rico

*José*

¿Qué tal? Me llamo José. Vivo en San Juan, Puerto Rico. Todos los domingos, mi familia y yo comemos el almuerzo en un restaurante. Nos gusta comer carne asada[5]. Es muy, muy buena. También me gustan los tostones[6]. ¡Pero los tostones de mi madre son más ricos que los tostones en un restaurante!

[5] barbecued      [6] fried plantains

# Repaso inclusivo
## ♻ Options for Review

¡AvanzaRap!
DVD
Sing and Learn

## 1 | Listen, understand, and compare

**Escuchar**

Listen to this episode from a call-in radio show giving advice to teens. Then answer the questions.

1. ¿Cómo es Diana? ¿Qué problema tiene?
2. ¿Por qué tiene que estudiar Diana?
3. ¿Qué le gusta hacer a Diana? ¿Y a Óscar?
4. ¿Óscar es mayor o menor que Diana? ¿Cuántos años tienen?
5. ¿Qué va a hacer Diana?

Do you have siblings or cousins? Do you have a lot in common or are you very different? Explain.

## 2 | Present a friend

**Hablar**

Bring in a photo or drawing of your best friend or a person you admire. Introduce the person to the class and talk about what personality traits, favorite activities, and favorite foods you have in common. Then mention your differences. Prepare to talk for at least two minutes.

## 3 | Get to know a new student

**Hablar**

Role-play a conversation in which you are an exchange student from Puerto Rico, and your partner is your host brother or sister. Introduce yourself and ask about his or her classes, likes and dislikes, and what his or her family is like. Then answer his or her questions for you. Your conversation should be at least three minutes long.

¿Cómo es tu familia?

Mi familia es grande.

## 4 | Plan a family reunion

**Escribir**

Your family is hosting a reunion with all of your extended family members. You are in charge of organizing a breakfast for everyone. Create a seating chart, and label each seat with the person's name, age, and relation to you. Write what breakfast foods and drinks each person likes and doesn't like.

## 5 | Display your family tree

**Hablar**
**Escribir**

Work with a partner to create a poster of your family tree or that of a TV family. Use photos or make drawings of each family member. Copy this chart on a piece of paper and use it to organize your information. Label each person's name, age, birthday, favorite activity, and favorite food. Use the family tree to describe your family to your partner, making comparisons between family members. Then present your partner's family to the class.

| Nombre | Edad | Cumpleaños | Actividad favorita | Comida favorita |
|--------|------|------------|--------------------|-----------------|
|        |      |            |                    |                 |

## 6 | Compare twins

**Leer**
**Escribir**

Read this chart from a magazine article about Manolo and Martín Santos, twins that were recently reunited after being separated at birth. Then write a paragraph comparing the two men. Include at least six comparisons.

### MUCHAS COINCIDENCIAS

**Manolo**

**Nacimiento:** 30/7, a las 2:20 de la tarde
**Personalidad:** serio, muy artístico
**Profesión:** Maestro de español. Enseña cuatro clases. Trabaja 45 horas en la semana.
**Familia:** dos hijos (Enrique y Arturo) y una hija (Rebeca)
**Actividades:** Le gusta practicar deportes: correr, montar en bicicleta, jugar al fútbol.

**Martín**

**Nacimiento:** 30/7, a las 2:22 de la tarde
**Personalidad:** cómico, muy artístico
**Profesión:** Maestro de español. Enseña seis clases. Trabaja 52 horas en la semana.
**Familia:** dos hijos (Eduardo y Ángel) y dos hijas (Rebeca y Rosa)
**Actividades:** Le gusta practicar deportes: andar en patineta, jugar al fútbol, jugar al golf.

### La historia increíble de los hermanos Santos

# España

## En el centro

## Lección 1

*Tema: ¡Vamos de compras!*

## Lección 2

*Tema: ¿Qué hacemos esta noche?*

Islas Canarias

« **¡Hola!**
Somos Maribel y Enrique.
Vivimos en Madrid, la capital. »

Francia

España

León

Andorra

• Salamanca

Barcelona •

Madrid ★

Portugal

Valencia

Islas Baleares

Océano
Atlántico

• Sevilla

Granada •

Mar Mediterráneo

Ceuta

Melilla

Argelia

Marruecos

**Población:** 40.491.052

**Área:** 194.897 millas cuadradas

**Capital:** Madrid

**Moneda:** el euro (comparte con otros 11 países)

**Idiomas:** castellano (español), catalán, gallego, vasco

**Comida típica:** tortilla española, paella, gazpacho

**Gente famosa:** Carmen Amaya (bailaora), Francisco de Goya (artista), Ana María Matute (escritora), Severo Ochoa (bioquímico)

*Paella*

*Un jugador de fútbol del Real Madrid*

◀ **Aficionados del fútbol** Official songs, or **himnos oficiales,** are an important part of the Spanish soccer experience. Fans of the Real Madrid team sing **¡Hala Madrid!** *(Let's go, Madrid!)*, especially during games against rival team FC Barcelona, known as **El Barça.** *What teams have sports rivalries where you live?*

**El arte y la literatura** Pablo Picasso, one of the 20th century's greatest artists, portrayed traditional Spanish themes in his work. He made this print of fictional characters Don Quijote and Sancho Panza exactly 350 years after Cervantes wrote his famous novel, *El ingenioso hidalgo Don Quijote de la Mancha. What other works of Picasso are you familiar with?* ▶

Don Quijote *(1955), Pablo Picasso*

*Bailarinas de flamenco en Sevilla*

◀ **Las costumbres regionales** During the **Feria de Abril** celebration, girls wear Seville's traditional costume, **el traje de sevillana. Sevillanas** are similar to **flamenco,** which involves singing, dance, and guitar as well as rhythmic clapping or foot taps. *What type of music and dress would be considered typically American?*

# España

## Lección 1

**Tema:**

# ¡Vamos de compras!

## In this lesson you will learn to

- talk about what clothes you want to buy
- say what you wear in different seasons

### using

- **tener** expressions
- stem-changing verbs: **e → ie**
- direct object pronouns

### ♻ ¿Recuerdas?

- numbers from 11 to 100
- the verb **tener**
- after-school activities

## Comparación cultural

### In this lesson you will learn about

- surrealism and Salvador Dalí
- climates around the world
- Spanish poet and novelist Antonio Colinas

### Compara con tu mundo

These teenagers are shopping for clothes in Madrid, Spain. While there are department stores (**almacenes**) and some shopping centers (**centros comerciales**) in Madrid, many people also shop at small stores like the one pictured here. *Where do you like to shop for clothes?*

### ¿Qué ves?

*Mira la foto*

¿La chica está al lado del chico?

¿Quién es más alto, el chico o la chica?

¿Cómo están ellos?

## Una tienda de ropa
*Madrid, España*

# Presentación de VOCABULARIO

**Goal:** Learn about the clothes Enrique and Maribel like to wear. Then practice what you have learned to talk about clothes and how much they cost. *Actividades 1–2*

 *¿Recuerdas?* Numbers from 11 to 100 p. 94

VIDEO
DVD

AUDIO

**A** ¡Hola! Me llamo Enrique. **Voy de compras** al **centro comercial** con mi amiga, Maribel. **Queremos** comprar **ropa nueva.** A Maribel le gusta ir a todas **las tiendas.**

la tienda

ir de compras

el centro comercial

**B** Voy a comprar **una camisa** y **unos jeans. Cuestan** treinta **euros.** El **vestido** de Maribel **cuesta** veinte euros. Es un buen **precio.**

Enrique

la camisa

la chaqueta

los jeans

los calcetines

Maribel

la blusa

los pantalones

los zapatos

el vestido

el precio

22€

**En España se dice...**

In Spain the word for *jeans* is **los vaqueros.** They also use **los tejanos.**

**C** Me gusta **llevar** ropa **blanca, roja** y **marrón.** A Maribel le gusta llevar **una camiseta verde** y **unos pantalones cortos azules.**

roja

verde

amarilla

anaranjada

la camiseta

marrones

azules

blancos

negros

los pantalones cortos

**D** Maribel **piensa** que **el vestido** es un poco **feo.** Ella **tiene razón;** no es muy bonito. Ella compra otro vestido que le gusta más.

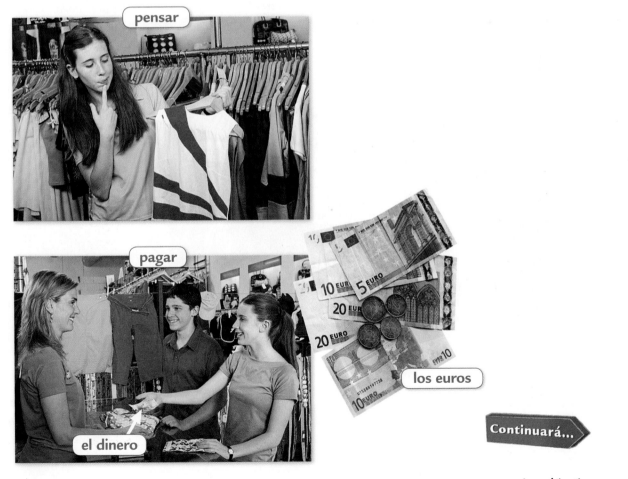

pensar

pagar

los euros

el dinero

# Presentación de VOCABULARIO
*(continuación)*

**E** En España hay cuatro **estaciones**. Maribel siempre **tiene calor durante el verano**. Me gusta **el invierno,** pero siempre **tengo frío**.

las estaciones

la primavera

el verano

el otoño

el invierno

### Más vocabulario

**cerrar** *to close*
**¿Cuánto cuesta(n)?**
  *How much does it
  (do they) cost?*
**el dólar** *dollar*
**empezar** *to begin*
**entender** *to understand*
**preferir** *to prefer*
**tener suerte** *to be lucky*
*Expansión de vocabulario*
  p. R5

tener calor

tener frío

el sombrero

el gorro

**¡A responder!** Escuchar

Listen to the following descriptions of clothes. Raise your hand if you are wearing that item.

**@HomeTutor** VideoPlus
**Interactive Flashcards**
ClassZone.com

# Práctica de VOCABULARIO

## 1 | Los precios de la ropa ♻ *¿Recuerdas?* Numbers from 11 to 100 p. 94

Hablar
Escribir

Tell how much the clothing items cost.

> **modelo:** la camisa
> La camisa cuesta veintiocho euros.

1. el vestido
2. los jeans
3. los zapatos
4. la chaqueta
5. la camiseta
6. los pantalones cortos
7. la blusa

## 2 | Ropa de muchos colores

Hablar

Ask a partner what color the clothing items are.

**A** ¿De qué color son los zapatos?

**B** Los zapatos son rojos.

1.

2.

3.

4.

5.

6.

7.

8.

*Más práctica*   Cuaderno *pp. 151–153*   Cuaderno para hispanohablantes *pp. 151–154*

PARA Y PIENSA

**Did you get it?** Ask how much the following items cost.
1. the white socks
2. the blue dress
3. the orange jacket
4. the red shorts

💫 **Get Help Online**
ClassZone.com

# VOCABULARIO *en contexto*

**¡AVANZA!** **Goal:** Pay attention to the different articles of clothing Enrique and Maribel talk about. Then practice these words and **tener** expressions to say what you wear in different seasons. *Actividades 3–4*

 *¿Recuerdas?* The verb **tener** p. 100, after-school activities p. 32

## Telehistoria escena 1

 **@HomeTutor** VideoPlus
**View, Read and Record**
ClassZone.com

### STRATEGIES

**Cuando lees**

**Scan for details** Before reading, quickly scan the scene to discover basic details: Who's in the scene? What are they doing? Where are they? What time is it? What's the season?

**Cuando escuchas**

**Listen for wishes** Listen to Maribel and Enrique express where they want to go. Who gets his or her way in this scene? How does this happen?

**Enrique**

**Maribel**

*Maribel is opening a package from Alicia.*

**Enrique:** ¿Es una camiseta?

**Maribel:** *(reading a flyer from the package)* Sí. Y Trini está en el centro comercial del Parque de las Avenidas de las doce a la una de la tarde.

**Enrique:** ¿Dónde está el Parque de las Avenidas?

**Maribel:** Necesito un mapa. ¿Vamos?

*They start walking. Enrique stops and points at a store.*

**Enrique:** ¡Una tienda de ropa! ¡Y yo necesito comprar una chaqueta! ¡Tengo frío!

**Maribel:** ¡Eres muy cómico! En el verano, cuando hace calor, ¿necesitas una chaqueta?

**Enrique:** ¿Hace calor? Yo no tengo calor.

**Maribel:** En el invierno, cuando hace frío, llevas pantalones cortos. Y durante la primavera, ¡nunca llevas calcetines!

**Enrique:** ¡Me gusta ser diferente! ¿No necesitas unos zapatos nuevos?

**Maribel:** *(reluctantly)* ¡Vale! Diez minutos. **Continuará...** p. 228

---

### También se dice

**España** Maribel uses the word **vale** to say *OK*. In other Spanish-speaking countries you might hear:
• **México** órale, sale, ándale
• **Cuba** dale

Escuchar
Leer

Complete the sentences by choosing the correct word or phrase, according to the episode.

1. Maribel tiene _____ .
2. Trini está en _____ .
3. Enrique necesita comprar _____ .
4. Enrique lleva _____ en el invierno.
5. Enrique nunca lleva _____ en la primavera.
6. A Enrique le gusta ser _____ .

a. pantalones cortos
b. diferente
c. calcetines
d. una camiseta
e. el centro comercial
f. una chaqueta

---

**Nota gramatical**  *¿Recuerdas?* The verb **tener** p. 100

**Tener** is used to form many expressions that in English would use the verb *to be.*

| | | | |
|---|---|---|---|
| tener **calor** | *to be hot* | tener **razón** | *to be right* |
| tener **frío** | *to be cold* | tener **suerte** | *to be lucky* |

En el invierno **tengo frío,** y en el verano **tengo calor.**
*In winter, I'm cold, and in summer, I'm hot.*

---

**4** | **¿Qué ropa llevas?**  *¿Recuerdas?* After-school activities p. 32

Hablar

Ask a partner what he or she wears in these situations.

**A** ¿Qué ropa llevas cuando paseas?

**B** Llevo pantalones, una camiseta y un sombrero.

**Estudiante A**
1. montar en bicicleta
2. tener calor
3. practicar deportes
4. tener frío
5. ir a la escuela
6. ¿ ?

**Estudiante B**
gorro
pantalones cortos
chaqueta
camiseta
vestido
¿ ?

---

**PARA Y PIENSA**

**Did you get it?** Enrique likes to be different. Complete each sentence with the correct form of **tener calor** or **tener frío.**
1. En el verano, Enrique _____ y lleva una chaqueta.
2. En el invierno, él lleva pantalones cortos porque _____ .
3. Cuando Maribel tiene calor, Enrique _____ .

Get Help Online
ClassZone.com

# Presentación de GRAMÁTICA

**Goal:** Learn how to form **e → ie** stem-changing verbs. Then use these verbs to talk about clothes you and others want to buy. *Actividades 5–10*

**English Grammar Connection:** There are no stem-changing verbs in the present tense of English.

## Stem-Changing Verbs: e → ie

**Animated** Grammar
ClassZone.com

In Spanish, some verbs have a stem change in the present tense. How do you form the present tense of **e → ie** stem-changing verbs?

*Here's how:*

Stem-changing verbs have regular **-ar, -er,** and **-ir** present-tense endings. For **e → ie** stem-changing verbs, the **e** of the stem changes to **ie** in all forms except **nosotros(as)** and **vosotros(as).**

*stem changes to*

quer**er**     qu**ie**ro

| querer | *to want* |
|---------|-----------|
| quiero | queremos |
| quieres | queréis |
| quiere | quieren |

Other **e → ie** stem-changing verbs you have learned are **cerrar, empezar, entender, pensar,** and **preferir.** In stem-changing verbs, it is the next-to-last syllable that changes.

> Paula **prefiere** el vestido azul.
> *Paula **prefers** the blue dress.*

Notice that when one verb follows another, the **first verb** is conjugated and the second is in its **infinitive** form.

> ¿**Quieres** mirar la televisión o leer un libro?
> ***Do you want** to watch television or read a book?*

*Más práctica*
Cuaderno *pp. 154–156*  **Conjuguemos.com**
Cuaderno para hispanohablantes *pp. 155–157*

**@HomeTutor**
Leveled Practice
ClassZone.com

# Práctica de GRAMÁTICA

## 5 | Después de las clases

**Leer**  Enrique is talking to his parents after school. Match the sentences that he would logically say together.

1. La clase de matemáticas es difícil.
2. Tengo hambre.
3. No me gusta andar en patineta.
4. Tenemos sed.
5. Hace calor.
6. Queremos unos zapatos nuevos.

a. Prefiero montar en bicicleta.
b. Preferimos llevar pantalones cortos.
c. Quiero un sándwich.
d. No cuestan mucho dinero.
e. Queremos un refresco.
f. No entiendo la tarea.

## 6 | Todos quieren ropa

**Escribir**   Enrique and Maribel are looking at a clothes catalog. Use the pictures to write sentences about what clothing items they and other people want.

**modelo:**  la madre de Enrique
La madre de Enrique quiere la blusa anaranjada.

1. Maribel
2. tú
3. vosotros
4. usted
5. yo
6. los amigos de Maribel
7. mis amigos y yo
8. ustedes

## 7 | El regalo de cumpleaños

**Leer
Escribir**

Maribel wants to buy a present for her sister. Complete what she says with the correct form of the appropriate verb.

| querer | cerrar | preferir |
| entender | pensar | empezar |

Mañana celebramos el cumpleaños de mi hermana mayor. Voy a la tienda de ropa porque ella **1.** una chaqueta nueva. Ya tiene dos chaquetas, pero ella **2.** que los otras chaquetas son feas. Mis padres no **3.** por qué necesita tres chaquetas. Pero ahora el otoño **4.** y a ella no le gusta tener frío. Mis hermanos y yo vamos a la tienda Moda 16. Yo **5.** otra tienda pero ellos tienen el dinero. Tenemos que llegar antes de las ocho porque la tienda **6.** a las ocho.

## 8 | ¿Tiene suerte en la tienda?

**Escuchar
Escribir**

Enrique is at the mall. Listen to what he says, and answer the questions.

**1.** ¿Qué estación empieza?
**2.** ¿Qué quiere comprar Enrique?
**3.** ¿Prefiere tener frío o calor él?

**4.** ¿Qué quiere comprar Micaela?
**5.** ¿Qué no entiende Enrique?
**6.** ¿Quién tiene suerte?

**AUDIO**

### Pronunciación   La letra c con a, o, u

Before **a, o,** or **u,** the Spanish **c** is pronounced like the /k/ sound in the English word *call*. Listen and repeat.

**ca** → camisa    calor
         tocar     nunca

**co** → comprar   corto
         poco      blanco

**cu** → cumpleaños  cuando
         cuaderno    escuela

Carmen compra pantalones cortos.
Carlos tiene calor; quiere una camiseta.

Before a consonant other than **h,** it has the same sound: **clase, octubre.**

Soy Carlos. Compro una camiseta.

Unidad 4 España

**226** doscientos veintiséis

## 9 | ¿Qué piensas de la ropa?

**Hablar**

Talk with a classmate about your opinions on clothes.

Compra

**A** ¿Quieres comprar un sombrero marrón?

**B** No, pienso que los sombreros marrones son feos. Prefiero los sombreros negros. (Sí, quiero comprar un sombrero marrón.)

1.
Compra

2.
Compra

3.
Compra

4.
Compra

5.
Compra

6.
Compra

7.
Compra

8.
Compra

## 10 | ¿Y tú?

**Hablar**
**Escribir**

Answer the following questions in complete sentences.

**modelo:** ¿Qué piensas hacer este fin de semana?
Pienso montar en bicicleta y leer un libro.

1. ¿A qué hora empieza tu clase de español?
2. ¿Qué entiendes mejor, las matemáticas o las ciencias?
3. ¿Qué quieres hacer después de las clases hoy?
4. ¿Qué colores prefieren tú y tus amigos?
5. ¿Piensas que ir de compras es divertido o aburrido?
6. ¿Qué estación prefieres? ¿Por qué?

*Más práctica*   Cuaderno *pp. 154–156*   Cuaderno para hispanohablantes *pp. 155–157*

---

**PARA Y PIENSA**

**Did you get it?** Complete each sentence with the correct form of the appropriate verb: **empezar**, **cerrar**, or **pensar**.
1. Yo _____ que la blusa amarilla es bonita.
2. Ya hace frío cuando _____ el invierno.
3. El centro comercial _____ a las nueve de la noche.

**Get Help Online**
ClassZone.com

# GRAMÁTICA en contexto

**¡AVANZA!** **Goal:** Listen to the **e → ie** stem-changing verbs that Enrique and Maribel use while they are shopping for clothes. Then use the stem-changing verbs to talk about your clothing preferences. *Actividades 11–12*

## Telehistoria escena 2

**@HomeTutor** VideoPlus
**View, Read and Record**
ClassZone.com

### STRATEGIES

**Cuando lees**
**Look for color words** In this scene, Enrique and Maribel discuss colors and types of clothing. Which color words do you find?

**Cuando escuchas**
**Disregard stereotypes** Who wants to keep looking at clothes and who is worried about being late? Is this expected? Why or why not?

VIDEO DVD

AUDIO

**Maribel:** Tenemos que estar en el centro comercial a las doce, ¿entiendes?

**Enrique:** Sí, entiendo. Dos minutos más. ¿Prefieres los vaqueros negros o los pantalones verdes?

**Maribel:** Prefiero ir al centro comercial, ¡ahora!

**Enrique:** Quiero la camisa blanca.

**Vendedora:** Tenemos camisas en color azul y en verde. ¿Queréis ver?

**Maribel:** *(to the clerk)* No, gracias. *(to Enrique, frustrated)* Pero Enrique, ¿una tienda de ropa? ¿No prefieres ir de compras al centro comercial?

**Enrique:** No. No quiero comprar la ropa en el centro comercial. Los precios no son buenos. *(still shopping)* ¿Te gustan los pantalones cortos azules?

**Maribel:** *(rushing him)* Sí, sí. Y me gustan los calcetines rojos, la camisa amarilla y los zapatos marrones...

**Enrique:** No, no, no. ¿Rojo, amarillo y marrón? No, no me gustan.

**Continuará...** p. 234

## 11 En la tienda de ropa *Comprensión del episodio*

Escuchar
Leer

Who prefers the following things: Maribel or Enrique?

**1.** ir de compras en una tienda de ropa
**2.** la camisa amarilla
**3.** la camisa blanca
**4.** los calcetines rojos
**5.** los zapatos marrones
**6.** ir al centro comercial temprano

**Maribel**

**Enrique**

## 12 La ropa y las estaciones

Hablar

Talk with a partner about what you prefer to wear and not wear during each season.

**A** ¿Qué prefieres llevar durante el verano?

**B** Prefiero llevar pantalones cortos. Nunca llevo chaqueta durante el verano.

---

## Comparación cultural

### El arte surrealista de España

*How might dreams influence an artist's work?* Artist Salvador Dalí from **Spain** is well known for his surrealist paintings. In surrealist art, the imagery reflects an artist's imagination and is often inspired by dreams. *La persistencia de la memoria,* considered one of Dalí's masterpieces, shows pocket watches that appear to be melting. Many interpret this painting as a commentary about the nature of time. What do you think Dalí's message is?

La persistencia de la memoria *(1931),*
*Salvador Dalí*

**Compara con tu mundo** *Can you think of a dream you had that would make an interesting painting? What would your painting look like?*

---

PARA Y PIENSA

**Did you get it?** Complete each sentence based on the Telehistoria with the correct form of the verb in parentheses.

**1.** Enrique _____ que van al centro comercial. (entender)
**2.** Maribel _____ ir al centro comercial. (preferir)
**3.** Enrique _____ comprar la camisa blanca. (querer)

# Presentación de GRAMÁTICA

**Goal:** Learn how to use direct object pronouns. Then practice using them to talk about the clothes you wear and those you want to buy. *Actividades 13–18*

**English Grammar Connection: Direct objects** receive the action of the verb in a sentence. They answer the question *whom?* or *what?* about the verb. The direct object can be a **noun** or a **pronoun**.

Luisa is buying the **blouse.** Luisa is buying **it.**    Luisa compra la **blusa.** Luisa **la** compra.

| noun | pronoun | | noun | pronoun |

## Direct Object Pronouns

Direct object **pronouns** can be used to replace **direct object nouns.**

*Here's how:*

| | Singular | | | Plural | |
|---|---|---|---|---|---|
| | **me** | *me* | | **nos** | *us* |
| | **te** | *you (familiar)* | | **os** | *you (familiar)* |
| *masculine* | **lo** | *you (formal), him, it* | | **los** | *you, them* | *masculine* |
| *feminine* | **la** | *you (formal), her, it* | | **las** | *you, them* | *feminine* |

The **direct object noun** is placed *after* the **conjugated verb.**

The **direct object pronoun** is placed directly *before* the **conjugated verb.**

*replaced by*

**Quiero** la **camisa** azul.    **La quiero.**

*I want the blue **shirt.***    *I want **it.***

When an **infinitive** follows the **conjugated verb,** the **direct object pronoun** can be placed *before* the **conjugated verb** or be *attached* to the **infinitive.**

*replaced by*

Quiero comprar **zapatos** negros.    Y **los** quiero **comprar** hoy.

*I want to buy black **shoes.***    *or* Y **quiero** comprar**los** hoy.

*And I want to buy **them** today.*

*Más práctica*
Cuaderno *pp. 157–159*
Cuaderno para hispanohablantes *pp. 158–161*

**@HomeTutor**
**Leveled Practice**
ClassZone.com

# *Práctica de* GRAMÁTICA

## 13 | Ropa para una fiesta

Leer | Maribel and her friend are talking about the clothes they want to buy for a party on Saturday. Complete their instant messages with the correct direct object pronouns.

---

**mensajero instantáneo**

**pelirroja16:** Quiero comprar un vestido azul pero no tengo mucho dinero. ¿ __1.__ (Lo/La) compro?

**busco_rebaja:** Mmm... __2.__ (me/te) entiendo. Bueno, ¿cuánto cuesta el vestido?

**pelirroja16:** Veintinueve euros. Y tú, ¿qué necesitas comprar? ¿Una blusa blanca?

**busco_rebaja:** Ya __3.__ (la/los) tengo. Necesito unos zapatos. Los zapatos negros son más elegantes. ¿ __4.__ (Me/Os) entiendes?

**pelirroja16:** Sí, tienes razón. Si quieres zapatos negros, __5.__ (nos/los) venden en la Tienda Betún.

**busco_rebaja:** ¡Vale! También venden vestidos azules. __6.__ (Nos/Los) tienen por veinte euros.

---

## 14 | Lo que Enrique quiere

Escribir | Use direct object pronouns to tell what Enrique wants or doesn't want to buy.

> **modelo:** No le gustan **los zapatos anaranjados.**
> No **los** quiere comprar. (No quiere comprar**los.**)

1. Los pantalones son feos.
2. No le gusta la camiseta.
3. Le gustan mucho las camisas.
4. Prefiere los calcetines verdes.
5. El sombrero es horrible.
6. Prefiere los zapatos azules.
7. No necesita pantalones cortos.
8. Prefiere la chaqueta blanca.
9. Le gusta el gorro rojo.
10. Los jeans son feos.

## 15 | Unos modelos cómicos

Hablar

Enrique and Maribel are trying on all kinds of clothes at the store. Ask a partner about what they are wearing.

**modelo:** gorro

**A** ¿Quién lleva el **gorro verde**?

**B** Enrique **lo** lleva.

1. zapatos
2. camisa
3. chaqueta
4. pantalones cortos
5. jeans
6. ¿ ?

## 16 | En la tienda de ropa

Hablar

Ask a partner about what people are buying or wearing in the picture. Your partner will use direct object pronouns to answer.

**A** ¿Compra el señor Costa un sombrero rojo?

**B** Sí, el señor Costa lo compra.

la Sra. Oliva

el Sr. Costa

Martina

Daniel

Adriana

Andrea

Leonardo

# 17 | ¿Cuándo lo usas?

**Hablar**

Work with a partner to name as many situations as you can in which you use the following items.

modelo: un lápiz

**A** ¿Cuándo usas un lápiz?

**B** Lo uso cuando hago la tarea y cuando escribo.

1. una chaqueta
2. el dinero
3. los pantalones cortos
4. un sombrero
5. una computadora

6. un gorro
7. el teléfono
8. un libro
9. una calculadora
10. un cuaderno

# 18 | ¿Qué llevas en julio?

**Hablar**

**Comparación cultural**

## Climas diferentes

*How does geography affect a country's climate?* Countries near the equator have rainy and dry seasons, but have warm temperatures year-round. Countries in the northern and southern hemispheres have opposite seasons. For example, in **Spain,** July is a summer month and the weather is often hot, but in **Chile** it is a winter month. Chile's varied terrain, from beaches to mountains, and length (over 2,600 miles) create many different climates.

Barcelona, España

**Compara con tu mundo** *How does the geography of your area affect the climate? Is there a large body of water or a mountain range that influences the weather?*

Los Andes en Chile

Ask a partner about the clothing items he or she wears in the following places in July: Chile, Mexico, Spain, Puerto Rico, Argentina, and New York.

**A** ¿Llevas una camiseta en Chile en julio?

**B** No, no la llevo. Llevo una chaqueta y...

*Más práctica* Cuaderno *pp. 157–159* Cuaderno para hispanohablantes *pp. 158–161*

**PARA Y PIENSA**

**Did you get it?** In each sentence, use the correct direct object pronoun.
1. Luisa quiere los pantalones blancos. Ella _____ compra.
2. No quiero la blusa nueva. ¿ _____ quieres tú?
3. Nosotros preferimos las camisas azules. _____ compramos.

**Get Help Online**
ClassZone.com

# Todo junto

**¡AVANZA!**

**Goal:** *Show what you know* Listen to Maribel and Enrique talk to the salesclerk about what Enrique wants to buy. Then use **e → ie** stem-changing verbs and direct object pronouns to talk about clothing preferences. *Actividades 19–23*

## Telehistoria completa

**@HomeTutor** VideoPlus
**View, Read and Record**
ClassZone.com

**STRATEGIES**

**Cuando lees**
**Discover what's forgotten** Enrique forgets something in this scene. Find out what he forgot. How does this create a problem?

**Cuando escuchas**
**Take the "emotional temperature"** Find out who has the greatest intensity of feeling by listening to voices. Who is the most upset and why?

**Escena 1** *Resumen*
Maribel tiene que ir al centro comercial porque necesita el autógrafo de Trini. Pero Enrique quiere ir de compras en una tienda.

**Escena 2** *Resumen*
Enrique y Maribel están en una tienda, y Enrique quiere comprar mucha ropa. Maribel prefiere ir al centro comercial.

VIDEO
DVD

AUDIO

**Escena 3**

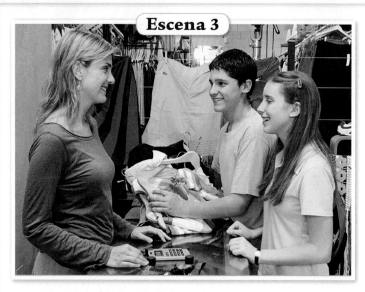

**Enrique:** Tienes razón. La chaqueta... la necesito. *(to the salesclerk)* ¿Vende chaquetas?

**Vendedora:** ¿En verano? No. Las vendo en el otoño.

**Enrique:** ¿Cuánto cuesta todo?

**Vendedora:** Los pantalones cuestan treinta euros, la camisa cuesta veinticinco, y el gorro, quince. Son setenta euros.

**Enrique:** ¡Mi dinero! ¡No lo tengo!

**Maribel:** Enrique, tienes que pagar. Son las once y media.

**Enrique:** Un gorro verde. ¡Lo quiero comprar! ¡Tengo que comprarlo!

**Maribel:** Enrique, ¡pero tú ya tienes un gorro verde!

**Enrique:** Sí, pero nunca lo llevo.

**Maribel:** Quieres una chaqueta, ¿no?

**Maribel:** ¡No te entiendo! ¿Quieres ir de compras y no tienes dinero?

**Enrique:** Está en mi mochila. ¿Dónde está mi mochila? ¿Tienes dinero? En el centro comercial yo compro la comida.

**Maribel:** ¿Con qué piensas pagar? No tienes dinero.

# 19 | ¿Cierto o falso? *Comprensión de los episodios*

Escuchar
Leer

Read the sentences and say whether they are true or false. Correct the false statements.

1. Enrique piensa que los precios son buenos en el centro comercial.
2. Maribel prefiere llegar al centro comercial a las doce.
3. Maribel necesita comprar una chaqueta.
4. Enrique tiene setenta euros para comprar su ropa.
5. A Maribel le gusta ser diferente.
6. Enrique prefiere llevar una chaqueta en el invierno.
7. Enrique compra una chaqueta en la tienda de ropa.

# 20 | Analizar la historia *Comprensión de los episodios*

Escuchar
Leer

Answer the questions about the episodes in complete sentences.

1. ¿Qué estación es?
2. ¿Dónde quiere comprar ropa Enrique?
3. ¿De qué color es el gorro?
4. ¿Cuánto cuestan los pantalones? ¿La camisa? ¿El gorro?
5. ¿Qué problema tiene Enrique?

# 21 | ¡A jugar! Un juego de quién

Hablar

> **STRATEGY Hablar**
> **Prepare and don't stress out** Create a list of useful questions and possible answers. Include various types of clothes. Review your verb endings. Then just talk!

Work in a group of three. Give a clue about someone in your Spanish class. The other members of your group will ask you yes/no questions to identify who it is. Follow the model.

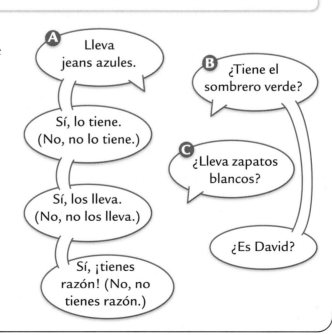

A Lleva jeans azules.

Sí, lo tiene. (No, no lo tiene.)

B ¿Tiene el sombrero verde?

C ¿Lleva zapatos blancos?

Sí, los lleva. (No, no los lleva.)

¿Es David?

Sí, ¡tienes razón! (No, no tienes razón.)

## 22 | Integración

Leer
Escuchar
Hablar

Read the discount coupon and listen to the store ad. Describe four items you want to buy for your friends and how much each item costs.

**Fuente 1  Cupón**

ALTA MODA
¡Descuentos de otoño!

**Ropa de chicos**
• pantalones
• chaquetas
• jeans
Descuento de 5€

**Ropa de chicas**
• zapatos
• blusas
• vestidos
Descuento de 10€

Calle Toro, 38 • Avenida de las Américas, 440  Madrid

**Fuente 2  Anuncio**

**Listen and take notes**
• ¿Qué venden en la tienda?
• ¿Cuánto cuesta la ropa?

**modelo:**  Quiero comprar un vestido verde para Emily. Cuesta...

## 23 | Un poema de la estación

Escribir

Write a poem about one of the seasons. Include the following elements.

**Para organizarte:**
• *el nombre de la estación* ⟶
• *dos colores que describen la estación* ⟶
• *tres cosas que quieres* ⟶
• *cuatro actividades que prefieres hacer* ⟶
• *una descripción de cómo estás* ⟶

**modelo:**
verano
verde, azul
quiero zapatos, helado, camisetas
prefiero jugar, pasear, leer, descansar
tengo calor

| Writing Criteria | Excellent | Good | Needs Work |
|---|---|---|---|
| **Content** | Your poem includes all of the elements. | Your poem includes some of the elements. | Your poem includes a few of the elements. |
| **Communication** | Most of your poem is easy to follow. | Parts of your poem are easy to follow. | Your poem is hard to follow. |
| **Accuracy** | Your poem has very few mistakes in grammar and vocabulary. | Your poem has some mistakes in grammar and vocabulary. | Your poem has many mistakes in grammar and vocabulary. |

**Más práctica**  Cuaderno *pp. 160–161*  Cuaderno para hispanohablantes *pp. 162–163*

**PARA Y PIENSA**

**Did you get it?** Answer each question based on the Telehistoria with **sí,** using direct object pronouns.
1. ¿Necesita Enrique la chaqueta?
2. ¿Prefiere Enrique el gorro verde?
3. ¿Quiere comprar Enrique la comida?

**Get Help Online**
ClassZone.com

# Juegos y diversiones

Review vocabulary by playing a game.

# Pasa la bola

### The Setup

Everyone should stand up and form a circle.

### Playing the Game

**First:** One of you will start by saying a vocabulary word from this lesson and tossing a small foam ball to another player. The player catching the ball will have five seconds to think of a word in the same category as the one just said (another color, clothing item, shopping word, or season). Your teacher will be the timekeeper and judge.

**Then:** Once the player has thought of a word and said it correctly, he or she will toss the ball to another player. That player then has to come up with another word in the same category as the first player's word. Players who cannot think of a valid answer in the allotted time must sit down.

### The Winner!

The winner is the last person standing.

dinero

precio

# Lectura

**Goal:** Read a poem by a Spanish poet. Then talk about what you have read and describe winter in your region.

**AUDIO**

# Las memorias del invierno

Antonio Colinas is a poet and novelist from León, in northern Spain. He published the following poem in 1988.

**STRATEGY Leer**

**Find the feelings** Find phrases that show the poet's feelings and write them in a chart like the one below. Write the feeling after each phrase.

Emotions in *Invierno tardío* by Colinas

Phrase: es como primavera temprana

Feeling: happiness

Phrase:
Feeling:

Phrase:
Feeling:

Antonio Colinas nació[1] en 1946 en La Bañeza, en la provincia de León, España. Escribe poesía, novelas, ensayos[2] y crítica. También estudia literatura italiana y la adapta al español. Su poesía ha ganado[3] muchos premios[4] en España, como el Premio Nacional de Literatura, en 1982. Ahora vive en Salamanca, España.

---

[1] was born   [2] essays   [3] has won   [4] awards

## Invierno tardío

No es increíble cuanto ven mis ojos[5];

nieva sobre el almendro florido[6],

nieva sobre la nieve.

Este invierno mi ánimo[7]

es como primavera temprana,

es como almendro florido

bajo la nieve.

Hay demasiado[8] frío

esta tarde en el mundo[9].

Pero abro la puerta a mi perro

y con él entra en casa[10] calor,

entra la humanidad.

---

[5] **ven...** my eyes see

[6] **sobre...** on the flowery almond tree

[7] spirit      [8] too much      [9] world      [10] house

∼56∼

### PARA Y PIENSA

## ¿Comprendiste?

1. ¿De dónde es Antonio Colinas? ¿Qué escribe? ¿Dónde vive ahora?

2. ¿Dónde está la persona en el poema? ¿Qué mira? En tu opinión, ¿está triste o contenta la persona?

3. ¿Piensas que el perro es un buen amigo? ¿Por qué?

## ¿Y tú?

¿Cómo es el invierno en tu región? ¿Qué te gusta hacer?

# Conexiones *El arte*

## Los árabes en España

For almost 800 years, from 711 to 1492, the Moors, Arab Muslims from northern Africa, occupied an area in southern Spain called **Al-Andalus,** now known as **Andalucía.** This was a period of rich cultural exchange in the arts, sciences, mathematics, agriculture, and architecture.

The Alhambra palace in Granada is a notable example of Moorish architecture in Spain. The interior is exquisitely detailed, bright, and airy. Ornately carved pillars and arches open onto sunny courtyards. The walls and ceilings are decorated with intricate geometric designs.

Design a courtyard based on the architectural styles illustrated in these pictures of the Alhambra. Create a drawing or model to show your design.

*El patio de los leones*

**La Alhambra**

*Un arco musulmán*

*Los jardines del Generalife*

### Proyecto 1 *La música*

Moorish civilization had a lasting influence on the music of Spain. The guitar may be derived from the oud, a type of lute and a classic Arab instrument. The word **guitarra** comes from the Arabic *qithara*. Some contemporary music is similar to the music played during the Moorish rule. Research and write about the musical group *Al-Andalus*. Include the members of the group, the places where they perform, and a description of their music.

### Proyecto 2 *La salud*

Olives have always been a part of Spanish tradition. Olive seeds that date back 8,000 years have been found in Spain. The majority of olive trees grown in the country are found in **Andalucía.** Spain is also one of the world's foremost producers of olive oil. Research and write about the health and beauty benefits of olives and olive oil. Describe how they are used on a daily basis.

### Proyecto 3 *El lenguaje*

The Moors brought many concepts and inventions to Spain. The Arabic words for many of these things still exist in Spanish. Often these words begin with **al-** or **a-.** Some examples are **almohada, álgebra, algodón,** and **ajedrez.** Using a Spanish-English dictionary, write the meanings of these words. Then find three more Spanish words that begin with **al-,** write their English definitions, and use the Internet or the library to find out if they have Arabic origin.

# *En resumen*
## Vocabulario y gramática

**Animated** Grammar
**Interactive Flashcards**
ClassZone.com

## Vocabulario

### Talk About Shopping

| | | | |
|---|---|---|---|
| el centro comercial | shopping center, mall | el dólar | dollar |
| ¿Cuánto cuesta(n)? | How much does it (do they) cost? | el euro | euro |
| | | ir de compras | to go shopping |
| Cuesta(n)... | It costs . . . (They cost . . .) | pagar | to pay |
| | | el precio | price |
| el dinero | money | la tienda | store |

### Describe Clothing

| | | | |
|---|---|---|---|
| la blusa | blouse | nuevo(a) | new |
| los calcetines | socks | los pantalones | pants |
| la camisa | shirt | los pantalones cortos | shorts |
| la camiseta | T-shirt | | |
| la chaqueta | jacket | la ropa | clothing |
| feo(a) | ugly | el sombrero | hat |
| el gorro | winter hat | el vestido | dress |
| los jeans | jeans | los zapatos | shoes |
| llevar | to wear | | |

### Colors

| | | | |
|---|---|---|---|
| amarillo(a) | yellow | marrón (pl. marrones) | brown |
| anaranjado(a) | orange | | |
| azul | blue | negro(a) | black |
| blanco(a) | white | rojo(a) | red |
| | | verde | green |

### Expressions with *tener*

| | |
|---|---|
| tener calor | to be hot |
| tener frío | to be cold |
| tener razón | to be right |
| tener suerte | to be lucky |

### Discuss Seasons

| | |
|---|---|
| la estación (pl. las estaciones) | season |
| el invierno | winter |
| el otoño | autumn, fall |
| la primavera | spring |
| el verano | summer |

### Other Words and Phrases

| | |
|---|---|
| durante | during |
| cerrar (ie) | to close |
| empezar (ie) | to begin |
| entender (ie) | to understand |
| pensar (ie) | to think, to plan |
| preferir (ie) | to prefer |
| querer (ie) | to want |

## Gramática

**Nota gramatical:** tener expressions *p. 223*

### Stem-Changing Verbs: e → ie

For **e → ie** stem-changing verbs, the **e** of the stem changes to **ie** in all forms except **nosotros(as)** and **vosotros(as)**.

| querer | to want |
|---|---|
| quiero | queremos |
| quieres | queréis |
| quiere | quieren |

### Direct Object Pronouns

**Direct object pronouns** can be used to replace **direct object nouns.**

| Singular | | Plural | |
|---|---|---|---|
| **me** | me | **nos** | us |
| **te** | you (familiar) | **os** | you (familiar) |
| **lo** | you (formal), him, it | **los** | you, them |
| **la** | you (formal), her, it | **las** | you, them |

# Repaso de la lección

**¡LLEGADA!**

**Now you can**
- talk about what clothes you want to buy
- say what you wear in different seasons

**Using**
- **tener** expressions
- stem-changing verbs: **e → ie**
- direct object pronouns

---

**To review**
- stem-changing verbs: **e → ie** p. 224
- direct object pronouns p. 230

AUDIO

## 1 | Listen and understand

Listen to Paula talk about clothes. Tell whether she wants to buy each article of clothing or not. Use direct object pronouns.

**1.**

**2.**

**3.**

**4.**

**5.**

**6.**

---

**To review**
- stem-changing verbs: **e → ie** p. 224

## 2 | Talk about what clothes you want to buy

Fernando is going shopping with his parents. What does he say?

**preferir**  **cerrar**  **entender**

**empezar**  **pensar**  **querer**

Las clases ___**1.**___ el lunes y necesito ropa. Yo ___**2.**___ comprar unas camisetas y unos pantalones pero no tengo mucho dinero. Yo ___**3.**___ las camisetas a las camisas. Yo no ___**4.**___ por qué una camiseta cuesta más en el centro comercial que en otras tiendas. Mi amiga Carla ___**5.**___ que hay ropa más bonita y menos cara en la tienda Moda Zaragoza. Necesito ir hoy porque la tienda ___**6.**___ los domingos.

**Talk about what clothes you want to buy**

**To review**
• **tener** expressions p. 223
• stem-changing verbs: **e → ie** p. 224

Tell whether these people are hot or cold, based on what they are thinking about buying.

> **modelo:** Ana / blusa de verano
> Ana piensa comprar una blusa de verano porque tiene calor.

**1.** Juan y yo / gorros
**2.** yo / pantalones cortos
**3.** tú / chaqueta
**4.** Laura y Carlos / camisetas de verano
**5.** ustedes / calcetines de invierno
**6.** Pilar / vestido de primavera

**4** **Say what you wear in different seasons**

**To review**
• direct object pronouns p. 230

Write sentences telling who prefers to wear these clothing items.

> **modelo:** los zapatos negros (Juan)
> Juan los prefiere llevar. (Juan prefiere llevarlos.)

**1.** los pantalones cortos (Rosa)
**2.** las camisas azules (ellas)
**3.** el sombrero rojo (yo)
**4.** la camiseta anaranjada (Carlos)
**5.** el gorro negro (ellos)
**6.** la blusa amarilla (nosotros)
**7.** los calcetines blancos (ustedes)
**8.** la chaqueta marrón (tú)
**9.** los zapatos marrones (usted)
**10.** el vestido verde (Amanda)

**5** **Spain and Chile**

**Comparación cultural**

**To review**
• **Sevillanas** p. 215
• Comparación cultural pp. 229, 233
• Lectura pp. 238–239

Answer these culture questions.

**1.** What are the characteristics of **sevillanas**?
**2.** How do the climates of Spain and Chile differ in July and why?
**3.** What are some characteristics of surrealist art?
**4.** What season is represented in Antonio Colinas' poem? How does the speaker of the poem feel and why?

*Más práctica* Cuaderno *pp. 162–173* Cuaderno para hispanohablantes *pp. 164–173*

**Get Help Online**
ClassZone.com

temporada

Compañía nacional de
TEATRO CLÁSICO

CLÁSICO

Lección

2

**Tema:**

## ¿Qué hacemos esta noche?

¡AVANZA!

## In this lesson you will learn to
- describe places and events in town
- talk about types of transportation
- say what you are going to do
- order from a menu

### using
- the verb **ver, ir a** + infinitive
- stem-changing verbs: **o → ue**
- stem-changing verbs: **e → i**

♲ *¿Recuerdas?*
- present tense of **-er** verbs
- the verb **ir, tener** expressions
- direct object pronouns

## Comparación cultural

### In this lesson you will learn about
- local markets
- art from Spain and Chile
- weekend activities in Spain, Guatemala, and Chile

### Compara con tu mundo
Maribel and Enrique are near the Teatro de la Comedia, where many traditional Spanish plays are performed. *What do you and your friends like to do on weekends?*

### ¿Qué ves?
*Mira la foto*
¿Es viejo el teatro?

¿Lleva pantalones o un vestido Maribel?

¿De qué color es la camisa de Enrique?

**TEATRO DE LA COMEDIA**

El castigo sin vengan...

**El Teatro de la Comedia
en la calle Príncipe**
*Madrid, España*

# Presentación de VOCABULARIO

**¡AVANZA!**

**Goal:** Learn about what Enrique and Maribel do when they go out. Then practice what you have learned to describe places and events in town. **Actividades 1–2**

♻ *¿Recuerdas?* Present tense of **-er** verbs p. 168

**VIDEO DVD**

**AUDIO**

**A** En **el centro** de Madrid hay muchos **lugares** para comer. Maribel y yo queremos ir a **la calle** de Alcalá para **encontrar** un buen **restaurante.** ¿Vamos **a pie, en coche** o **en autobús?**

a pie

en coche

en autobús

**B** En **el menú** hay muchos **platos principales.** Si te gusta **la carne,** hay **bistec.** Si no, también hay **pescado.**

las patatas

el brócoli

el camarero

el pollo

el bistec

el menú

el arroz

el pescado

la ensalada

las verduras

el tomate

**C** La cuenta es veinticinco euros. ¿Cuánto dinero necesitamos para la propina?

la cuenta

**D** Tomamos el autobús para ir al **cine.** Vamos al Cine Ideal para ver una película.

el cine

la ventanilla

las entradas

**E** Aquí en Madrid también hay **teatros** y **parques** pero yo prefiero ir a **un concierto** para escuchar música.

el teatro

el parque

el concierto

Continuará...

**F** Vamos a **un café. De postre** nos gusta **pedir un pastel.** Después, Maribel está muy cansada. Es la hora de **dormir.**

el café

la mesa

el pastel

**En España se dice...**

In Spain the word for *cake* is **la tarta.** The word for *beans* is **las alubias.**

dormir

## Más vocabulario

**allí** *there*
**almorzar** *to eat lunch*
**costar** *to cost*
**los frijoles** *beans*
**la música rock** *rock music*
**poder** *to be able, can*
**servir** *to serve*
**tal vez** *perhaps, maybe*
**volver** *to return, to come back*
*Expansión de vocabulario* p. R5

**¡A responder!** Escuchar

Listen to the waiter. Point to the photo with the food that he mentions.

**@HomeTutor** VideoPlus
**Interactive Flashcards**
ClassZone.com

# Práctica de VOCABULARIO

## 1 | Diversiones en el centro

**Leer** | Read each description and look for the matching word.

1. Es una persona que trabaja en un café.
2. Es el lugar adonde vas para comer.
3. Vas aquí para ver una película.
4. La necesitas para ir a un concierto.
5. Lo comes después del plato principal.
6. Compras entradas aquí.

a. la ventanilla
b. el restaurante
c. la camarera
d. la entrada
e. el cine
f. el postre

---

**Nota gramatical** ♻ **¿Recuerdas?** Present tense of **-er** verbs p. 168

**Ver** has an irregular **yo** form in the present tense: **veo.**

**Veo** muchos autobuses en el centro.     *I **see** a lot of buses downtown.*

---

## 2 | ¿Qué ves en el restaurante?

**Hablar**

Señor and Señora Ortiz are at the restaurant Los Reyes. Ask a partner what he or she sees.

**A** ¿Qué ves en el restaurante?

**B** Allí veo una silla.

---

*Más práctica*    Cuaderno *pp. 174–176*    Cuaderno para hispanohablantes *pp. 174–177*

---

**PARA Y PIENSA**

### Did you get it?

1. Name three things you would find in a restaurant.
2. Name three places where you and your friends might go to have fun.

**Get Help Online**
ClassZone.com

# VOCABULARIO *en contexto*

**¡AVANZA!** **Goal:** Focus on how Maribel and Enrique talk about where they go and how they get there. Then practice these words and **ir a** + infinitive to talk about types of transportation and what you are going to do. *Actividades 3–4*

 *¿Recuerdas?* The verb **ir** p. 134

## Telehistoria escena 1

@*HomeTutor* VideoPlus
**View, Read and Record**
ClassZone.com

**STRATEGIES**

**Cuando lees**

**Think about timing** Consider timing while reading. How long will Enrique's plan take? Will they see Trini? Why or why not?

**Cuando escuchas**

**Enter the scene** As you listen to Enrique's travel plan, enter the scene. If you were Maribel, would you feel calm or nervous about Enrique's ideas? Why?

VIDEO DVD

AUDIO

Enrique

Maribel

**Enrique:** ¿Trini Salgado está en el centro comercial del Parque de las Avenidas a las doce?

**Maribel:** Sí. Y ya es tarde. Enrique, ¡por favor!

**Enrique:** ¡Vale! ¿Y cómo vamos a llegar allí? ¿En autobús?

*Enrique puts the T-shirt in his bag so that Maribel can open the map.*

**Maribel:** Podemos empezar aquí en el parque. El centro comercial está allí. ¿Cuál es la calle?

**Enrique:** Calle Poveda. ¡Es fácil! Tomamos el autobús al centro. Vamos a pie a la biblioteca —aquí. Mi madre está allí. Ella tiene coche. ¡Llegamos al centro comercial en coche!

**Maribel:** ¡Pero, Enrique! Son las once y cuarenta y cinco. Vamos a llegar tarde. ¿Qué voy a hacer?

**Enrique:** ¡Ah! El autobús setenta y cuatro va al centro comercial. Llega aquí a las doce y llega al centro comercial a las doce y media.

**Maribel:** ¡Vale! **Continuará...** p. 256

### También se dice

**España** Enrique says **el autobús** to talk about taking the bus. In other Spanish-speaking countries you might hear:
• **Puerto Rico, República Dominicana, Cuba** **la guagua**
• **México el camión**
• **muchos países el colectivo, el micro**

## 3 ¿Cómo piensan llegar? *Comprensión del episodio*

Escuchar
Leer

Read the sentences and tell whether they are true or false.

1. Maribel y Enrique no tienen mapa.
2. La madre de Enrique está en la biblioteca.
3. El centro comercial está en la calle Poveda.
4. Enrique quiere ir a pie al centro comercial.
5. El autobús llega al centro comercial a las doce.

---

**Nota gramatical** ♻ *¿Recuerdas?* The verb **ir** p. 134

To talk about what you are going to do, use a form of **ir a** + **infinitive.**

¿Qué **van a hacer** ustedes?
*What **are you going to do**?*

**Vamos a mirar** una película.
***We're going to watch** a movie.*

**Vamos a** can also mean *Let's*.

---

## 4 ¿Qué vas a comer?

Hablar

Ask a partner what he or she is going to eat this week. Your partner should explain his or her answers.

**A** ¿Vas a comer carne?

**B** Sí, voy a comer carne. Es rica.
(No, no voy a comer carne. Es horrible.)

1.
2.
3.
4.

5.
6.
7.
8.

---

**PARA Y PIENSA**

**Did you get it?** Complete each sentence with the correct phrase to tell what form of transportation is used.

1. Maribel va a la escuela _____ ; va a tomar el cuarenta y dos.
2. Enrique y su hermano van a ir _____ al parque; les gusta pasear.
3. Maribel y su mamá van al concierto _____ porque no quieren llegar tarde.

**Get Help Online**
ClassZone.com

# Presentación de GRAMÁTICA

 **¡AVANZA!** **Goal:** Learn how to form o → ue stem-changing verbs. Then practice using these verbs to talk about going out with friends. *Actividades 5–10*

**English Grammar Connection:** Remember that there are no stem-changing verbs in the present tense of English (see p. 224). In Spanish, **o → ue** stem changes happen in all three classes of verbs: **-ar, -er,** and **-ir.**

## Stem-Changing Verbs: o → ue

Some verbs have an **o → ue** stem change in the present tense. How do you form the present tense of these verbs?

*Here's how:*

Remember that stem-changing verbs have regular **-ar, -er,** and **-ir** endings. For **o → ue** stem-changing verbs, the last **o** of the stem changes to **ue** in all forms except **nosotros(as)** and **vosotros(as).**

| poder | *to be able, can* |
|---|---|
| puedo | podemos |
| puedes | podéis |
| puede | pueden |

Carmen **puede** ir al concierto.
*Carmen **can** go to the concert.*

Other verbs you know that have this stem change are **almorzar, costar, dormir, encontrar,** and **volver.**

**Almuerzo** a la una.
***I eat lunch** at one o'clock.*

Antonio, ¿cuándo **vuelves**?
*Antonio, when **are you coming back**?*

*Más práctica*
Cuaderno *pp. 177–179*   **Conjuguemos.com**
Cuaderno para hispanohablantes *pp. 178–180*

**@HomeTutor**
Leveled Practice
ClassZone.com

# Práctica de GRAMÁTICA

## 5 | Un concierto de música rock

Leer
Escribir

Maribel is talking with her friend Toni about when they can go to a concert. Complete what she says with forms of **poder,** and use the poster to answer her question.

Presenta **Los Rebeldes**

en el Centro Cívico, Madrid
**Entrada: 18€ en la ventanilla**
**Fecha: 22–23 de abril**
Hora: el viernes por la tarde
(19:00) y por la noche (22:00)
el sábado por la tarde
(14:00) y por la noche (21:00)

Nosotros queremos ir a un concierto el viernes o el sábado, pero ¿cuándo? Yo no __1.__ ir el viernes en la noche porque tengo que trabajar. Manolo no __2.__ ir el sábado en la noche. Ana y Miguel no __3.__ ir el viernes en la noche y el sábado en la tarde no van a estar aquí. Enrique y su hermano no __4.__ ir el sábado en la tarde porque van a un restaurante con su primo. Y Toni, tú no __5.__ ir el sábado en la noche. ¿Cuándo __6.__ ir todos nosotros?

## 6 | ¿Quieres ir?

Leer
Escribir

Complete the conversation between Enrique and Maribel by choosing the correct verb and conjugating it in the appropriate form.

**Enrique:** Yo __1.__ (dormir / almorzar) en el café Mariposa hoy. La comida es muy rica y no __2.__ (volver / costar) mucho. ¿Quieres ir?

**Maribel:** Gracias, pero yo no __3.__ (encontrar / poder) comer ahora. Mis padres __4.__ (volver / dormir) de sus vacaciones en México. Necesito ir a la tienda ahora para comprar comida.

**Enrique:** Tú __5.__ (poder / dormir) ir a pie porque la tienda está cerca de aquí.

**Maribel:** Mis padres quieren comer unas verduras y nosotros siempre __6.__ (costar / encontrar) buenas verduras allí.

**Enrique:** ¿Tú y tus padres __7.__ (poder / volver) ir al cine esta noche? Yo voy a las siete y media.

**Maribel:** Gracias, Enrique, pero mis padres siempre están muy cansados después de sus vacaciones y __8.__ (dormir / almorzar) mucho.

# 7 | Las actividades en el centro

**Escribir** Combine phrases from the three puzzle pieces to describe activities downtown. Use the correct verb forms to write your sentences.

**modelo:** el camarero / no poder trabajar / en el restaurante
El camarero no puede trabajar en el restaurante.

| | | |
|---|---|---|
| las entradas para el concierto | almorzar | en el mapa |
| yo | costar | con amigos en el parque |
| vosotros | encontrar la calle | después de comer mucho |
| tú | poder jugar al fútbol | quince euros |
| usted | dormir bien | en el café con mi familia |
| nosotros | volver al centro | en autobús |

# 8 | Todos tienen excusas

**Hablar** Talk with another student about the activities that you can't do this weekend. Say that you can't do something and make up an excuse.

**modelo:** ir a un concierto

**A** ¿Vas a ir a un concierto?

**B** No, no puedo ir a un concierto. Voy a ir al cine con mi hermano.

1. ir al teatro
2. dormir diez horas
3. practicar deportes
4. almorzar en un café
5. pasar un rato con los amigos
6. ver una película en el cine
7. ir al centro
8. comprar ropa
9. montar en bicicleta
10. preparar la comida

# 9 | ¡Vamos a ir de compras!

## Comparación cultural

*Chichicastenango, Guatemala*

### Los mercados

*How do local markets reflect the culture of an area?* Every Sunday, tourists and locals head to El Rastro, one of the oldest flea markets in Madrid, **Spain,** to search for bargains amid the hundreds of stalls. Vendors offer a wide variety of items such as antiques, secondhand clothing, CDs, books, maps, and art.

In **Guatemala,** the town of Chichicastenango hosts a popular market in which you can find handicrafts from the Maya-Quiché culture. Many vendors wear the traditional dress of their region and sell colorful textiles including Mayan blouses called *huipiles.* Other common items include fruits and vegetables, masks, baskets, candles, and flowers.

*El Rastro en Madrid, España*

**Compara con tu mundo** *What type of souvenir might a visitor to your community purchase? Why is it popular?*

Ask a partner where you can find books, CDs, fruit, art, vegetables, maps, and **huipiles.**

**A** ¿Dónde puedo encontrar libros?

**B** Encuentras libros en El Rastro.

# 10 | ¿Y tú?

Answer the following questions in complete sentences.

1. ¿A qué hora almuerzas?
2. ¿Cuánto cuesta el almuerzo en la cafetería de tu escuela?
3. ¿A qué hora vuelves de la escuela?
4. ¿Cuándo puedes pasar un rato con los amigos?
5. ¿Cuántas horas duermes los sábados?
6. ¿En qué tiendas encuentras tu ropa?

*Más práctica*    Cuaderno *pp. 177–179*    Cuaderno para hispanohablantes *pp. 178–180*

**PARA Y PIENSA**

**Did you get it?** Complete each sentence with the correct form of the appropriate verb: **poder, costar, almorzar,** or **dormir.**

1. El pescado _____ diez dólares.
2. Nosotros _____ a la una en el café.
3. Yo _____ ocho horas.
4. Ellos no _____ contestar.

**Get Help Online**
ClassZone.com

# GRAMÁTICA *en contexto*

**¡AVANZA!** **Goal:** Identify the **o → ue** stem-changing verbs Enrique and Maribel use to talk about things to do in the city. Then practice using these verbs to talk about where you go. *Actividades 11–12*

## Telehistoria escena 2

 **@HomeTutor** VideoPlus
**View, Read and Record**
ClassZone.com

**STRATEGIES**

**Cuando lees**

**Compare scenes** As you read this scene, compare it to Scene 1. How are these scenes alike in terms of Enrique's promises and his behavior? What trends do you find?

**Cuando escuchas**

**Identify causes** A negative feeling can have more than one cause. Listen for the causes of Maribel's anxiety and concerns. How many causes are there? What are they?

VIDEO
DVD

AUDIO

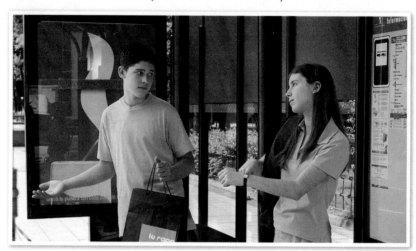

**Enrique:** ¿Qué vas a hacer hoy por la tarde?

**Maribel:** Después de ir de compras, quiero volver al centro. Hay un concierto de música rock, o puedo ir al cine a ver una película... ¡o puedo ir al teatro!

**Enrique:** ¡Un concierto de rock! ¿Puedo ir?

**Maribel:** Mmm... ¡quiero ir al teatro! Vamos al teatro.

**Enrique:** ¿Al teatro? Pero las entradas cuestan mucho, y...

*After the trouble he caused, Enrique decides to go along with Maribel's idea.*

**Enrique:** ¡Vale! Vamos al teatro.

**Maribel:** *(amused)* No, vamos al concierto.

**Enrique:** ¡Muy bien! Voy a comprar las entradas.

**Maribel:** ¡Pero, Enrique! El autobús...

**Enrique:** La ventanilla está allí, cerca del café. Vuelvo en dos minutos.

*As he runs to buy the tickets, Maribel sees the bus approaching. She decides to go alone, but realizes she no longer has the T-shirt.*

**Maribel:** ¡La camiseta! ¡No encuentro la camiseta! ¡Enrique!

**Continuará...** p. 262

## 11 | Planes para la tarde  *Comprensión del episodio*

Escuchar
Leer

Match phrases to complete the sentences.

1. Después de ir de compras, Maribel quiere...
2. Enrique no quiere ir al teatro porque...
3. Maribel y Enrique van...
4. El autobús llega...
5. Enrique va a comprar las entradas...

**a.** cuando Enrique va a comprar las entradas.
**b.** volver al centro.
**c.** a un concierto de música rock en la tarde.
**d.** y tiene la camiseta.
**e.** las entradas cuestan mucho.

## 12 | ¿Qué encuentras?

Hablar

Talk with a partner about what you find in these places.

**A** ¿Qué encuentras en una biblioteca?

**B** Encuentro libros y computadoras allí.

**1.**

**2.**

**3.**

**4.**

**5.**

**6.**

**PARA Y PIENSA**

**Did you get it?**  Complete each sentence based on the Telehistoria with the correct form of the verb in parentheses.
1. Maribel _____ ir al cine o al teatro. (poder)
2. Maribel no _____ la camiseta. (encontrar)
3. Enrique _____ tarde y los dos no van al centro comercial. (volver)

**Get Help Online**
ClassZone.com

# Presentación de GRAMÁTICA

**¡AVANZA!**

**Goal:** Learn how to form **e → i** stem-changing verbs. Then practice using these verbs to order from a menu. *Actividades 13–18*

♻ *¿Recuerdas?* Direct object pronouns p. 230, **tener** expressions p. 223

**English Grammar Connection:** Remember that there are no stem-changing verbs in the present tense of English (see p. 224). There are, however, a number of stem-changing verbs in Spanish.

## Stem-Changing Verbs: e → i

**Animated** Grammar
ClassZone.com

Some **-ir** verbs have an **e → i** stem change in the present tense. How do you form the present tense of these verbs?

**Here's how:**

For **e → i** stem-changing verbs, the last **e** of the stem changes to **i** in all forms except **nosotros(as)** and **vosotros(as).**

| **servir** *to serve* | |
|---|---|
| si**rvo** | servimos |
| si**rves** | servís |
| si**rve** | si**rven** |

El camarero **sirve** la comida.
*The waiter **serves** the food.*

Another verb you know with this stem change is **pedir.**

¿**Pides** una ensalada?
*Are you **ordering** a salad?*

Siempre **pedimos** pollo.
*We always **order** chicken.*

*Más práctica*
Cuaderno *pp. 180–182*
Cuaderno para hispanohablantes *pp. 181–184*

**Conjuguemos.com**

**@HomeTutor**
Leveled Practice
ClassZone.com

# Práctica de GRAMÁTICA

## 13 | ¿Qué piden?

**Hablar
Escribir**

Tell what these people are ordering.

**modelo:** yo
Yo pido carne.

**1.** tú

**2.** mis amigas

**3.** yo

**4.** vosotros

**5.** mi madre

**6.** Maribel

**7.** mis abuelos y yo

**8.** ustedes

## 14 | ¿Quién sirve la comida?  ¿*Recuerdas?* Direct object pronouns p. 230

**Hablar
Escribir**

Tell what these people ask for and who serves it.

**modelo:** Maribel: bebida (la camarera)
Maribel pide una bebida y la camarera la sirve.

**1.** yo: ensalada (Enrique)

**2.** mi amigo: pollo (sus padres)

**3.** tú: pescado (yo)

**4.** mis amigas y yo: verduras (vosotros)

**5.** usted: patatas (nosotros)

**6.** vosotros: postre (el camarero)

**AUDIO**

### Pronunciación   La letra c con e, i

Before **e** and **i**, the Spanish **c**
is pronounced like the *c* in *city*.

Listen and repeat.

ce → cero  centro
cerrar  quince

ci → cien  cine
precio  estación

In many regions of Spain, the **c** before **e** and **i** is
pronounced like the *th* of the English word *think*.

Necesitamos
cinco lápices para
hacer la tarea de
ciencias.

## 15 | Una cena especial

**Hablar**
**Escribir**

Enrique and his family are going out to dinner. Complete what he says with the correct form of **servir** or **pedir.**

Mi familia __**1.**__ una mesa cerca de la ventana. Mis padres __**2.**__ ensaladas y pollo con arroz. Yo __**3.**__ bistec. Los camareros __**4.**__ las ensaladas y los platos principales. Todos nosotros __**5.**__ helado. El camarero __**6.**__ los postres.

## 16 | ¿Qué sirven en el café?

**Escuchar**
**Escribir**

Enrique is in a café and is talking to the waiters and waitresses. Write sentences to tell what these people are serving.

**1.** los camareros       **3.** el camarero       **5.** Luis y José
**2.** el señor Fuentes     **4.** la camarera       **6.** Ana

## 17 | En el restaurante

**Hablar**
**Escribir**

Look at the restaurant scene below. Tell what the people are ordering or serving.

## 18 | ¿Qué pides del menú?  *¿Recuerdas?* tener expressions p. 223

**Hablar**

Ask a partner what he or she orders in a restaurant in the following situations.

modelo: bebida / en el almuerzo

**A** ¿Qué bebida pides en el almuerzo?

**B** Pido leche o un refresco.

1. comida / en el almuerzo
2. bebida / cuando tienes frío
3. bebida / en el desayuno
4. comida / cuando tienes calor
5. comida / cuando tienes hambre
6. bebida / cuando tienes mucha sed

## Comparación cultural

### Las meninas

*Why might an artist create a version of another artist's masterpiece?* Diego Velázquez served as the official painter for King Philip IV of **Spain** and painted many portraits of the royal family. *Las meninas* shows the *Infanta* (princess) and her attendants. Velázquez included himself in the painting. Three centuries later, Pablo Picasso, also from Spain, completed 58 interpretations of this painting. What similarities and differences do you notice?

*Las meninas (1656), Diego Velázquez*

Las meninas (Infanta Margarita) (1957), Pablo Picasso

### Compara con tu mundo

*What famous artwork would you like to try to re-create and why? How would your version be different from the original?*

*Más práctica*  Cuaderno *pp. 180–182*  Cuaderno para hispanohablantes *pp. 181–184*

**PARA Y PIENSA**

**Did you get it?** Complete each sentence with the correct form of **pedir** or **servir**.

1. En la cena los camareros _____ arroz con pollo.
2. Mi madre hace un pastel y lo _____ de postre.
3. Nosotros no _____ mucho porque no tenemos mucha hambre.

> **Get Help Online** ClassZone.com

# Todo junto

**¡AVANZA!**

**Goal:** *Show what you know* Pay attention to how Maribel and Enrique tell the waiter what they would like to eat. Then practice using **o → ue** and **e → i** stem-changing verbs to order food and give your opinion on restaurants. *Actividades 19–23*

## Telehistoria completa

**@HomeTutor** VideoPlus
**View, Read and Record**
ClassZone.com

### STRATEGIES

**Cuando lees**

**Analyze the communication** Analyze this scene's communication by answering these questions: Why does Maribel order so much food? What is the effect?

**Cuando escuchar**

**Listen for contrasts** Listen for contrasts during the scene. Examples: What do Maribel and Enrique order? Who promises to pay, and who actually pays?

**Escena 1** *Resumen*

Enrique y Maribel pueden tomar el autobús setenta y cuatro al centro comercial. Piensan llegar a las doce y media.

**Escena 2** *Resumen*

Enrique va a comprar las entradas para un concierto. El autobús llega pero Enrique no está. Maribel no tiene la camiseta.

VIDEO
DVD

AUDIO

**Escena 3**

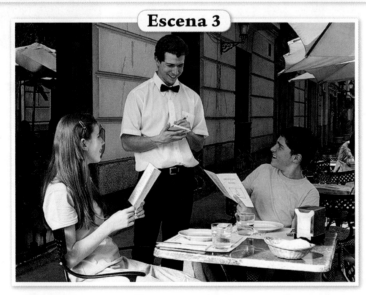

*They arrive at an outdoor restaurant.*

**Enrique:** Es un restaurante muy bonito.

**Maribel:** Pero no tengo el autógrafo de Trini.

**Enrique:** Vamos a pedir la comida. ¡Yo pago!

**Maribel:** Ah, ¿pagas tú? Ahora pido toda la comida del menú.

*The waiter arrives.*

**Maribel:** Señor, ¿sirven pescado hoy?

**Camarero:** No, hoy no tenemos pescado.

**Maribel:** Quiero empezar con una ensalada. De plato principal quiero el pollo con verduras y... Sí, y filete con patatas.

**Camarero:** ¿Dos platos principales? ¿Filete y pollo?

**Enrique:** Es mucho, ¿no?

**Maribel:** Sí. Y de postre quiero un arroz con leche.

**Enrique:** *(nervously)* Pan y agua, por favor.

**Maribel:** Él va a pagar la cuenta.

**Enrique:** *(nods, then remembers)* ¡Maribel! ¡Mi mochila! ¡No tengo dinero!

**Maribel:** *(smiling)* Ay, Enrique, yo sí tengo dinero.

**¿Quién lo hace?** *Comprensión de los episodios*

Escuchar
Leer

Read these sentences and tell whether they are about Enrique or Maribel.

**1.** Quiere volver al centro después de ir de compras.
**2.** Piensa que las entradas cuestan mucho.
**3.** No encuentra la camiseta.
**4.** Piensa que el restaurante es muy bonito.
**5.** Pide mucha comida.

---

**20** **Problemas en el centro** *Comprensión de los episodios*

Escuchar
Leer

Answer the questions according to the episodes.

**1.** ¿Cómo quieren ir Maribel y Enrique al centro comercial?
**2.** ¿Adónde va el autobús setenta y cuatro?
**3.** ¿Por qué no quiere ir al teatro Enrique?
**4.** ¿Por qué está enojada Maribel?
**5.** ¿Qué pide Maribel en el restaurante?

---

**21** **Clientes y camareros**

Hablar

**STRATEGY**

**Plan the whole scene** Plan the whole scene from start to finish. What would the waiter or waitress say before, during, and after the meal? What would the customers say at each stage?

Work in a group of three. Prepare a scene in a café with customers and a waiter or waitress. Present your scene to the class.

**Para organizarte:**
- qué comidas y bebidas piden
- qué sirve el (la) camarero(a)
- cuánto cuesta la comida (la cuenta y la propina)

**Camarero(a)** Buenas tardes. ¿Quieren ver el menú?

**Cliente 1** Buenas tardes. Sí, por favor. Tenemos mucha hambre.

Ustedes pueden pedir el pollo con patatas. Es mucha comida.

**Cliente 2** Tal vez, pero hoy tengo ganas de comer...

## 22 | Integración

Leer
Escuchar
Hablar

Read the pamphlet and listen to the guide. Describe five activities you are going to do, where, and how you can get there.

**Fuente 1 Folleto del hotel**

*Lugares de interés*

| | TRANSPORTE | | |
|---|:---:|:---:|:---:|
| Biblioteca Nacional | ■ | | 45 |
| Café Almagro | | | 7 |
| Centro Comercial ABC Serrano | | ■ | 19 |
| Cine Ábaco | | ■ | |
| Parque del Buen Retiro | ■ | | |
| Plaza de la Moncloa | | ■ | 133 |
| Restaurante Oberón | ■ | ■ | |
| Teatro Marquina | ■ | | |

PUERTA DEL SOL, 2 MADRID

**Fuente 2 Anuncio del guía turístico**

**Listen and take notes**

• ¿Qué actividades menciona el guía?
• ¿En qué lugares puedes hacer las actividades?

**modelo:** Voy a comer pescado. Voy al Restaurante Oberón. Puedo ir a pie o en coche...

## 23 | Una crítica culinaria

Escribir

You are a newspaper food critic. Write a short review of your favorite restaurant. Explain what the waiters are like, what they serve, what you order, what the food is like, and how much it costs.

**modelo:** El restaurante Salazar es muy bueno. Los camareros son trabajadores. De plato principal sirven...

| Writing Criteria | Excellent | Good | Needs Work |
|---|---|---|---|
| **Content** | Your review includes a lot of information. | Your review includes some information. | Your review includes little information. |
| **Communication** | Most of your review is organized and easy to follow. | Parts of your review are organized and easy to follow. | Your review is disorganized and hard to follow. |
| **Accuracy** | Your review has few mistakes in grammar and vocabulary. | Your review has some mistakes in grammar and vocabulary. | Your review has many mistakes in grammar and vocabulary. |

*Más práctica*  Cuaderno *pp. 183–184*  Cuaderno para hispanohablantes *pp. 185–186*

**PARA Y PIENSA**

**Did you get it?** Choose the correct verb to make each sentence logical according to the Telehistoria.

**Get Help Online**
ClassZone.com

1. Maribel y Enrique (almuerzan / encuentran) en un restaurante bonito.
2. Maribel (sirve / pide) mucha comida.
3. Enrique no (puede / vuelve) pagar.

# Juegos y diversiones

Review vocabulary by playing a game.

# CUATRO RINCONES

## The Setup

Your teacher will label a poster for each corner of the room: **el restaurante, el cine, el parque,** and **el centro.** Form two teams.

## Playing the Game

Your teacher will give each of you in turn an index card with a Spanish word or phrase on it. Go to the corner of the room for the place related to the word or phrase on your card. Then use the word(s) on your card and the location name in a sentence.

Your team will receive one point for each player who goes to the correct corner and a second point for each player to use the words correctly in a sentence.

## The Winner!

The team with the most points at the end wins.

### Materials

- index cards with Spanish words and phrases
- four posters representing places in a city

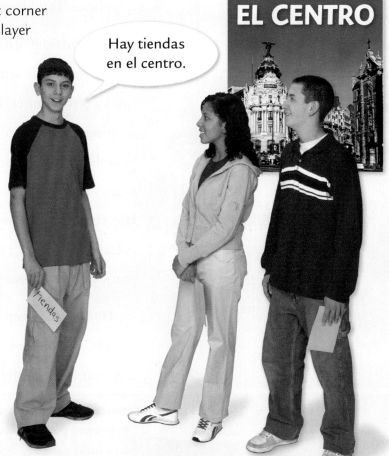

Hay tiendas en el centro.

EL CENTRO

# Lectura cultural

**¡AVANZA!**

**Goal:** Read about weekend activities in Spain and Chile. Then talk about what each city offers and compare these activities with what you do on weekends.

## Comparación cultural

AUDIO

# El fin de semana en España y Chile

**STRATEGY Leer**

**List attractions and places**
Use a table like the one below to list attractions and the places where they can be found.

|  | conciertos | zoológico | botes |
|---|---|---|---|
| **Madrid** | Parque del Buen Retiro |  |  |
| **Santiago de Chile** |  |  |  |

España

Los habitantes de Madrid, España, y Santiago de Chile hacen muchas actividades en el fin de semana. Van a parques, restaurantes, teatros, cines y otros lugares divertidos. También van de compras.

En Madrid hay muchos lugares interesantes para pasar los fines de semana. La Plaza Mayor tiene muchos cafés y restaurantes. Hay un mercado de sellos [1] los domingos. El Parque del Buen Retiro es un lugar perfecto para descansar y pasear. En este parque hay jardines [2], cafés y un lago [3] donde las personas pueden alquilar botes. Hay conciertos allí en el verano. Otro parque popular es la Casa de Campo. Hay un zoológico, una piscina [4], un parque de diversiones [5] y un lago para botes.

Hay muchas tiendas en el centro. El almacén [6] más grande es El Corte Inglés: allí los madrileños [7] pueden comprar ropa, comida y mucho más.

---

[1] **mercado...** stamp market    [2] gardens    [3] lake
[4] swimming pool    [5] **parque...** amusement park
[6] department store    [7] people of Madrid

*El Parque del Buen Retiro en Madrid*

En Santiago de Chile las personas pasan los fines de semana en muchos lugares. Siempre hay mucha actividad en la Plaza de Armas, la parte histórica de Santiago. Hay conciertos allí los domingos.

El parque del Cerro Santa Lucía es perfecto para pasear. Los santiaguinos[8] pueden ver jardines y el panorama de Santiago. El Cerro San Cristóbal en el Parque Metropolitano es un lugar favorito para comer, correr y montar en bicicleta. Hay jardines, piscinas, un zoológico, cafés y restaurantes en el parque.

Los santiaguinos van a tiendas en el centro y a centros comerciales como Alto Las Condes. En el Mercado Central pueden comprar pescado y frutas y comer en restaurantes con precios baratos[9].

---

[8] people of Santiago, Chile    [9] inexpensive

*La Plaza de Armas*

Chile

*Cerro San Cristóbal*

PARA
Y
PIENSA

**¿Comprendiste?**
1. ¿Qué hay en la Plaza Mayor y la Plaza de Armas los domingos?
2. ¿A qué parques van los madrileños y los santiaguinos?
3. ¿Dónde pueden ir de compras los habitantes de Madrid y Santiago?

**¿Y tú?**
¿Cuál(es) de estos lugares en Madrid y Santiago quieres visitar? ¿Adónde vas los fines de semana donde vives? ¿Qué haces allí?

# Proyectos culturales

## Pinturas de España y Chile

*What messages can an artist communicate through a painting?* When you look at a painting, you might see something different than what the artist originally intended when he or she painted it. In fact, a single work of art can have a number of different interpretations.

**España** *Landscape near El Escorial (1932), Ignacio Zuloaga y Zabaleta*

**Chile** La Siesta *(1872), Pedro Lira*

### Proyecto 2 *Your own painting*

Now try your hand at being an artist.

**Materials for your own painting**
Construction paper
Charcoal pencil, colored pencils or pens, watercolor paint, paintbrushes

**Instructions**
Create a landscape scene on construction paper. Use the paintings above as an inspiration.

### Proyecto 1 *Interpret and investigate*

Interpreting the two paintings above from **Spain** and **Chile.**

**Instructions**
1. After looking at each painting, describe it to yourself. What message do you get from it? As you scan the painting, does any particular point draw your attention?
2. Use the Internet or your school's library to learn more about the two paintings. You might look up information about the artists and whether the paintings reflect personal events in their lives.

## En tu comunidad

Visit the website of a museum in your community or area that contains works of art from a Spanish-speaking country. What can you learn about that country by examining the artwork? Record your impressions in a journal.

## Lección 2

# En resumen
## Vocabulario y gramática

**Animated** Grammar

**Interactive Flashcards**
ClassZone.com

## Vocabulario

### Describe Places in Town

| | |
|---|---|
| el café | café |
| el centro | center, downtown |
| el cine | movie theater; the movies |
| el parque | park |
| el restaurante | restaurant |
| el teatro | theater |

### Describe Events in Town

| | |
|---|---|
| el concierto | concert |
| las entradas | tickets |
| la música rock | rock music |
| la película | movie |
| la ventanilla | ticket window |

### Getting Around Town

| | |
|---|---|
| a pie | by foot |
| la calle | street |
| en autobús | by bus |
| en coche | by car |
| encontrar (ue) | to find |
| tomar | to take |

### In a Restaurant

| | |
|---|---|
| el (la) camarero(a) | (food) server |
| costar (ue) | to cost |
| la cuenta | bill |
| de postre | for dessert |
| el menú | menu |
| la mesa | table |
| el plato principal | main course |
| la propina | tip |

### For Dinner

| | |
|---|---|
| el arroz | rice |
| el bistec | beef |
| el brócoli | broccoli |
| la carne | meat |
| la ensalada | salad |
| los frijoles | beans |
| el pastel | cake |
| la patata | potato |
| el pescado | fish |
| el pollo | chicken |
| el tomate | tomato |
| las verduras | vegetables |

### Ordering from a Menu

| | |
|---|---|
| pedir (i) | to order, to ask for |
| servir (i) | to serve |

### Other Words and Phrases

| | |
|---|---|
| allí | there |
| almorzar (ue) | to eat lunch |
| aquí | here |
| dormir (ue) | to sleep |
| el lugar | place |
| poder (ue) | to be able, can |
| tal vez | perhaps, maybe |
| ver | to see |
| volver (ue) | to return, to come back |

## Gramática

**Notas gramaticales:** The verb **ver** *p. 249,* **ir a** + infinitive *p. 251*

### Stem-Changing Verbs: o → ue

For **o → ue** stem-changing verbs, the last **o** of the stem changes to **ue** in all forms except **nosotros(as)** and **vosotros(as).**

| **poder** *to be able, can* | |
|---|---|
| puedo | podemos |
| puedes | podéis |
| puede | pueden |

### Stem-Changing Verbs: e → i

For **e → i** stem-changing verbs, the last **e** of the stem changes to **i** in all forms except **nosotros(as)** and **vosotros(as).**

| **servir** *to serve* | |
|---|---|
| sirvo | servimos |
| sirves | servís |
| sirve | sirven |

# Repaso de la lección

**¡LLEGADA!**

**@HomeTutor**
ClassZone.com

**¡AvanzaRap!**
DVD
**Sing and Learn**

## Now you can

- describe places and events in town
- talk about types of transportation
- say what you are going to do
- order from a menu

## Using

- **ir a** + infinitive
- stem-changing verbs: **o → ue**
- stem-changing verbs: **e → i**

---

**To review**
- stem-changing verbs: **o → ue** p. 252
- **ir a** + infinitive p. 251
- stem-changing verbs: **e → i** p. 258

## 1 | Listen and understand

**AUDIO**

Listen to the conversation in a restaurant. Then answer the questions.

**1.** ¿Cuántas personas van a comer?

**2.** ¿Cómo son los platos principales?

**3.** ¿Qué pide Raúl con el bistec?

**4.** ¿Qué pide Raúl para beber?

**5.** ¿Qué pide Tere de plato principal?

**6.** ¿Quién pide el pastel de postre?

---

**To review**
- **ir a** + infinitive p. 251

## 2 | Say what you are going to do

Tell what people are going to do on Saturday and how they plan to get there.

**modelo:** Angélica / almorzar en un restaurante
Angélica va a almorzar en un restaurante.
Va a ir en autobús.

**1.** Gilberto / pasear en el parque

**2.** yo / volver al centro

**3.** las chicas / beber refrescos en un café

**4.** tú / ver una película en el cine

**5.** nosotros / escuchar música rock

**6.** vosotros / ir al teatro

**To review**
• stem-changing verbs: **o → ue** p. 252

## 3 | Describe places and events in town

Tomás is describing his activities. Complete his e-mail message with the correct form of the appropriate verb.

| encontrar | almorzar | volver | poder | costar | dormir |

Los domingos por la tarde, yo __1.__ en el restaurante Casa Serrano con mi familia. Nosotros __2.__ platos muy buenos en el menú y la comida no __3.__ mucho. Yo nunca __4.__ comer todo porque sirven mucha comida. Nosotros __5.__ a casa a las tres o a las cuatro. Muchas veces mis hermanos menores están cansados y __6.__ dos horas. Me gusta pasar los domingos con mi familia. Es un día muy tranquilo.

**To review**
• stem-changing verbs: **e → i** p. 258

## 4 | Order from a menu

Describe the problems in the restaurant.

**modelo:** Leonor: carne / el camarero: pescado
Leonor pide carne, pero el camarero sirve pescado.

1. tú: agua / la camarera: leche
2. yo: brócoli / el camarero: patatas
3. ustedes: bistec / los camareros: pollo
4. Nicolás: ensalada / el camarero: tomates
5. nosotros: arroz / los camareros: verduras
6. vosotros: pastel / la camarera: helado

**To review**
• Comparación cultural pp. 244, 255, 261
• Lectura cultural pp. 266–267

## 5 | Spain, Guatemala, and Chile

**Comparación cultural**

Answer these culture questions.

1. What is featured at Madrid's Teatro de la Comedia?
2. What can you find at Madrid's Rastro and Chichicastenango's market?
3. Who is depicted in *Las meninas*?
4. What can you see and do in Madrid's Parque del Buen Retiro and Santiago's Parque Metropolitano?

*Más práctica* Cuaderno *pp. 185–196* Cuaderno para hispanohablantes *pp. 187–196*

**Get Help Online** ClassZone.com

Guatemala

España

Chile

AUDIO

# ¿Adónde vamos el sábado?

## Lectura y escritura

**WebQuest**
ClassZone.com

**①** **Leer** Activities that young people do vary around the world. Read what Anita, Rodrigo, and Armando do for fun on Saturdays.

**②** **Escribir** Using the three descriptions as models, write a short paragraph about what you like to do on Saturdays.

**STRATEGY   Escribir**
**Create an activity chart**
To write about what you do for fun on Saturdays, use an activity chart like the one shown.

| Categoría | Detalles |
|---|---|
| lugares | |
| ropa | |
| actividades | |

**Step 1** Complete the chart with details about where you go, what you wear, and what you do for fun on Saturdays.

**Step 2** Write your paragraph. Make sure to include all the information from your chart. Check your writing by yourself or with help from a friend. Make final corrections.

### Compara con tu mundo

Use the paragraph you wrote to compare the activities you do for fun to the activities described by *one* of the three students. How are the activities similar? How are they different?

Cuaderno *pp. 197–199*   Cuaderno para hispanohablantes *pp. 197–199*

## Guatemala

### Anita

¿Qué tal? Soy Anita y me gusta escuchar música folklórica. El sábado mis amigos y yo pensamos ir a un concierto de marimba[1] en el centro. Las entradas no cuestan mucho y los conciertos son muy buenos. ¿Qué ropa voy a llevar? Quiero llevar un vestido porque es primavera y hace calor. Mis amigos prefieren llevar camisetas y jeans.

[1] musical instrument resembling a xylophone

## España

### Rodrigo

¡Hola! Me llamo Rodrigo y vivo en Madrid. El sábado quiero ir de compras con mi hermano. Siempre necesito comprar camisetas y calcetines. Muchas veces los encuentro en el centro comercial. Se llama Xanadú y tiene tiendas, restaurantes y ¡un parque de nieve! Allí puedes practicar deportes de invierno durante todo el año. A mi hermano le gusta la nieve en el verano, pero a mí no. En el verano ¡prefiero tener calor!

## Chile

### Armando

¡Hola! Me llamo Armando y soy de Santiago, Chile. En septiembre puedes ir a muchos rodeos porque hay muchas fiestas nacionales en Chile. El sábado voy a ir a un rodeo con mis amigos para ver a los huasos[2]. Pienso llevar unos jeans nuevos y una chaqueta porque no quiero tener frío. Quiero llevar un sombrero de vaquero[3], pero no puedo. ¡Cuestan mucho!

[2] Chilean cowboys    [3] cowboy

# Repaso inclusivo
♻ Options for Review

## 1 | Listen, understand, and compare

Escuchar

Listen to Mrs. Estrada and her son, Carlitos, order a meal at a restaurant. Then answer the questions.

1. ¿Qué tiene ganas de comer Carlitos?
2. ¿Qué pide para empezar? ¿Y de plato principal?
3. ¿Qué plato pide la señora Estrada para empezar?
4. ¿Qué no sirven hoy en el restaurante?
5. ¿Qué van a beber ellos?

Which order most resembles what you like to eat? What foods and drinks do you order when you go to restaurants?

## 2 | Present a family outing

Hablar

Prepare a presentation about a family outing to a restaurant. Bring in a photo of your own or one from a magazine. Talk about the clothes each person is wearing, what food the restaurant serves, what each person orders, and how much it costs. You should talk for at least two minutes.

## 3 | Compare school days

Hablar

Interview a partner about his or her day at school. Ask about the classes your partner prefers, what he or she eats for lunch and at what time, and what he or she is going to do after school today. Finish by comparing your days. Your conversation should be at least three minutes long.

¿A qué hora almuerzas?

Almuerzo a las doce.

## 4 | Help find a lost child

**Hablar**

Role-play a situation in which you are a mall employee in customer service. Your partner is at the mall with a younger cousin, but can't find him or her. Ask your partner about age, physical characteristics, and clothing. Copy this chart on a piece of paper and use it to organize your information. Your conversation should be at least two minutes long.

| Edad | |
|------|---|
| Características físicas | |
| Ropa | |

## 5 | Create a fashion show

**Hablar**
**Escribir**

Work in a group of five. Individually, write a description of the clothes you are wearing. Include color, where you can buy each item, how much they cost, and in what season(s) you can wear them. Your description should have at least eight sentences. Then perform the fashion show for the class, reading each other's descriptions as each "model" walks down the runway.

## 6 | Plan a weekend with family

**Leer**
**Escribir**

You are studying in Barcelona, Spain, for the summer and your parents are coming to visit. Read this newspaper supplement to find out about the weekend's events. Then write an e-mail to your parents, and suggest what you can do and where you can go together or separately during the weekend. Keep in mind everyone's likes and dislikes. Your e-mail should have at least six suggestions.

**Suplemento especial – fin de semana**

### GUÍA DEL OCIO - BARCELONA

**VIERNES**

**Cena especial**
Comida española típica, con música de flamenco.
Restaurante Casals (de las 21.30 a las 23.30 h)

**Concierto**
Los hermanos Pujols tocan música rock.
Plaza Cataluña (a las 14.30 h)

**SÁBADO**

**Películas**
*Terror en el centro*
Hollywood. Película de terror. Dos chicos de Nueva York van en autobús cuando llegan unos extraterrestres horribles.
Cines Maremagnum (a las 16.00 y 18.30 h)

*Mi tía loca*
España. Película cómica. La historia de una chica y su tía favorita.
Cine Diagonal Mar (a las 13.30 y 21.00 h)

**Comprar y pasear**
La calle que lo tiene todo: libros, ropa, comida ¡y más!
Las Ramblas (todo el día)

**DOMINGO**

**Eliminar el cáncer**
Puedes pasear y donar dinero para combatir el cáncer.
Parque Güell (a las 10.00 h)

**Compras**
Los mejores precios del verano en las tiendas de ropa.
Centro Comercial Barcelona Glorias (de las 10.30 a las 20.30 h)

**Concierto de Beethoven**
La orquesta de Barcelona toca música clásica. Un concierto para toda la familia.
Teatro Liceu (a las 20.00 h)

## ¿?Entre dos

**Pair Activities**

## ¿Qué les gusta hacer?

### Estudiante A

Ricardo

Ricardo and Isabel like to do many things. Look at the pictures on the right to find out what Ricardo likes to do. (Your partner has pictures showing what Isabel likes to do.) Take turns asking each other questions to discover what Ricardo and Isabel like to do.

**Estudiante A:** A Ricardo le gusta... ¿Y a Isabel?

**Estudiante B:** A Isabel también le gusta... ¿A Ricardo le gusta...?

*What activities do Ricardo and Isabel both like to do?*

---

## ¿Qué les gusta hacer?

### Estudiante B

Isabel

Ricardo and Isabel like to do many things. Look at the pictures on the right to find out what Isabel likes to do. (Your partner has pictures showing what Ricardo likes to do.) Take turns asking each other questions to discover what Ricardo and Isabel like to do.

**Estudiante A: A Ricardo le gusta... ¿Y a Isabel?**

**Estudiante B: A Isabel también le gusta... ¿A Ricardo le gusta...?**

*What activities do Ricardo and Isabel both like to do?*

# Entre dos • Lección 2

## ¿Cómo se llaman?

**Estudiante A**

You and your partner want to know the names of the people in the picture.
Your picture has the names of three people and your partner's picture has
the names of three other people. Take turns asking each other questions and
describing people to find out the names of all the people.

**Estudiante A:** ¿Cómo se llama la chica rubia?

**Estudiante B:** ¿La chica pequeña y joven?

**Estudiante A:** Sí.

**Estudiante B:** Se llama Gabi.
¿Cómo se llama...?

Who in the picture
do you think is
*artístico(a)*? Why?

## ¿Cómo se llaman?

**Estudiante B**

You and your partner want to know the names of the people in the picture.
Your picture has the names of three people and your partner's picture has
the names of three other people. Take turns asking each other questions and
describing people to find out the names of all the people.

**Estudiante A:** ¿Cómo se llama la chica rubia?

**Estudiante B:** ¿La chica pequeña y joven?

**Estudiante A:** Sí.

**Estudiante B:** Se llama Gabi.
¿Cómo se llama...?

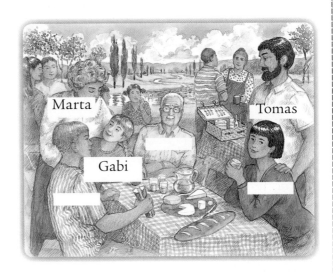

*Who in the picture
do you think is
**artístico(a)**? Why?*

Unidad 1  Entre dos · Lección 2
doscientos setenta y nueve

**279**

## Estudiante A

**¿ What classes do you and your partner have at the same time?**

You and your partner want to compare class schedules. Look at your class schedule on the right. Your partner has a different schedule. Ask each other questions to find out what classes you have at various times of the day.

**Estudiante A:** A las… tengo… ¿Y tú?
**Estudiante B:** Yo (también) tengo… ¿Qué clase tienes a las…?

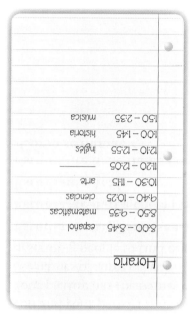

### Horario

| | |
|---|---|
| 8:00 – 8:45 | español |
| 8:50 – 9:35 | matemáticas |
| 9:40 – 10:25 | ciencias |
| 10:30 – 11:15 | arte |
| 11:20 – 12:05 | —— |
| 12:10 – 12:55 | inglés |
| 1:00 – 1:45 | historia |
| 1:50 – 2:35 | música |

---

## Horario de clases

## Estudiante B

You and your partner want to compare class schedules. Look at your class schedule on the right. Your partner has a different schedule. Ask each other questions to find out what classes you have at various times of the day.

**Estudiante A:** A las… tengo… ¿Y tú?
**Estudiante B:** Yo (también) tengo… ¿Qué clase tienes a las…?

### Horario

| | |
|---|---|
| 8:00 – 8:45 | español |
| 8:50 – 9:35 | historia |
| 9:40 – 10:25 | ciencias |
| 10:30 – 11:15 | arte |
| 11:20 – 12:05 | inglés |
| 12:10 – 12:55 | —— |
| 1:00 – 1:45 | matemáticas |
| 1:50 – 2:35 | música |

*What classes do you and your partner have at the same time?*

# Entre dos • Lección 2

¿? Did you and your partner leave some of the supplies in the same places?

## ¿Dónde están?

**Estudiante A**

You and your partner have borrowed some school supplies from friends but have forgotten them at different places in school. Ask your partner where the following friends' supplies are:

Alejo's and Marta's calculators

Sergio's paper

Julia's pencil

Then, answer your partner's questions based on the images and cues. Take turns doing this activity.

**Estudiante A: ¿Dónde está el borrador de la maestra?**

**Estudiante B: Está en la clase.**

---

## ¿Dónde están?

**Estudiante B**

You and your partner have borrowed some school supplies from friends but have forgotten them at different places in school. Ask your partner where the following friends' supplies are:

Daniel's backpack

Florencia's and Luis's pens

Félix's notebook

Then, answer your partner's questions based on the images and cues. Take turns doing this activity.

**Estudiante A: ¿Dónde está el borrador de la maestra?**

**Estudiante B: Está en la clase.**

 Did you and your partner leave some of the supplies in the same places?

*(Estudiante A — esta sección está impresa al revés)*

**¿Qué le gusta comer?**

**Estudiante A**

You and your partner are discussing what Elena and Mario like and don't like to eat. Look at the pictures below to find out what Elena likes and dislikes. (Your partner has pictures showing what Mario likes and dislikes.) Talk to your partner about Elena's and Mario's favorite foods.

Estudiante A: **A Elena le gusta(n)…, pero no le gusta(n)… ¿Y a Mario?**

Estudiante B: **A Mario no le gusta(n)…, pero le gusta(n)… ¿A Elena le gusta(n)…?**

A Elena no le gusta(n)…

A Elena le gusta(n)…

¿? What foods do Elena and Mario both like? What foods do they both dislike?

---

**¿Qué le gusta comer?**

**Estudiante B**

You and your partner are discussing what Elena and Mario like and don't like to eat. Look at the pictures below to find out what Mario likes and dislikes. (Your partner has pictures showing what Elena likes and dislikes.) Talk to your partner about Elena's and Mario's favorite foods.

Estudiante A: **A Elena le gusta(n)…, pero no le gusta(n)… ¿Y a Mario?**

Estudiante B: **A Mario no le gusta(n)…, pero le gusta(n)… ¿A Elena le gusta(n)…?**

A Mario le gusta(n)…

A Mario no le gusta(n)…

*What foods do Elena and Mario both like? What foods do they both dislike?* ¿?

# Entre dos • Lección 2

## ¿Cuántos años tienen?

**Estudiante A**

You and your partner are looking at Pedro's family tree. You know the age of some of Pedro's family members and your partner knows the age of the other members of Pedro's family. Take turns asking each other how old Pedro's family members are.

Estudiante A: **¿Cuántos años tiene su...?**

Estudiante B: **Su... tiene...**

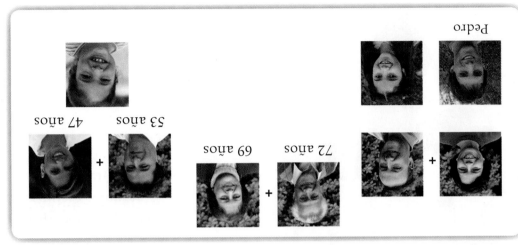

Pedro

53 años    47 años

72 años    69 años

*Which family members are the same age?*

## ¿Cuántos años tienen?

**Estudiante B**

You and your partner are looking at Pedro's family tree. You know the age of some of Pedro's family members and your partner knows the age of the other members of Pedro's family. Take turns asking each other how old Pedro's family members are.

Estudiante A: **¿Cuántos años tiene su...?**

Estudiante B: **Su... tiene...**

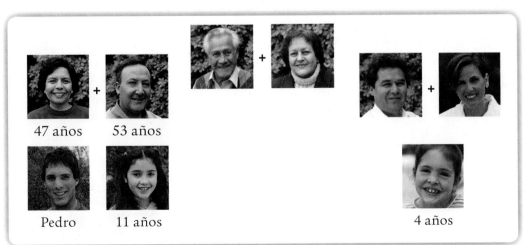

47 años    53 años

Pedro    11 años

4 años

*Which family members are the same age?*

## Estudiante A

145 €
113 €
12 €
35 €
23 €

¿Cuánto cuesta la ropa de Éster en total? ¿Y de Eduardo?

### En la tienda de ropa

Eduardo and Éster are shopping for clothes. Look at the pictures on the right to find out what Eduardo wants to buy. (Your partner has pictures showing what Éster wants to buy.) Take turns asking each other what Éster and Eduardo are buying, in what color, and how much each item costs. Note the cost of each item.

Estudiante A: **¿Qué quiere comprar Éster?**
Estudiante B: **Éster quiere comprar...**
Estudiante A: **¿Cuánto cuesta(n)...?**

---

### En la tienda de ropa

**Estudiante B**

Eduardo and Éster are shopping for clothes. Look at the pictures on the right to find out what Éster wants to buy. (Your partner has pictures showing what Eduardo wants to buy.) Take turns asking each other what Éster and Eduardo are buying, in what color, and how much each item costs. Note the cost of each item.

Estudiante A: **¿Qué quiere comprar Eduardo?**
Estudiante B: **Eduardo quiere comprar...**
Estudiante A: **¿Cuánto cuesta(n)...?**

¿Cuánto cuesta la ropa de Éster en total? ¿Y de Eduardo?

49 €
33 €
9 €
89 €
38 €

# Entre dos • Lección 2

## ¿Qué van a pedir?

**Estudiante A**

You and your partner are supposed to meet some friends at a restaurant. They are late and they asked you to order for them. Take turns asking each other what your friends are going to order.

Estudiante A: **¿Qué va a pedir Tom?**

Estudiante B: **Tom va a pedir...**

*Are any of your friends ordering the same thing?*

Tom

Julie

---

## ¿Qué van a pedir?

**Estudiante B**

You and your partner are supposed to meet some friends at a restaurant. They are late and they asked you to order for them. Take turns asking each other what your friends are going to order.

Estudiante A: **¿Qué va a pedir Sara?**

Estudiante B: **Sara va a pedir...**

Sara

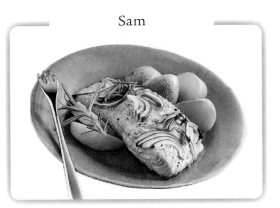

Sam

*Are any of your friends ordering the same thing?*

# Recursos

## Lección 1
# ¿Qué te gusta hacer?

### Talk About Activities

| | |
|---|---|
| **cuidar niños** | to baby-sit |
| **pintar** | to paint |
| **la reunión** | meeting |
| **el club** | club |
| **manejar** | to drive |
| **trabajar a tiempo parcial** | to work part-time |
| **trabajar de voluntario** | to volunteer |
| **tocar un instrumento** | to play an instrument |
| *Instruments* | |
| **el piano** | piano |
| **el clarinete** | clarinet |
| **la flauta** | flute |
| **el saxofón** | saxophone |
| **el tambor** | drum |
| **la trompeta** | trumpet |
| **la viola** | viola |
| **el violín** | violin |

### Snack Foods and Beverages

| | |
|---|---|
| **la merienda** | snack |
| **las papitas** | chips |
| **las galletas saladas** | crackers |
| **las galletitas** | cookies |
| **el chicle** | chewing gum |
| **los dulces** | candy |
| **la limonada** | lemonade |

## Lección 2
# Mis amigos y yo

### Describe Yourself and Others

| *Personality* | |
|---|---|
| **listo(a)** | clever / smart |
| **callado(a)** | quiet |
| **extrovertido(a)** | outgoing |
| **tímido(a)** | shy |
| **sincero(a)** | sincere |
| **tonto(a)** | silly |
| **travieso(a)** | mischievous |
| **paciente** | patient |
| **talentoso(a)** | talented |
| **creativo(a)** | creative |
| **ambicioso(a)** | ambitious |
| *Appearance* | |
| **el pelo oscuro** | dark hair |
| **el pelo rizado** | curly hair |
| **el pelo lacio** | straight hair |
| **calvo(a)** | bald |
| **los frenillos** | braces |

### People

| | |
|---|---|
| **el (la) policía** | police officer |
| **el actor** | actor |
| **la actriz** | actress |
| **el (la) compañero(a) de clase** | classmate |
| **el (la) bombero(a)** | firefighter |
| **el (la) secretario(a)** | secretary |
| **el jefe, la jefa** | boss |

# Unidad 2

## Expansión de vocabulario

## Lección 1
### Somos estudiantes

### *Tell Time and Discuss Daily Schedules*

| la medianoche | midnight |
|---|---|
| el mediodía | noon |

### *Describing Classes*

| School Subjects | |
|---|---|
| la asignatura | school subject |
| la educación física | physical education |
| las ciencias sociales | social studies |
| la geometría | geometry |
| la geografía | geography |
| el álgebra | algebra |
| la lengua, el idioma | language |
| la literatura | literature |
| la biología | biology |
| la química | chemistry |
| la banda | band |
| el coro | choir |
| la orquesta | orchestra |
| la hora de estudio | study hall |
| In School | |
| la asamblea | assembly |
| el recreo | recess, break |
| Classroom Activities | |
| preguntar | to ask |
| la respuesta | answer |
| la prueba | test, quiz |

### *Describe Frequency*

| cada | each |
|---|---|
| a veces | sometimes |
| ¿Con qué frecuencia...? | How often. . . ? |
| rara vez | rarely |

### *Other Words and Phrases*

| terminar | to finish |
|---|---|
| esperar | to wait (for) |
| mientras | while |
| otra vez | again |

## Lección 2
### En la escuela

### *Describe Classroom Objects*

| la carpeta | folder |
|---|---|
| las tijeras | scissors |
| la regla | ruler |
| el diccionario | dictionary |
| la impresora | printer |
| la bandera | flag |
| el globo | globe |

### *Places in School*

| la sala de clase | classroom |
|---|---|
| el casillero | locker |
| el auditorio | auditorium |

### *Say Where Things Are Located*

| entre | between |
|---|---|
| fuera (de) | out / outside (of) |
| (a la) derecha (de) | (to the) right (of) |
| (a la) izquierda (de) | (to the) left (of) |
| aquí | here |
| allí | there |
| enfrente (de) | across from, facing |

### *Talk About How You Feel*

| feliz, alegre | happy |
|---|---|
| preocupado(a) | worried |
| listo(a) | ready |
| Estoy de acuerdo. | I agree. |

### *Other Words and Phrases*

| mismo(a) | same |
|---|---|
| según | according to |
| creer | to think, to believe |
| especialmente | especially |
| olvidar | to forget |
| sobre | about |
| además | besides, further |
| suficiente, bastante | enough |
| sin | without |

## Lección 1
# Mi comida favorita

### *Talk About Foods and Beverages*

| *For Breakfast* | |
|---|---|
| **desayunar** | to have breakfast |
| **la mantequilla** | butter |
| **la miel** | honey |
| **el pan tostado** | toast |
| **el batido** | milkshake, smoothie |
| *For Lunch* | |
| **la bolsa** | bag |
| **la mantequilla de cacahuate** | peanut butter |
| **la jalea** | jelly |
| **el atún** | tuna |
| **la ensalada** | salad |
| *Fruit* | |
| **el plátano** | banana; plantain |
| **la toronja** | grapefruit |
| **la piña** | pineapple |
| **el durazno** | peach |
| **el limón** | lemon |
| **la sandía** | watermelon |

## Lección 2
# En mi familia

### *Talk About Family*

| | |
|---|---|
| **el esposo** | husband |
| **la esposa** | wife |
| **la hermanastra** | stepsister |
| **el hermanastro** | stepbrother |
| **la media hermana** | half-sister |
| **el medio hermano** | half-brother |
| **el nieto** | grandson |
| **la nieta** | granddaughter |
| **el sobrino** | nephew |
| **la sobrina** | niece |
| **el (la) bebé** | baby |

### *Pets*

| | |
|---|---|
| **el pájaro** | bird |
| **el pez (*pl.* los peces)** | fish |
| **el conejo** | rabbit |
| **el lagarto** | lizard |
| **la rana** | frog |
| **el hámster** | hamster |

# Unidad 4 — Expansión de vocabulario

## Lección 1
## ¡Vamos de compras!

### Describe Clothing

| | |
|---|---|
| **las botas** | boots |
| **el impermeable** | raincoat |
| **la falda** | skirt |
| **el suéter** | sweater |
| **la sudadera (con capucha)** | (hooded) sweatshirt |
| **los pantalones deportivos** | sweatpants |
| **el abrigo** | coat |
| **los zapatos de tenis** | tennis shoes, sneakers |
| **el pijama** | pajamas |
| **las sandalias** | sandals |
| **la gorra** | baseball cap |
| **las gafas de sol** | sunglasses |
| **los guantes** | gloves |
| **la bufanda** | scarf |
| **el paraguas** | umbrella |
| **la bolsa** | bag, purse |
| *Colors* | |
| **morado(a)** | purple |
| **rosado(a)** | pink |
| **gris** | gray |

### Discuss Seasons

| | |
|---|---|
| **el norte** | north |
| **el sur** | south |
| **el este** | east |
| **el oeste** | west |

## Lección 2
## ¿Qué hacemos esta noche?

### Describe Places In Town

| | |
|---|---|
| **la iglesia** | church |
| **el edificio** | building |
| **el centro de videojuegos** | arcade |
| **la piscina** | pool |
| **la acera** | sidewalk |
| **el correo** | post office |
| **la librería** | bookstore |
| **la zapatería** | shoe store |
| **el templo** | temple |
| **la tienda de discos** | music store |
| *Music* | |
| **el rap** | rap |
| **alternativa** | alternative |
| **la música electrónica** | electronic music, techno |
| **la canción** | song |
| **la letra** | lyrics |

### In a Restaurant

| | |
|---|---|
| **la cuchara** | spoon |
| **el cuchillo** | knife |
| **el tenedor** | fork |
| **el vaso** | glass |
| **la servilleta** | napkin |
| **el tazón** | bowl |
| **la taza** | cup |
| *For Dinner* | |
| **el puerco** | pork |
| **el pavo** | turkey |
| **los fideos** | noodles |
| **la salsa** | sauce |
| **la pimienta** | pepper |
| **la sal** | salt |
| **los mariscos** | seafood |
| *Vegetables* | |
| **la zanahoria** | carrot |
| **la lechuga** | lettuce |
| **el maíz** | corn |

## Para y piensa
# Self-Check Answers

### Lección preliminar

**p. 5**
1. Buenos días.
2. ¿Cómo estás?
*Answers may vary but can include:*
3. Adiós, hasta mañana, hasta luego.

**p. 9**
1. c.
2. a.
3. b.

**p. 11**
1. See p. 10

**p. 15**
1. b.
2. a.
3. c.

**p. 17**
1. seis - dos - cinco - uno - cuatro - dos - cero - nueve
2. tres - siete - cero - ocho - nueve - dos - seis - tres
3. cuatro - uno - ocho - cinco - dos - siete - seis - cero

**p. 19**
1. lunes
2. mañana

**p. 21**
1. b.
2. a.
3. c.

**p. 24**
1. ¿Cómo se dice *please*?
2. ¿Comprendes?

### Unidad 1 Estados Unidos

#### Lección 1
**p. 35 Práctica de vocabulario**
1. escuchar música
2. hacer la tarea

**p. 37 Vocabulario en contexto**
1. jugar
2. música
3. comer

**p. 41 Práctica de gramática**
1. Cristóbal y yo somos de Honduras.
2. Tomás es de la República Dominicana.
3. Yo soy de México.

**p. 43 Gramática en contexto**
1. El Sr. Costas es de la Florida.
2. Alicia es de Miami.
3. Teresa y Miguel son de Honduras y Cuba.

**p. 47 Práctica de gramática**
1. Le gusta
2. Te gusta
3. Nos gusta

**p. 50 Todo junto**
1. Teresa es de Honduras.
   Le gusta tocar la guitarra.
2. Alicia es de Miami.
   Le gusta comer.
3. Miguel es de Cuba.
   Le gusta mirar la televisión.

#### Lección 2
**p. 63 Práctica de vocabulario**
1. Juan es bajo.
2. David es artístico.
3. Carlos es serio.

**p. 65 Vocabulario en contexto**
1. perezoso
2. atlético
3. estudioso

**p. 69 Práctica de gramática**
1. la televisión
2. unas frutas
3. el libro
4. unos hombres

**p. 71 Gramática en contexto**
1. Ricardo es un amigo de Alberto.
2. Marta y Carla son unas chicas de la clase de la señora García.
3. Ana es una chica muy inteligente.

**p. 75 Práctica de gramática**
1. una estudiante desorganizada
2. unos chicos simpáticos
3. unas mujeres trabajadoras
4. un hombre grande

**p. 78 Todo junto**
1. Alberto es un chico simpático.
2. Ricardo es un estudiante trabajador.
3. Sandra es una persona organizada.

# Unidad 2 México

## Lección 1

**p. 97 Práctica de vocabulario**
1. Me gusta dibujar en la clase de arte.
2. Hay veintitrés chicos en la clase de matemáticas.

**p. 99 Vocabulario en contexto**
1. a las diez y cuarto
   (a las diez y quince)
2. las ocho y veinte
3. a las siete

**p. 103 Práctica de gramática**
1. Juan nunca tiene que preparar la comida.
2. Tenemos la clase de inglés todos los días.
3. Siempre tengo que usar la computadora.

**p. 105 Gramática en contexto**
1. tienen
2. tiene que
3. tienen

**p. 109 Práctica de gramática**
1. usamos
2. preparo
3. dibujan
4. Necesitas

**p. 112 Todo junto**
1. toma
2. practicar
3. estudian

## Lección 2

**p. 125 Práctica de vocabulario**
*Answers may vary but can include:*
1. el baño, el gimnasio, la cafetería, la biblioteca, etc.
2. el mapa, el escritorio, la silla, el reloj, etc.

**p. 127 Vocabulario en contexto**
1. la biblioteca
2. el gimnasio
3. la biblioteca

**p. 131 Práctica de gramática**
1. Estoy cerca de las ventanas.
2. Pablo, ¿estás nervioso?

**p. 133 Gramática en contexto**
*Answers may vary but can include:*
1. Pablo y Claudia están en la biblioteca.
2. Pablo está nervioso.
3. Pablo tiene que estar en el gimnasio a las cinco.

**p. 137 Práctica de gramática**
1. Teresa va a la cafetería.
2. Los estudiantes van a la oficina del director.
3. Nosotros vamos al gimnasio.
4. Yo voy a la clase de matemáticas.

**p. 140 Todo junto**
1. está; va a
2. están; van a
3. está; va a

# Unidad 3 Puerto Rico

## Lección 1

**p. 159 Práctica de vocabulario**
*Answers may vary but can include:*
1. los huevos, el cereal, el yogur, la fruta
2. el sándwich, la sopa, la hamburguesa

**p. 161 Vocabulario en contexto**
1. Quiénes
2. Cuándo
3. Por qué

**p. 165 Práctica de gramática**
1. Me gustan los huevos para el desayuno.
2. A José le gusta la pizza con jamón.
3. ¿Por qué no te gusta la fruta?

**p. 167 Gramática en contexto**
1. gusta
2. gusta
3. gustan

**p. 171 Práctica de gramática**
1. hacen; comen       3. hace; bebe
2. haces; leo

**p. 174 Todo junto**
1. gusta; come
2. gustan; comparten

## Lección 2

**p. 187 Práctica de vocabulario**
1. hijo            3. hermanas
2. padres

**p. 189 Vocabulario en contexto**
1. Marisol tiene catorce años.
2. El gato de la familia Vélez tiene ocho años.
3. Los padres de Marisol tienen cincuenta y dos años.

**p. 193 Práctica de gramática**
1. mi; el seis de septiembre
2. nuestro; el veinticinco de enero.
3. su; el diecisiete de abril.

**p. 195 Gramática en contexto**
1. El cumpleaños de Camila es el doce de junio.
2. El cumpleaños de Ester es el primero de octubre.
3. El cumpleaños de Tito es el veintiocho de marzo.
4. El cumpleaños de Celia es el diecisiete de enero.

**p. 199 Práctica de gramática**
1. Mi hermano es más alto que mi padre.
2. Me gustan las manzanas tanto como las bananas.
3. La clase de matemáticas es mejor que la clase de arte.

**p. 202 Todo junto**
1. Sus perros son tan grandes como Marisol.
2. Su primo es menor que él.
3. Sus perros son más perezosos que los gatos.

## Unidad 4 España

### Lección 1

**p. 221 Práctica de vocabulario**
1. ¿Cuánto cuestan los calcetines blancos?
2. ¿Cuánto cuesta el vestido azul?
3. ¿Cuánto cuesta la chaqueta anaranjada?
4. ¿Cuánto cuestan los pantalones cortos rojos?

**p. 223 Vocabulario en contexto**
1. tiene frío
2. tiene calor
3. tiene frío

**p. 227 Práctica de gramática**
1. pienso
2. empieza
3. cierra

**p. 229 Gramática en contexto**
1. entiende
2. prefiere
3. quiere

**p. 233 Práctica de gramática**
1. los
2. La
3. Las

**p. 236 Todo junto**
1. Sí, Enrique la necesita.
2. Sí, Enrique lo prefiere.
3. Sí, Enrique la quiere comprar. (Sí, Enrique quiere comprarla.)

### Lección 2

**p. 249 Práctica de vocabulario**
*Answers may vary but can include:*
1. El menú, el (la) camarero(a), la cuenta, los platos principales, etc.
2. El teatro, el parque, el cine, etc.

**p. 251 Vocabulario en contexto**
1. en autobús
2. a pie
3. en coche

**p. 255 Práctica de gramática**
1. cuesta
2. almorzamos
3. duermo
4. pueden

**p. 257 Gramática en contexto**
1. puede
2. encuentra
3. vuelve

**p. 261 Práctica de gramática**
1. sirven
2. sirve
3. pedimos

**p. 264 Todo junto**
1. almuerzan
2. pide
3. puede

# Resumen de gramática

## Nouns, Articles, and Pronouns

RESUMEN DE GRAMÁTICA

### Nouns

**Nouns** identify people, animals, places, and things. All Spanish nouns, even if they refer to objects, are either **masculine** or **feminine.** They are also either **singular** or **plural.**

Nouns ending in **-o** are usually masculine; nouns ending in **-a** are usually feminine.

To form the **plural** of a noun, add **-s** if the noun ends in a vowel; add **-es** if it ends in a consonant.

| Singular Nouns | | Plural Nouns | |
|---|---|---|---|
| **Masculine** | **Feminine** | **Masculine** | **Feminine** |
| abuelo | abuela | abuelo**s** | abuela**s** |
| chico | chica | chico**s** | chica**s** |
| hombre | mujer | hombre**s** | mujer**es** |
| papel | pluma | papel**es** | pluma**s** |
| zapato | blusa | zapato**s** | blusa**s** |

### Articles

**Articles** identify the class of a noun: masculine or feminine, singular or plural. **Definite articles** are the equivalent of the English word *the.* **Indefinite articles** are the equivalent of *a, an,* or *some.*

**Definite Articles**

| | Masculine | Feminine |
|---|---|---|
| **Singular** | **el** chico | **la** chica |
| **Plural** | **los** chicos | **las** chicas |

**Indefinite Articles**

| | Masculine | Feminine |
|---|---|---|
| **Singular** | **un** chico | **una** chica |
| **Plural** | **unos** chicos | **unas** chicas |

## Pronouns

**Pronouns** take the place of nouns. The pronoun used is determined by its function or purpose in a sentence.

### Subject Pronouns

| | |
|---|---|
| yo | nosotros(as) |
| tú | vosotros(as) |
| usted | ustedes |
| él, ella | ellos(as) |

### Direct Object Pronouns

| | |
|---|---|
| me | nos |
| te | os |
| lo, la | los, las |

## Adjectives

**Adjectives** describe nouns. In Spanish, adjectives match the **gender** and **number** of the nouns they describe. To make an adjective plural, add **-s** if it ends in a vowel; add **-es** if it ends in a consonant. The adjective usually comes after the noun in Spanish.

### Adjectives

| | Masculine | Feminine |
|---|---|---|
| **Singular** | el chico alt**o** | la chica alt**a** |
| | el chico inteligente | la chica inteligente |
| | el chico joven | la chica joven |
| | el chico trabajador | la chica trabajador**a** |
| **Plural** | los chicos alto**s** | las chicas alta**s** |
| | los chicos inteligente**s** | las chicas inteligente**s** |
| | los chicos jóven**es** | las chicas jóven**es** |
| | los chicos trabajador**es** | las chicas trabajora**s** |

Sometimes adjectives are shortened when they are placed in front of a masculine singular noun.

### Shortened Forms

| | |
|---|---|
| bueno | **buen** chico |
| malo | **mal** chico |

**Possessive adjectives** indicate who owns something or describe a relationship between people or things. They agree in number with the nouns they describe. **Nuestro(a)** and **vuestro(a)** must also agree in gender with the nouns they describe.

### Possessive Adjectives

|  | Masculine | | Feminine | |
|---|---|---|---|---|
| **Singular** | **mi** amigo | **nuestro** amigo | **mi** amiga | **nuestra** amiga |
|  | **tu** amigo | **vuestro** amigo | **tu** amiga | **vuestra** amiga |
|  | **su** amigo | **su** amigo | **su** amiga | **su** amiga |
| **Plural** | **mis** amigos | **nuestros** amigos | **mis** amigas | **nuestras** amigas |
|  | **tus** amigos | **vuestros** amigos | **tus** amigas | **vuestras** amigas |
|  | **sus** amigos | **sus** amigos | **sus** amigas | **sus** amigas |

# Comparatives

**Comparatives** are used to compare two people or things.

### Comparatives

| **más (+)** | **menos (–)** | **tan, tanto (=)** |
|---|---|---|
| **más** serio **que...** | **menos** serio **que...** | **tan** serio **como...** |
| Me gusta leer **más que** pasear. | Me gusta pasear **menos que** leer. | Me gusta hablar **tanto como** escuchar. |

There are a few irregular comparative words. When talking about the age of people, use **mayor** and **menor.** When talking about qualities, use **mejor** and **peor.**

| Age | Quality |
|---|---|
| mayor | mejor |
| menor | peor |

# Verbs: Present Tense

## Regular Verbs

**Regular verbs** ending in **-ar, -er,** or **-ir** always have regular endings in the present tense.

| -ar Verbs | | -er Verbs | | -ir Verbs | |
|---|---|---|---|---|---|
| hablo | hablamos | vendo | vendemos | comparto | compartimos |
| hablas | habláis | vendes | vendéis | compartes | compartís |
| habla | hablan | vende | venden | comparte | comparten |

## Verbs with Irregular yo Forms

Some verbs have regular forms in the present tense except for the **yo** form.

**hacer**

| | |
|---|---|
| hago | hacemos |
| haces | hacéis |
| hace | hacen |

**ver**

| | |
|---|---|
| veo | vemos |
| ves | veis |
| ve | ven |

## Stem-Changing Verbs

**e → ie**

| | |
|---|---|
| qu**ie**ro | queremos |
| qu**ie**res | queréis |
| qu**ie**re | qu**ie**ren |

Other **e → ie** stem-changing verbs are **cerrar, comenzar, despertarse, empezar, entender, pensar,** and **preferir.**

**o → ue**

| | |
|---|---|
| p**ue**do | podemos |
| p**ue**des | podéis |
| p**ue**de | p**ue**den |

Other **o → ue** stem-changing verbs are **almorzar, costar, dormir, encontrar,** and **volver.**

**e → i**

| | |
|---|---|
| s**i**rvo | servimos |
| s**i**rves | servís |
| s**i**rve | s**i**rven |

Another **e → i** stem-changing verb is **pedir.**

## Irregular Verbs

The following verbs are irregular in the present tense.

**estar**

| | |
|---|---|
| estoy | estamos |
| estás | estáis |
| está | están |

**ir**

| | |
|---|---|
| voy | vamos |
| vas | vais |
| va | van |

**ser**

| | |
|---|---|
| soy | somos |
| eres | sois |
| es | son |

**tener**

| | |
|---|---|
| tengo | tenemos |
| tienes | tenéis |
| tiene | tienen |

RESUMEN DE
GRAMÁTICA

# Glosario
# español-inglés

This Spanish-English glossary contains all the active vocabulary words that appear in the text as well as passive vocabulary lists. **LP** refers to the Lección preliminar.

 **A**

**a** to, at
  **A la(s)...** At... o'clock. **2.1**
  **a pie** on foot **4.2**
  **¿A qué hora es/son...?** At what time is/are...? **2.1**
**abril** April **3.2**
**la abuela** grandmother **3.2**
**el abuelo** grandfather **3.2**
**los abuelos** grandparents **3.2**
**aburrido(a)** boring **2.2**
**acabar de...** to have just... **5.2**
**la actividad** activity **1.1**
**Adiós.** Goodbye. **LP**
**adónde** (to) where **2.2**
  **¿Adónde vas?** Where are you going? **2.2**
**agosto** August **3.2**
**el agua** (fem.) water **1.1**
**ahora** now **3.1**
**al** to the **2.2**
  **al lado (de)** next to **2.2**
**allí** there **4.2**
**el almacén** (*pl.* **los almacenes**) department store
**almorzar (ue)** to eat lunch **4.2**
**el almuerzo** lunch **3.1**
**alquilar** to rent **1.1**
  **alquilar un DVD** to rent a DVD **1.1**
**alto(a)** tall **1.2**
**amarillo(a)** yellow **4.1**
**el (la) amigo(a)** friend **1.2**
**anaranjado(a)** orange (color) **4.1**
**andar en patineta** to skateboard **1.1**
**el ánimo** spirit
**antes (de)** before **1.1**
**la antorcha** torch
**el anuncio** advertisement; announcement

**el año** year **3.2**
  **el Año Nuevo** New Year
  **¿Cuántos años tienes?** How old are you? **3.2**
  **tener... años** to be... years old **3.2**
**aprender** to learn **1.1**
  **aprender el español** to learn Spanish **1.1**
**los apuntes** notes **2.1**
  **tomar apuntes** to take notes **2.1**
**aquí** here **4.2**
**el arrecife de coral** coral reef
**el arroz** rice **4.2**
**el arte** art **2.1**
**el artículo** article
**artístico(a)** artistic **1.2**
**atlético(a)** athletic **1.2**
**el autobús** (*pl.* **los autobuses**) bus **4.2**
  **en autobús** by bus **4.2**
**avanzar** to advance, to move ahead
  **¡Avanza!** Advance!, Move ahead!
  **avancemos** let's advance, let's move ahead
**el aymara** indigenous language of Bolivia and Peru
**azul** blue **4.1**

 **B**

**bailar** to dance
**el (la) bailarín(ina)** (*pl.* **los bailarines**) dancer
**el baile** dance
**bajo(a)** short (height) **1.2**
**la banana** banana **3.1**
**la banda** musical band
**el baño** bathroom **2.2**
**la batalla** battle
**beber** to drink **1.1**
**la bebida** beverage, drink **3.1**
**la biblioteca** library **2.2**
**la bicicleta** bicycle **1.1**

**bien** well, fine **LP**
  **Bien. ¿Y tú/usted?** Fine. And you? (familiar/formal) **LP**
  **Muy bien. ¿Y tú/usted?** Very well. And you? (familiar/formal) **LP**
**el bistec** beef **4.2**
**blanco(a)** white **4.1**
**la blusa** blouse **4.1**
**bonito(a)** pretty **1.2**
**el borrador** eraser **2.2**
**el brindis** celebratory toast
**el brócoli** broccoli **4.2**
**bueno(a)** good **1.2**
  **Buenos días.** Good morning. **LP**
  **Buenas noches.** Good evening; Good night. **LP**
  **Buenas tardes.** Good afternoon. **LP**

**C**

**cada** each; every
**el café** coffee; café **3.1, 4.2**
**la cafetería** cafeteria **2.2**
**la calavera** skull
**el calcetín** (*pl.* **los calcetines**) sock **4.1**
**la calculadora** calculator **2.2**
**caliente** hot
**la calle** street **4.2**
**el (la) camarero(a)** (food) server **4.2**
**el cambio** change
**la camisa** shirt **4.1**
**la camiseta** T-shirt **4.1**
**cansado(a)** tired **2.2**
**Carnaval** Carnival
**la carne** meat **4.2**
**la carreta** horse-drawn carriage
**la casa** house
**el cascarón** (*pl.* **los cascarones**) confetti-filled egg

**la caseta** small house or tent
**casi** almost **2.1**
**castaño(a)** brown (hair) **1.2**
**catorce** fourteen **2.1**
**el cementerio** cemetery
**la cena** dinner **3.1**
**el centro** center, downtown **4.2**
   **el centro comercial** shopping center, mall **4.1**
**cerca (de)** near (to) **2.2**
**el cereal** cereal **3.1**
**cero** zero **LP**
**cerrar (ie)** to close **4.1**
**la chaqueta** jacket **4.1**
**la chica** girl **1.2**
**el chico** boy **1.2**
**cien** one hundred **2.1**
**las ciencias** science **2.1**
**cierto(a)** true
**cinco** five **LP**
**cincuenta** fifty **2.1**
**el cine** movie theater; the movies **4.2**
**la clase** class, classroom **LP**; kind, type
**el coche** car **4.2**
   **en coche** by car **4.2**
**el colegio** high school
**comer** to eat **1.1**
**cómico(a)** funny **1.2**
**la comida** meal; food **1.1, 3.1**
**como** as, like
**¿Cómo...?** How...? **3.1**
   **¿Cómo eres?** What are you like? **1.2**
   **¿Cómo estás?** How are you? (familiar) **LP**
   **¿Cómo está usted?** How are you? (formal) **LP**
   **¿Cómo se llama?** What's his/her/your (formal) name? **LP**
   **¿Cómo te llamas?** What's your name? (familiar) **LP**
**comparar** to compare
**compartir** to share **3.1**
**comprar** to buy **1.1**
**¿Comprendiste?** Did you understand?
**la computadora** computer **2.1**
**común** common
**el concierto** concert **4.2**
**contento(a)** happy **2.2**
**contestar** to answer **2.1**
**el correo electrónico** e-mail **1.1**
**correr** to run **1.1**

**costar (ue)** to cost **4.2**
   **¿Cuánto cuesta(n)?** How much does it (do they) cost? **4.1**
   **Cuesta(n)...** It (They) cost... **4.1**
**la Cremà** burning of papier-mâché figures during Las Fallas
**el cuaderno** notebook **2.2**
**el cuadro** painting
**¿Cuál(es)?** Which?; What? **3.1**
   **¿Cuál es la fecha?** What is the date? **3.2**
   **¿Cuál es tu/su número de teléfono?** What is your phone number? (familiar/formal) **LP**
**cuando** when **2.2**
**¿Cuándo?** When? **2.2**
**cuánto(a)** how much **3.2**
   **¿Cuánto cuesta(n)?** How much does it (do they) cost? **4.1**
**cuántos(as)** how many **3.2**
   **¿Cuántos(as)...?** How many...? **2.1**
   **¿Cuántos años tienes?** How old are you? **3.2**
**cuarenta** forty **2.1**
**cuatro** four **LP**
**cuatrocientos(as)** four hundred **3.2**
**la cuenta** bill (in a restaurant) **4.2**
**el cumpleaños** birthday **3.2**
   **¡Feliz cumpleaños!** Happy birthday! **3.2**

**de** of, from **1.1**
   **de la mañana** in the morning (with a time) **2.1**
   **De nada.** You're welcome. **LP**
   **de la noche** at night (with a time) **2.1**
   **¿De qué color es/son...?** What color is/are...?
   **de la tarde** in the afternoon (with a time) **2.1**
   **de vez en cuando** once in a while **2.1**
**debajo (de)** underneath, under **2.2**
**del (de la)** of *or* from the **2.2**
**delante (de)** in front (of) **2.2**
**demasiado** too much
**dentro (de)** inside (of) **2.2**
**los deportes** sports **1.1**
**deprimido(a)** depressed **2.2**
**el desayuno** breakfast **3.1**

**descansar** to rest **1.1**
**desear** to wish, to want
**el desfile** parade
**desorganizado(a)** disorganized **1.2**
**después (de)** afterward; after **1.1**
**detrás (de)** behind **2.2**
**el día** day **LP**
   **Buenos días.** Good morning. **LP**
   **¿Qué día es hoy?** What day is today? **LP**
   **todos los días** every day **2.1**
**dibujar** to draw **1.1**
**el dibujo** drawing
**diciembre** December **3.2**
**diecinueve** nineteen **2.1**
**dieciocho** eighteen **2.1**
**dieciséis** sixteen **2.1**
**diecisiete** seventeen **2.1**
**diez** ten **LP**
**diferente** different
**difícil** difficult **2.1**
**el difunto** deceased
**el dinero** money **4.1**
**el (la) director(a)** principal **2.2**
**el disfraz (*pl.* los disfraces)** costume
**divertido(a)** fun **2.2**
**doce** twelve **2.1**
**el dólar** dollar **4.1**
**domingo** Sunday **LP**
**donde** where
**¿Dónde?** Where? **2.2**
   **¿De dónde eres?** Where are you from? (familiar) **LP**
   **¿De dónde es?** Where is he/she from? **LP**
   **¿De dónde es usted?** Where are you from? (formal) **LP**
**dormir (ue)** to sleep **4.2**
**dos** two **LP**
**doscientos(as)** two hundred **3.2**
**durante** during **4.1**
**el DVD** DVD **1.1**

**el ejército** army
**él** he **1.1**
**ella** she **1.1**
**ellos(as)** they **1.1**
**emocionado(a)** excited **2.2**
**empezar (ie)** to begin **4.1**
**en** in **2.1**; on
   **en autobús** by bus **4.2**
   **en coche** by car **4.2**

**Encantado(a).** Delighted; Pleased to meet you. **LP**

**encima (de)** on top (of) **2.2**

**encontrar (ue)** to find **4.2**

**la encuesta** survey

**enero** January **3.2**

**enojado(a)** angry **2.2**

**la ensalada** salad **4.2**

**enseñar** to teach **2.1**

**entender (ie)** to understand **4.1**

**la entrada** ticket **4.2**

**entrar** to enter

**el equipo** team

**la escena** scene

**escribir** to write **1.1**

    **escribir correos electrónicos** to write e-mails **1.1**

**el escritorio** desk **2.2**

**la escritura** writing

**escuchar** to listen (to) **1.1**

    **escuchar música** to listen to music **1.1**

**la escuela** school **1.1**

    **la escuela secundaria** high school

**el español** Spanish **2.1**

**especial** special

**el esqueleto** skeleton

**la estación** (*pl.* **las estaciones**) season **4.1**

**estar** to be **2.2**

    **¿Está bien?** OK?

**el (la) estudiante** student **1.2**

**estudiar** to study **1.1**

**estudioso(a)** studious **1.2**

**el euro** euro **4.1**

**el examen** (*pl.* **los exámenes**) test, exam **2.1**

**fácil** easy **2.1**

**las fallas** displays of large papier-mâché figures

**el (la) fallero(a)** celebrant of Las Fallas

**falso(a)** false

**la familia** family **3.2**

**febrero** February **3.2**

**la fecha** date **3.2**

    **¿Cuál es la fecha?** What is the date? **3.2**

    **la fecha de nacimiento** birth date **3.2**

**feo(a)** ugly **4.1**

**la fiesta** party; holiday

    **la fiesta nacional** national holiday

    **la fiesta patria** patriotic holiday

**el fin de semana** weekend

**el (la) francés(esa)** (*pl.* **los franceses**) French

**los frijoles** beans **4.2**

**la fruta** fruit **1.1**

**los fuegos artificiales** fireworks

**la fuente** source; fountain

**el fútbol** soccer (the sport) **1.1**

**la galleta** cookie **1.1**

**el (la) gato(a)** cat **3.2**

**el gimnasio** gymnasium **2.2**

**el gorro** winter hat **4.1**

**Gracias.** Thank you. **LP**

    **Muchas gracias.** Thank you very much. **LP**

**la gramática** grammar

**grande** big, large; great **1.2**

**el grito** shout

**guapo(a)** good-looking **1.2**

**la guitarra** guitar **1.1**

**gustar**

    **Me gusta...** I like... **1.1**

    **No me gusta...** I don't like... **1.1**

    **¿Qué te gusta hacer?** What do you like to do? **1.1**

    **¿Te gusta...?** Do you like...? **1.1**

**el gusto** pleasure

    **El gusto es mío.** The pleasure is mine. **LP**

    **Mucho gusto.** Nice to meet you. **LP**

**hablar** to talk, to speak **1.1**

    **hablar por teléfono** to talk on the phone **1.1**

**hacer (hago)** to make, to do **3.1**

    **Hace calor.** It is hot. **LP**

    **Hace frío.** It is cold. **LP**

    **Hace sol.** It is sunny. **LP**

    **Hace viento.** It is windy. **LP**

    **hacer la tarea** to do homework **1.1**

**¿Qué tiempo hace?** What is the weather like? **LP**

**la hamburguesa** hamburger **3.1**

**hasta** until

    **Hasta luego.** See you later. **LP**

    **Hasta mañana.** See you tomorrow. **LP**

**hay...** there is/are... **2.1**

**el helado** ice cream **1.1**

**la hermana** sister **3.2**

**el hermano** brother **3.2**

**los hermanos** brothers, brother(s) and sister(s) **3.2**

**la hija** daughter **3.2**

**el hijo** son **3.2**

**los hijos** children, son(s) and daughter(s) **3.2**

**la hispanidad** cultural community of Spanish speakers

**la historia** history **2.1**

**Hola.** Hello; Hi. **LP**

**el hombre** man **1.2**

**la hora** hour; time **2.1**

    **¿A qué hora es/son...?** At what time is/are...? **2.1**

    **¿Qué hora es?** What time is it? **2.1**

**el horario** schedule **2.1**

**horrible** horrible **3.1**

**hoy** today **LP**

    **¿Qué día es hoy?** What day is today? **LP**

    **Hoy es...** Today is... **LP**

**el huevo** egg **3.1**

**el idioma** language

**Igualmente.** Same here; Likewise. **LP**

**importante** important **3.1**

    **Es importante.** It's important. **3.1**

**los incas** Incas, an indigenous South American people

**la independencia** independence

**la información** information

**el inglés** English **2.1**

**inteligente** intelligent **1.2**

**interesante** interesting **2.2**

**el invierno** winter **4.1**

**ir** to go **2.2**
   **ir a...** to be going to... **4.2**
   **ir de compras** to go shopping **4.1**
   **Vamos a...** Let's... **4.2**

**el jamón** (*pl.* **los jamones**) ham **3.1**
**el jardín** (*pl.* **los jardines**) garden
**los jeans** jeans **4.1**
**joven** (*pl.* **jóvenes**) young **1.2**
**jueves** Thursday **LP**
**jugar (ue)** to play (sports or games)
   **jugar al fútbol** to play soccer **1.1**
**el jugo** juice **1.1**
   **el jugo de naranja** orange
      juice **3.1**
**julio** July **3.2**
**junio** June **3.2**

**el lado** side
   **al lado (de)** next to **2.2**
**el lago** lake
**el lápiz** (*pl.* **los lápices**) pencil **2.2**
**la lección** (*pl.* **las lecciones**) lesson
**la leche** milk **3.1**
**la lectura** reading
**leer** to read **1.1**
   **leer un libro** to read a book **1.1**
**lejos (de)** far (from) **2.2**
**las lentejas** lentils
**el libertador** liberator
**el libro** book **1.1**
**llamarse** to be called
   **¿Cómo se llama?** What's his/her/
      your (formal) name? **LP**
   **¿Cómo te llamas?** What's your
      name? (familiar) **LP**
   **Me llamo...** My name is... **LP**
   **Se llama...** His/Her name is... **LP**
**la llegada** arrival
**llegar** to arrive **2.1**
**llevar** to wear **4.1**
**llover (ue)** to rain
   **Llueve.** It is raining. **LP**
**el lugar** place **4.2**
**lunes** Monday **LP**

**la madrastra** stepmother **3.2**
**la madre** mother **3.2**
**el (la) maestro(a)** teacher **LP**
**malo(a)** bad **1.2**
   **Mal. ¿Y tú/usted?** Bad. And you?
      (familiar/formal) **LP**
**la manzana** apple **3.1**
**mañana** tomorrow **LP**
   **Hasta mañana.** See you
      tomorrow. **LP**
   **Mañana es...** Tomorrow is... **LP**
**la mañana** morning **2.1**
   **de la mañana** in the morning
      (with a time) **2.1**
**el mapa** map **2.2**
**marrón** (*pl.* **marrones**) brown **4.1**
**martes** Tuesday **LP**
**marzo** March **3.2**
**más** more **1.1**
   **Más o menos. ¿Y tú/usted?** So-
      so. And you? (familiar/
      formal) **LP**
   **más que...** more than... **3.2**
   **más... que** more... than **3.2**
**la máscarà** mask
**la mascleta** firecracker explosions
   during Las Fallas
**las matemáticas** math **2.1**
**mayo** May **3.2**
**mayor** older **3.2**
**la medianoche** midnight
**medio(a)** half
   **...y media** half past... (the
      hour) **2.1**
**mejor** better **3.2**
**menor** younger **3.2**
**menos** less
   **...menos (diez)** (ten) to/before...
      (the hour) **2.1**
   **menos que...** less than... **3.2**
   **menos... que** less... than **3.2**
**el mensaje instantáneo** instant
   message
**el menú** menu **4.2**
**el mercado** market
   **el mercado al aire libre** open-air
      market
**el mes** month **3.2**
**la mesa** table **4.2**
**mi** my **3.2**
**miércoles** Wednesday **LP**
**mil** thousand, one thousand **3.2**

**un millón (de)** million, one
   million **3.2**
**el minuto** minute **2.1**
**mirar** to watch **1.1**; to look at
   **mirar la televisión** to watch
      television **1.1**
**mismo(a)** same
**la mochila** backpack **2.2**
**montar** to ride **1.1**
   **montar en bicicleta** to ride a
      bike **1.1**
**mucho** a lot **2.1**
   **Mucho gusto.** Nice to meet
      you. **LP**
**muchos(as)** many **2.1**
   **muchas veces** often, many
      times **2.1**
**la mujer** woman **1.2**
**el mundo** world
**el museo** museum
**la música** music **1.1**
   **la música folklórica** folk music
   **la música rock** rock music **4.2**
**el (la) músico(a)** musician
**muy** very **1.2**
   **Muy bien. ¿Y tú/usted?** Very well.
      And you? (familiar/formal) **LP**

**nacer** to be born
**nada** nothing
   **De nada.** You're welcome. **LP**
**la naranja** orange (fruit) **3.1**
**necesitar** to need **2.1**
**negro(a)** black **4.1**
**nervioso(a)** nervous **2.2**
**nevar (ie)** to snow
   **Nieva.** It is snowing. **LP**
**la nieve** snow
**el ninot** (*pl.* **los ninots**) large papier-
   mâché figure
**no** no **LP**
**la noche** night **2.1**; evening **LP**
   **Buenas noches.** Good evening;
      Good night. **LP**
   **de la noche** at night (with a
      time) **2.1**
**la Nochebuena** Christmas Eve
**la Nochevieja** New Year's Eve
**el nombre** name
**nosotros(as)** we **1.1**

**la nota** grade (on a test) **2.1**
    **sacar una buena/mala nota** to get a good/bad grade **2.1**
**novecientos(as)** nine hundred **3.2**
**noventa** ninety **2.1**
**noviembre** November **3.2**
**nuestro(a)** our **3.2**
**nueve** nine **LP**
**nuevo(a)** new **4.1**
**el número** number **LP**
    **el número de teléfono** phone number **LP**
**nunca** never **2.1**
**nutritivo(a)** nutritious **3.1**

**o** or **1.1**
**ocho** eight **LP**
**ochocientos(as)** eight hundred **3.2**
**octubre** October **3.2**
**ocupado(a)** busy **2.2**
**la oficina** office **2.2**
    **la oficina del (de la) director(a)** principal's office **2.2**
**el ojo** eye
**once** eleven **2.1**
**la oración** (*pl.* **las oraciones**) sentence
**organizado(a)** organized **1.2**
**el otoño** autumn, fall **4.1**
**otro(a)** other **3.1**

**el padrastro** stepfather **3.2**
**el padre** father **3.2**
**los padres** parents **3.2**
**pagar** to pay **4.1**
**la página** page
**el país** country, nation **LP**
**el pan** bread **3.1**
    **el pan de muertos** special bread made for Día de los Muertos
**los pantalones** pants **4.1**
    **los pantalones cortos** shorts **4.1**
**la papa** potato **1.1**
    **las papas fritas** French fries **1.1**
**el papel** paper **2.2**
    **el papel picado** paper cutouts
**para** for; in order to **3.1**

**parar** to stop
    **Para y piensa.** Stop and think.
**la pareja** pair
**el párrafo** paragraph
**el parque** park **4.2**
    **el parque de diversiones** amusement park
**la parte** part
**el pasado** the past
**pasar** to happen
    **pasar un rato con los amigos** to spend time with friends **1.1**
    **¿Qué pasa?** What's happening? **LP**
    **¿Qué te pasa (a ti)?** What's the matter (with you)?
**pasear** to go for a walk **1.1**
**el paseo** walk, stroll; ride
**el pasillo** hall **2.2**
**el pastel** cake **4.2**
**la patata** potato **4.2**
**pedir (i)** to order, to ask for **4.2**
**la película** movie **4.2**
**pelirrojo(a)** red-haired **1.2**
**el pelo** hair **1.2**
    **el pelo castaño/rubio** brown/blond hair **1.2**
**pensar (ie)** to think; to plan **4.1**
**peor** worse **3.2**
**pequeño(a)** little, small **1.2**
**Perdón.** Excuse me. **LP**
**perezoso(a)** lazy **1.2**
**el periódico** newspaper
    **el periódico escolar** student newspaper
**pero** but **1.1**
**el (la) perro(a)** dog **3.2**
**la persona** person **1.2**
**el pescado** fish (as food) **4.2**
**el pie** foot
    **a pie** on foot **4.2**
**la piscina** swimming pool
**la pista** clue
**el pizarrón** (*pl.* **los pizarrones**) chalkboard, board **2.2**
**la pizza** pizza **1.1**
**la planta** plant
**el plato** plate; dish; course
    **el plato principal** main course **4.2**
**la playa** beach
**la pluma** pen **2.2**
**un poco** a little **1.2**
**pocos(as)** few
**poder (ue)** to be able, can **4.2**

**el pollo** chicken **4.2**
**por** for, per
    **Por favor.** Please. **LP**
    **¿Por qué?** Why? **3.1**
**porque** because **1.2**
**el postre** dessert **4.2**
    **de postre** for dessert **4.2**
**practicar** to practice **1.1**
    **practicar deportes** to play or practice sports **1.1**
**el precio** price **4.1**
**preferir (ie)** to prefer **4.1**
**la pregunta** question
**el premio** award
**preparar** to prepare **1.1**
    **preparar la comida** to prepare food, to make a meal **1.1**
**presentar** to introduce **LP**
    **Te/Le presento a...** Let me introduce you to... (familiar/formal) **LP**
**la primavera** spring **4.1**
**primero(a)** first
    **el primero de...** the first of... (date) **3.2**
**el (la) primo(a)** cousin **3.2**
**los primos** cousins **3.2**
**el problema** problem **2.2**
**la procesión** (*pl.* **las procesiones**) procession
**proclamar** to declare
**la propina** tip (in a restaurant) **4.2**
**el pueblo** town
**la puerta** door **2.2**

**¿Qué?** What? **3.1**
    **¿De qué color es/son...?** What color is/are...?
    **¿Qué día es hoy?** What day is today? **LP**
    **¿Qué hora es?** What time is it? **2.1**
    **¿Qué pasa?** What's happening? **LP**
    **¿Qué tal?** How's it going? **LP**
    **¿Qué te gusta hacer?** What do you like to do? **1.1**
    **¿Qué tiempo hace?** What is the weather like? **LP**
**el quechua** indigenous language from South America
**querer (ie)** to want **4.1**

**el queso** cheese **3.1**
   **el queso crema** cream cheese
**¿Quién(es)?** Who? **3.1**
   **¿Quién es?** Who is he/she/it? **LP**
**quince** fifteen **2.1**
**quinientos(as)** five hundred **3.2**

**un rato** a while, a short time
**la raza** (human) race
**la razón** (*pl.* **las razones**) reason
   **tener razón** to be right **4.1**
**la reconstrucción** (*pl.* **las reconstrucciones**) reenactment
**recordar (ue)** to remember
   **¿Recuerdas?** Do you remember?
**el recorrido** run, journey
**el recreo** recess
**el refresco** soft drink **1.1**
**regular** OK **LP**
   **Regular. ¿Y tú/usted?** OK. And you? (familiar/formal) **LP**
**el reloj** watch; clock **2.2**
**el repaso** review
**responder** to reply
**el restaurante** restaurant **4.2**
**el resultado** result
**el resumen** summary
   **en resumen** in summary
**los Reyes Magos** Three Kings
**rico(a)** tasty, delicious **3.1**
**rojo(a)** red **4.1**
**la rosca de reyes** sweet bread eaten on January 6
**la ropa** clothing **4.1**
**rubio(a)** blond **1.2**

**sábado** Saturday **LP**
**sacar una buena/mala nota** to get a good/bad grade **2.1**
**¡Saludos!** Greetings!
   **Saludos desde...** Greetings from...
**el sándwich** sandwich **3.1**
   **el sándwich de jamón y queso** ham and cheese sandwich **3.1**
**el santo** saint
**seis** six **LP**
**seiscientos(as)** six hundred **3.2**

**la semana** week **LP**
   **el fin de semana** weekend
   **Semana Santa** Holy Week
**Señor (Sr.)** Mr. **LP**
**Señora (Sra.)** Mrs. **LP**
**Señorita (Srta.)** Miss **LP**
**septiembre** September **3.2**
**ser** to be **1.1**
   **Es de...** He/She is from... **LP**
   **Es el... de...** It's the... of... (day and month) **3.2**
   **Es la.../Son las...** It is... o'clock. **2.1**
   **Soy de...** I'm from... **LP**
**serio(a)** serious **1.2**
**servir (i)** to serve **4.2**
**sesenta** sixty **2.1**
**setecientos(as)** seven hundred **3.2**
**setenta** seventy **2.1**
**si** if
**sí** yes **LP**
**siempre** always **2.1**
**siete** seven **LP**
**la silla** chair **2.2**
**simpático(a)** nice, friendly **1.2**
**sobre** about; on
**el sombrero** hat **4.1**
**la sopa** soup **3.1**
**su** his, her, its, their, your (formal) **3.2**
**el supermercado** supermarket

**tal vez** perhaps, maybe **4.2**
**también** also, too **1.1**
   **también se dice...** you can also say...
**tan... como** as... as **3.2**
**tanto como...** as much as... **3.2**
**tanto(a)** so much
**tantos(as)** so many
**tarde** late **2.1**
**la tarde** afternoon **2.1**
   **Buenas tardes.** Good afternoon. **LP**
   **de la tarde** in the afternoon (with a time) **2.1**
**la tarea** homework **1.1**
**la tarjeta postal** postcard
**el teatro** theater **4.2**

**el teléfono** telephone
   **¿Cuál es tu/su número de teléfono?** What is your phone number? (familiar/formal) **LP**
   **Mi número de teléfono es...** My phone number is... **LP**
**el tema** theme
**temprano** early **2.1**
**tener** to have **2.1**
   **¿Cuántos años tienes?** How old are you? **3.2**
   **tener... años** to be... years old **3.2**
   **tener calor** to be hot **4.1**
   **tener frío** to be cold **4.1**
   **tener ganas de...** to to feel like... **3.1**
   **tener hambre** to be hungry **3.1**
   **tener que...** to have to... **2.1**
   **tener razón** to be right **4.1**
   **tener sed** to be thirsty **3.1**
   **tener suerte** to be lucky **4.1**
**la tía** aunt **3.2**
**el tiempo** weather **LP**
   **¿Qué tiempo hace?** What is the weather like? **LP**
**la tienda** store **4.1**
**el tío** uncle **3.2**
**los tíos** uncles, uncle(s) and aunt(s) **3.2**
**típico(a)** typical
**el tipo** type
**la tiza** chalk **2.2**
**tocar** to play (an instrument) **1.1**
   **tocar la guitarra** to play the guitar **1.1**
**todo junto** all together
**todos(as)** all **1.2**
   **todos los días** every day **2.1**
**tomar** to take **4.2**
   **tomar apuntes** to take notes **2.1**
**el tomate** tomato **4.2**
**trabajador(a)** hard-working **1.2**
**trabajar** to work **1.1**
**tranquilo(a)** calm **2.2**
**trece** thirteen **2.1**
**treinta** thirty **2.1**
**treinta y uno** thirty-one **2.1**
**tres** three **LP**
**trescientos(as)** three hundred **3.2**
**triste** sad **2.2**
**tu** your (sing., familiar) **3.2**
**tú** you (sing., familiar) **1.1**
**el turismo** tourism
**el turrón** (*pl.* **los turrones**) almond nougat candy

**último(a)** last
**la unidad** unit
**uno** one **LP**
**usar** to use **2.1**
　**usar la computadora** to use the computer **2.1**
**usted** you (sing., formal) **1.1**
**ustedes** you (pl.) **1.1**
**la uva** grape **3.1**
　**las doce uvas** twelve grapes eaten on New Year's Eve

**¡Vale!** OK!
**varios(as)** various
**veinte** twenty **2.1**
**veintiuno** twenty-one **2.1**
**el (la) vendedor(a)** salesclerk
**vender** to sell **3.1**
**la ventana** window **2.2**
**la ventanilla** ticket window **4.2**
**ver (veo)** to see **4.2**

**el verano** summer **4.1**
**la verdad** truth
　**¿Verdad?** Really?; Right? **LP**
**verde** green **4.1**
**las verduras** vegetables **4.2**
**el vestido** dress **4.1**
**la vez** (*pl.* **las veces**) time
　**a veces** sometimes
　**de vez en cuando** once in a while **2.1**
　**muchas veces** often, many times **2.1**
　**tal vez** maybe **4.2**
**la vida** life
**el videojuego** video game
**viejo(a)** old **1.2**
**el viento** wind
　**Hace viento.** It is windy. **LP**
**viernes** Friday **LP**
**el villancico** seasonal children's song
**visitar** to visit
**vivir** to live **3.2**
**el vocabulario** vocabulary
**volver (ue)** to return, to come back **4.2**
**vosotros(as)** you (pl. familiar) **1.1**
**vuestro(a)** your (pl. familiar) **3.2**

**y** and
　**...y (diez)** (ten) past... (the hour) **2.1**
　**...y cuarto** quarter past... (the hour) **2.1**
　**...y media** half past... (the hour) **2.1**
　**¿Y tú?** And you? (familiar) **LP**
　**¿Y usted?** And you? (formal) **LP**
**ya** already **3.2**
**yo** I **1.1**
**el yogur** yogurt **3.1**

**el zapato** shoe **4.1**

# Glosario
## inglés-español

This English-Spanish glossary contains all the active vocabulary words that appear in the text as well as passive vocabulary lists. **LP** refers to Lección preliminar.

**about** sobre
**activity** la actividad **1.1**
**to advance** avanzar
**advertisement** el anuncio
**after** después (de) **1.1**
**afternoon** la tarde **2.1**
   **Good afternoon.** Buenas tardes. **LP**
   **in the afternoon** de la tarde **2.1**
**afterward** después **1.1**
**all** todos(as) **1.2**
**all together** todo junto
**almost** casi **2.1**
**already** ya **3.2**
**also** también **1.1**
**always** siempre **2.1**
**and** y
**angry** enojado(a) **2.2**
**announcement** el anuncio
**answer** la respuesta
**to answer** contestar **2.1**
**apple** la manzana **3.1**
**April** abril **3.2**
**arrival** la llegada
**to arrive** llegar **2.1**
**art** el arte **2.1**
**article** el artículo
**artistic** artístico(a) **1.2**
**as** como
   **as... as** tan... como **3.2**
   **as much as...** tanto como... **3.2**
**to ask for** pedir (i) **4.2**
**at** a
   **at night** de la noche **2.1**
   **At... o'clock.** A la(s)... **2.1**
   **At what time is/are...?** ¿A qué hora es/son...? **2.1**
**athletic** atlético(a) **1.2**
**August** agosto **3.2**
**aunt** la tía **3.2**
**autumn** el otoño **4.1**
**award** el premio

**backpack** la mochila **2.2**
**bad** malo(a) **1.2**
   **Bad. And you?** (familiar/formal) Mal. ¿Y tú/usted? **LP**
**banana** la banana **3.1**
**bathroom** el baño **2.2**
**to be** ser **1.1**; estar **2.2**
   **to be able** poder (ue) **4.2**
   **to be called** llamarse
   **to be cold** tener frío **4.1**
   **to be hot** tener calor **4.1**
   **to be hungry** tener hambre **3.1**
   **to be lucky** tener suerte **4.1**
   **to be right** tener razón **4.1**
   **to be thirsty** tener sed **3.1**
   **to be... years old** tener... años **3.2**
**beach** la playa
**beans** los frijoles **4.2**
**because** porque **1.2**
**beef** el bistec **4.2**
**before** antes (de) **1.1**; menos (with a time) **2.1**
**to begin** empezar (ie) **4.1**
**behind** detrás (de) **2.2**
**better** mejor **3.2**
**beverage** la bebida **3.1**
**bicycle** la bicicleta **1.1**
**big** grande **1.2**
**bill (in a restaurant)** la cuenta **4.2**
**birth date** la fecha de nacimiento **3.2**
**birthday** el cumpleaños **3.2**
   **Happy birthday!** ¡Feliz cumpleaños! **3.2**
**black** negro(a) **4.1**
**blond** rubio(a) **1.2**
**blouse** la blusa **4.1**
**blue** azul **4.1**
**board** el pizarrón (*pl.* los pizarrones) **2.2**
**boat** el bote
**book** el libro **1.1**
**boring** aburrido(a) **2.2**

**boy** el chico **1.2**
**bread** el pan **3.1**
**breakfast** el desayuno **3.1**
**broccoli** el brócoli **4.2**
**brother** el hermano **3.2**
**brown** marrón (*pl.* marrones) **4.1**
   **brown hair** el pelo castaño **1.2**
**bus** el autobús (*pl.* los autobuses) **4.2**
   **by bus** en autobús **4.2**
**busy** ocupado(a) **2.2**
**but** pero **1.1**
**to buy** comprar **1.1**

**café** el café **4.2**
**cafeteria** la cafetería **2.2**
**cake** el pastel **4.2**
**calculator** la calculadora **2.2**
**calm** tranquilo(a) **2.2**
**can (to be able)** poder (ue) **4.2**
**car** el coche **4.2**
   **by car** en coche **4.2**
**cat** el (la) gato(a) **3.2**
**center** el centro **4.2**
**cereal** el cereal **3.1**
**chair** la silla **2.2**
**chalk** la tiza **2.2**
**chalkboard** el pizarrón (*pl.* los pizarrones) **2.2**
**change** el cambio
**cheese** el queso **3.1**
   **cream cheese** el queso crema
**chicken** el pollo **4.2**
**children** los hijos **3.2**
**class** la clase **LP**
**classroom** la clase **LP**
**clock** el reloj **2.2**
**to close** cerrar (ie) **4.1**
**clothing** la ropa **4.1**
**clue** la pista
**coffee** el café **3.1**

**cold** el frío

    **It is cold.** Hace frío. **LP**

    **to be cold** tener frío **4.1**

**color** el color

    **What color is/are...?** ¿De qué
    color es/son...?

**to come back** volver (ue) **4.2**

**common** común

**to compare** comparar

**computer** la computadora **2.1**

**concert** el concierto **4.2**

**cookie** la galleta **1.1**

**coral reef** el arrecife de coral

**to correct** corregir

**to cost** costar (ue) **4.2**

    **How much does it (do they)
    cost?** ¿Cuánto cuesta(n)? **4.1**

    **It (They) cost...** Cuesta(n)... **4.1**

**costume** el disfraz (*pl.* los disfraces)

**country** el país **LP**

**course** el plato

    **main course** el plato
    principal **4.2**

**cousin** el (la) primo(a) **3.2**

**dance** el baile

**to dance** bailar

**date** la fecha **3.2**

    **birth date** la fecha de
    nacimiento **3.2**

    **What is the date?** ¿Cuál es la
    fecha? **3.2**

**daughter** la hija **3.2**

**day** el día **LP**

    **every day** todos los días **2.1**

    **What day is today?** ¿Qué día es
    hoy? **LP**

**December** diciembre **3.2**

**delicious** rico(a) **3.1**

**Delighted.** Encantado(a). **LP**

**department store** el almacén (*pl.*
los almacenes)

**depressed** deprimido(a) **2.2**

**desk** el escritorio **2.2**

**dessert** el postre **4.2**

    **for dessert** de postre **4.2**

**different** diferente

**difficult** difícil **2.1**

**dinner** la cena **3.1**

**dish** el plato

    **main dish** el plato principal **4.2**

**disorganized** desorganizado(a) **1.2**

**to do** hacer (hago) **3.1**

**dog** el (la) perro(a) **3.2**

**dollar** el dólar **4.1**

**door** la puerta **2.2**

**downtown** el centro **4.2**

**to draw** dibujar **1.1**

**drawing** el dibujo

**dress** el vestido **4.1**

**drink** la bebida **3.1**

**to drink** beber **1.1**

**during** durante **4.1**

**DVD** el DVD **1.1**

**each** cada

**early** temprano **2.1**

**easy** fácil **2.1**

**to eat** comer **1.1**

    **to eat lunch** almorzar (ue) **4.2**

**egg** el huevo **3.1**

**eight** ocho **LP**

**eight hundred** ochocientos(as) **3.2**

**eighteen** dieciocho **2.1**

**eleven** once **2.1**

**e-mail** el correo electrónico **1.1**

**English** el inglés **2.1**

**to enter** entrar

**eraser** el borrador **2.2**

**euro** el euro **4.1**

**evening** la noche **LP**

    **Good evening.** Buenas
    noches. **LP**

**every** cada

    **every day** todos los días **2.1**

**exam** el examen (*pl.* los
exámenes) **2.1**

**excited** emocionado(a) **2.2**

**Excuse me.** Perdón. **LP**

**eye** el ojo

**fall** el otoño **4.1**

**false** falso(a)

**family** la familia **3.2**

**far (from)** lejos (de) **2.2**

**father** el padre **3.2**

**February** febrero **3.2**

**to feel like...** tener ganas
de... **3.1**

**few** pocos(as)

**fifteen** quince **2.1**

**fifty** cincuenta **2.1**

**to find** encontrar (ue) **4.2**

**fine** bien **LP**

    **Fine. And you?** (familiar/ Bien.
    ¿Y tú/usted? formal) **LP**

**fireworks** los fuegos artificiales

**first** primero(a)

    **the first of...** el primero de... **3.2**

**fish** el pescado **4.2**

**five** cinco **LP**

**five hundred** quinientos(as) **3.2**

**food** la comida **1.1, 3.1**

**food server** el (la) camarero(a) **4.2**

**foot** el pie

    **on foot** a pie **4.2**

**for** para **3.1**; por

**forty** cuarenta **2.1**

**fountain** la fuente

**four** cuatro **LP**

**four hundred**
cuatrocientos(as) **3.2**

**fourteen** catorce **2.1**

**French fries** las papas fritas **1.1**

**Friday** viernes **LP**

**friend** el (la) amigo(a) **1.2**

    **to spend time with friends**
    pasar un rato con los amigos **1.1**

**from** de **1.1**

**fruit** la fruta **1.1**

**fun** divertido(a) **2.2**

**funny** cómico(a) **1.2**

**garden** el jardín (*pl.* los jardines)

**girl** la chica **1.2**

**to go** ir **2.2**

    **to be going to...** ir a... **4.2**

    **to go for a walk** pasear **1.1**

    **to go shopping** ir de
    compras **4.1**

**good** bueno(a) **1.2**

    **Good afternoon.** Buenas
    tardes. **LP**

    **Good evening.** Buenas
    noches. **LP**

    **Good morning.** Buenos
    días. **LP**

    **Good night.** Buenas noches. **LP**

**Goodbye.** Adiós. **LP**

**good-looking** guapo(a) **1.2**

**grade** la nota **2.1**

   **to get a good/bad grade** sacar una buena/mala nota **2.1**

**grammar** la grámatica

**grandfather** el abuelo **3.2**

**grandmother** la abuela **3.2**

**grandparents** los abuelos **3.2**

**grape** la uva **3.1**

**green** verde **4.1**

**Greetings!** ¡Saludos!

   **Greetings from...** Saludos desde...

**guitar** la guitarra **1.1**

**gymnasium** el gimnasio **2.2**

**hair** el pelo **1.2**

   **blond hair** pelo rubio **1.2**

   **brown hair** pelo castaño **1.2**

**half** medio(a)

   **half past...** ... y media **2.1**

**hall** el pasillo **2.2**

**ham** el jamón (*pl.* los jamones) **3.1**

**hamburger** la hamburguesa **3.1**

**to happen** pasar

   **What's happening?** ¿Qué pasa? **LP**

**happy** contento(a) **2.2**

**hard-working** trabajador(a) **1.2**

**hat** el sombrero **4.1**

   **winter hat** el gorro **4.1**

**to have** tener **2.1**

   **to have to...** tener que... **2.1**

**he** él **1.1**

**Hello.** Hola. **LP**

**her** su **3.2**

**here** aquí **4.2**

**Hi.** Hola. **LP**

**high school** el colegio, la escuela secundaria

**his** su **3.2**

**history** la historia **2.1**

**homework** la tarea **1.1**

   **to do homework** hacer la tarea **1.1**

**horrible** horrible **3.1**

**hot** caliente

   **It is hot.** Hace calor. **LP**

   **to be hot** tener calor **4.1**

**hour** la hora **2.1**

**How...?** ¿Cómo...? **3.1**

   **How are you?** ¿Cómo estás? (familiar); ¿Cómo está usted? (formal) **LP**

   **How many...?** ¿Cuántos(as)...? **2.1**

   **How old are you?** ¿Cuántos años tienes? **3.2**

   **How's it going?** ¿Qué tal? **LP**

**how many** cuántos(as) **3.2**

**how much** cuánto(a) **3.2**

   **How much does it (do they) cost?** ¿Cuánto cuesta(n)? **4.1**

**hungry: to be hungry** tener hambre **3.1**

**I** yo **1.1**

**ice cream** el helado **1.1**

**if** si

**important** importante **3.1**

   **It's important.** Es importante. **3.1**

**in** en **2.1**

   **in front (of)** delante (de) **2.2**

   **in order to** para **3.1**

   **in the afternoon** de la tarde **2.1**

   **in the morning** de la mañana **2.1**

**inexpensive** barato(a)

**information** la información

**inside (of)** dentro (de) **2.2**

**intelligent** inteligente **1.2**

**interesting** interesante **2.2**

**to introduce** presentar **LP**

   **Let me introduce you to...** Te/Le presento a... (familiar/formal) **LP**

**its** su **3.2**

**jacket** la chaqueta **4.1**

**January** enero **3.2**

**jeans** los jeans **4.1**

**juice** el jugo **1.1**

   **orange juice** el jugo de naranja **3.1**

**July** julio **3.2**

**June** junio **3.2**

**kind** amable

**lake** el lago

**language** el idioma, el lenguaje

**large** grande **1.2**

**late** tarde **2.1**

**later**

   **See you later.** Hasta luego. **LP**

**lazy** perezoso(a) **1.2**

**to learn** aprender **1.1**

   **to learn Spanish** aprender el español **1.1**

**less** menos

   **less than...** menos que... **3.2**

   **less... than** menos... que **3.2**

**lesson** la lección

**Let's...** Vamos a... **4.2**

**library** la biblioteca **2.2**

**life** la vida

**like** como

**to like**

   **Do you like...?** ¿Te gusta...? **1.1**

   **I don't like...** No me gusta... **1.1**

   **I like...** Me gusta... **1.1**

   **What do you like to do?** ¿Qué te gusta hacer? **1.1**

**Likewise.** Igualmente. **LP**

**to listen (to)** escuchar **1.1**

   **to listen to music** escuchar música **1.1**

**little** pequeño(a) **1.2**

   **a little** un poco **1.2**

**to live** vivir **3.2**

**to look (at)** mirar

**a lot** mucho **2.1**

**lunch** el almuerzo **3.1**

   **to eat lunch** almorzar (ue) **4.2**

**to make** hacer (hago) **3.1**

**mall** el centro comercial **4.1**

**man** el hombre **1.2**

**many** muchos(as) **2.1**

   **many times** muchas veces **2.1**

**map** el mapa **2.2**

**March** marzo **3.2**
**market** el mercado
  **open-air market** el mercado al aire libre
**math** las matemáticas **2.1**
**May** mayo **3.2**
**maybe** tal vez **4.2**
**meal** la comida **1.1, 3.1**
**meat** la carne **4.2**
**to meet**
  **Nice to meet you.** Mucho gusto. **LP**
**menu** el menú **4.2**
**milk** la leche **3.1**
**million** un millón (de) **3.2**
**minute** el minuto **2.1**
**Miss** Señorita (Srta.) **LP**
**Monday** lunes **LP**
**money** el dinero **4.1**
**month** el mes **3.2**
**more** más **1.1**
  **more than...** más que... **3.2**
  **more... than** más... que **3.2**
**morning** la mañana **2.1**
  **Good morning.** Buenos días. **LP**
  **in the morning** de la mañana **2.1**
**mother** la madre **3.2**
**movie** la película **4.2**
**movie theater** el cine **4.2**
**the movies** el cine **4.2**
**Mr.** Señor (Sr.) **LP**
**Mrs.** Señora (Sra.) **LP**
**museum** el museo
**music** la música **1.1**
  **folk music** la música folklórica
  **rock music** la música rock **4.2**
**my** mi **3.2**

**name** el nombre
  **His/Her name is...** Se llama... **LP**
  **My name is...** Me llamo... **LP**
  **What's his/her/your (formal) name?** ¿Cómo se llama? **LP**
  **What's your (familiar) name?** ¿Cómo te llamas? **LP**
**near (to)** cerca (de) **2.2**
**to need** necesitar **2.1**
**nervous** nervioso(a) **2.2**
**never** nunca **2.1**

**new** nuevo(a) **4.1**
  **New Year** el Año Nuevo
**newspaper** el periódico
  **student newspaper** el periódico escolar
**next to** al lado (de) **2.2**
**nice** simpático(a) **1.2**
  **Nice to meet you.** Mucho gusto. **LP**
**night** la noche **2.1**
  **at night** de la noche **2.1**
  **Good night.** Buenas noches. **LP**
**nine** nueve **LP**
**nine hundred** novecientos(as) **3.2**
**nineteen** diecinueve **2.1**
**ninety** noventa **2.1**
**no** no **LP**
**notebook** el cuaderno **2.2**
**notes** los apuntes **2.1**
  **to take notes** tomar apuntes **2.1**
**November** noviembre **3.2**
**now** ahora **3.1**
**number** el número **LP**
  **phone number** el número de teléfono **LP**
**nutritious** nutritivo(a) **3.1**

**o'clock: It is... o'clock.** Es la.../Son las... **2.1**
**October** octubre **3.2**
**of** de **1.1**
**office** la oficina **2.2**
  **principal's office** la oficina del (de la) director(a) **2.2**
**often** muchas veces **2.1**
**OK**
  **OK!** ¡Vale!
  **OK?** ¿Está bien?
  **OK. And you?** Regular. ¿Y tú/usted? (familiar/formal) **LP**
**old** viejo(a) **1.2**
  **How old are you?** ¿Cuántos años tienes? **3.2**
  **to be... years old** tener... años **3.2**
**older** mayor **3.2**
**on** en; sobre
  **on foot** a pie **4.2**
  **on top (of)** encima (de) **2.2**
**once: once in a while** de vez en cuando **2.1**
**one** uno **LP**
**one hundred** cien **2.1**

**one thousand** mil **3.2**
**or** o **1.1**
**orange (color)** anaranjado(a) **4.1**
**orange (fruit)** la naranja **3.1**
**to order** pedir (i) **4.2**
**organized** organizado(a) **1.2**
**other** otro(a) **3.1**
**our** nuestro(a) **3.2**

**page** la página
**painting** el cuadro
**pair** la pareja
**pants** los pantalones **4.1**
**paper** el papel **2.2**
**parade** el desfile
**paragraph** el párrafo
**parents** los padres **3.2**
**park** el parque **4.2**
  **amusement park** el parque de diversiones
**part** la parte
**party** la fiesta
**past**
  **half past...** ...y media **2.1**
  **quarter past...** ...y cuarto **2.1**
**the past** el pasado
**to pay** pagar **4.1**
**pen** la pluma **2.2**
**pencil** el lápiz (*pl.* los lápices) **2.2**
**perhaps** tal vez **4.2**
**person** la persona **1.2**
**phone** el teléfono **LP**
  **What is your phone number?** ¿Cuál es tu/su número de teléfono? (familiar/formal) **LP**
  **My phone number is...** Mi número de teléfono es... **LP**
**pizza** la pizza **1.1**
**place** el lugar **4.2**
**to plan** pensar (ie) **4.1**
**plant** la planta
**plate** el plato
**to play**
  **(an instrument)** tocar **1.1**
  **(games)** jugar (ue) **1.1**
  **(sports)** jugar (ue), practicar **1.1**
**Please.** Por favor. **LP**
  **Pleased to meet you.** Encantado(a). **LP**
**pleasure** el gusto
  **The pleasure is mine.** El gusto es mío. **LP**
**postcard** la tarjeta postal

**potato** la papa **1.1**; la patata **4.2**
**to practice** practicar **1.1**
**to prefer** preferir (ie) **4.1**
**to prepare** preparar **1.1**
  **to prepare food/a meal** preparar la comida **1.1**
**pretty** bonito(a) **1.2**
**price** el precio **4.1**
**principal** el (la) director(a) **2.2**
**problem** el problema **2.2**

**quarter (to)** (menos) cuarto **2.1**
**quarter past** ...y cuarto **2.1**

**to rain** llover (ue)
  **It is raining.** Llueve. **LP**
**to read** leer **1.1**
  **to read a book** leer un libro **1.1**
**reading** la lectura
**Really?** ¿Verdad?
**recess** el recreo
**red** rojo(a) **4.1**
**red-haired** pelirrojo(a) **1.2**
**to rent** alquilar **1.1**
  **to rent a DVD** alquilar un DVD **1.1**
**to reply** responder
**to rest** descansar **1.1**
**restaurant** el restaurante **4.2**
**result** el resultado
**to return** volver (ue) **4.2**
**review** el repaso
**rice** el arroz **4.2**
**to ride a bike** montar en bicicleta **1.1**
**right** derecho(a)
  **Right?** ¿Verdad? **LP**
  **to be right** tener razón **4.1**
**to run** correr **1.1**

**sad** triste **2.2**
**salad** la ensalada **4.2**
**salesclerk** el (la) vendedor(a)
**same** mismo(a)
  **Same here.** Igualmente. **LP**

**sandwich** el sándwich **3.1**
  **ham and cheese sandwich** el sándwich de jamón y queso **3.1**
**Saturday** sábado **LP**
**scene** la escena
**schedule** el horario **2.1**
**school** la escuela **1.1**
  **high school** el colegio, la escuela secundaria
**science** las ciencias **2.1**
**season** la estación (*pl.* las estaciones) **4.1**
**to see** ver (veo) **4.2**
  **See you later.** Hasta luego. **LP**
  **See you tomorrow.** Hasta mañana. **LP**
**to sell** vender **3.1**
**sentence** la oración (*pl.* las oraciones)
**September** septiembre **3.2**
**serious** serio(a) **1.2**
**to serve** servir (i) **4.2**
**seven** siete **LP**
**seven hundred** setecientos(as) **3.2**
**seventeen** diecisiete **2.1**
**seventy** setenta **2.1**
**to share** compartir **3.1**
**she** ella **1.1**
**shirt** la camisa **4.1**
**shoe** el zapato **4.1**
**shop: to go shopping** ir de compras **4.1**
**shopping center** el centro comercial **4.1**
**short (height)** bajo(a) **1.2**
**shorts** los pantalones cortos **4.1**
**sister** la hermana **3.2**
**six** seis **LP**
**six hundred** seiscientos(as) **3.2**
**sixteen** dieciséis **2.1**
**sixty** sesenta **2.1**
**to skateboard** andar en patineta **1.1**
**to sleep** dormir (ue) **4.2**
**small** pequeño(a) **1.2**
**snow** la nieve
**to snow** nevar (ie)
  **It is snowing.** Nieva. **LP**
**so**
  **so many** tantos(as)
  **so much** tanto(a)
**soccer** el fútbol **1.1**
**sock** el calcetín (*pl.* los calcetines) **4.1**
**soft drink** el refresco **1.1**
**sometimes** a veces
**son** el hijo **3.2**
**So-so. And you?** Más o menos. ¿Y tú/usted? (familiar/formal) **LP**

**soup** la sopa **3.1**
**source** la fuente
**Spanish** el español **2.1**
**to speak** hablar **1.1**
**special** especial
**to spend: to spend time with friends** pasar un rato con los amigos **1.1**
**spirit** el ánimo
**sports** los deportes **1.1**
**spring** la primavera **4.1**
**stepfather** el padrastro **3.2**
**stepmother** la madrastra **3.2**
**to stop** parar
**store** la tienda **4.1**
**street** la calle **4.2**
**student** el (la) estudiante **1.2**
**studious** estudioso(a) **1.2**
**to study** estudiar **1.1**
**summary** el resumen
  **in summary** en resumen
**summer** el verano **4.1**
**sun** el sol
  **It is sunny.** Hace sol. **LP**
**Sunday** domingo **LP**
**supermarket** el supermercado
**survey** la encuesta
**swimming pool** la piscina

**table** la mesa **4.2**
**to take** tomar **4.2**
  **to take notes** tomar apuntes **2.1**
**to talk** hablar **1.1**
  **to talk on the phone** hablar por teléfono **1.1**
**tall** alto(a) **1.2**
**tasty** rico(a) **3.1**
**to teach** enseñar **2.1**
**teacher** el (la) maestro(a) **LP**
**team** el equipo
**ten** diez **LP**
**test** el examen (*pl.* los exámenes) **2.1**
**Thank you.** Gracias. **LP**
  **Thank you very much.** Muchas gracias. **LP**
**theater** el teatro **4.2**
**their** su **3.2**
**them** ellos(as) **7.2**
**theme** el tema
**there** allí **4.2**
  **there is/are...** hay... **2.1**
**they** ellos(as) **1.1**

**to think** pensar (ie) **4.1**
**thirst** la sed
   **to be thirsty** tener sed **3.1**
**thirteen** trece **2.1**
**thirty** treinta **2.1**
**thirty-one** treinta y uno **2.1**
**thousand** mil **3.2**
**three** tres **LP**
**three hundred** trescientos(as) **3.2**
**Thursday** jueves **LP**
**ticket** la entrada **4.2**
**time** la hora **2.1**; la vez
   **At what time is/are...?** ¿A qué
      hora es/son...? **2.1**
   **What time is it?** ¿Qué hora
      es? **2.1**
**tip** la propina **4.2**
**tired** cansado(a) **2.2**
**to** menos (with a time) **2.1**; a
**today** hoy **LP**
   **Today is...** Hoy es... **LP**
   **What day is today?** ¿Qué día es
      hoy? **LP**
**tomato** el tomate **4.2**
**tomorrow** mañana **LP**
   **See you tomorrow.** Hasta
      mañana. **LP**
   **Tomorrow is...** Mañana es... **LP**
**too** también **1.1**
**too much** demasiado
**tourism** el turismo
**town** el pueblo
**true** cierto(a)
**T-shirt** la camiseta **4.1**
**Tuesday** martes **LP**
**twelve** doce **2.1**
**twenty** veinte **2.1**
**twenty-one** veintiuno **2.1**
**two** dos **LP**
**two hundred** doscientos(as) **3.2**
**type** el tipo; la clase
**typical** típico(a)

**ugly** feo(a) **4.1**
**uncle** el tío **3.2**
**under** debajo (de) **2.2**
**underneath** debajo (de) **2.2**
**to understand** entender (ie) **4.1**
   **Did you understand?**
      ¿Comprendiste?
**unit** la unidad

**to use** usar **2.1**
   **to use the computer** usar la
      computadora **2.1**

**various** varios(as)
**vegetables** las verduras **4.2**
**very** muy **1.2**
   **Very well. And you?** Muy bien.
      ¿Y tú/usted? (familiar/formal)
      **LP**
**video game** el videojuego
**to visit** visitar
**vocabulary** vocabulario

**waiter** el camarero **4.2**
**waitress** la camarera **4.2**
**to walk** caminar **6.2**
   **to go for a walk** pasear **1.1**
**to want** querer (ie) **4.1**; desear
**watch** el reloj **2.2**
**to watch** mirar **1.1**
   **to watch television** mirar la
      televisión **1.1**
**water** el agua (fem.) **1.1**
**we** nosotros(as) **1.1**
**to wear** llevar **4.1**
**weather** el tiempo **LP**
   **What is the weather like?** ¿Qué
      tiempo hace? **LP**
**Wednesday** miércoles **LP**
**week** la semana **LP**
**welcome: You're welcome.** De
   nada. **LP**
**well** bien **LP**
   **Very well. And you?** Muy bien.
      ¿Y tú/usted? (familiar/formal)
      **LP**
**what** qué
   **What?** ¿Qué?; ¿Cuál? **3.1**
   **What are you like?** ¿Cómo
      eres? **1.2**
   **What color is/are...?** ¿De qué
      color es/son...?
   **What day is today?** ¿Qué día es
      hoy? **LP**
   **What do you like to do?** ¿Qué
      te gusta hacer? **1.1**
   **What is the date?** ¿Cuál es la
      fecha? **3.2**

**What is the weather like?** ¿Qué
   tiempo hace? **LP**
**What is your phone number?**
   ¿Cuál es tu/su número de
   teléfono? (familiar/formal) **LP**
**What time is it?** ¿Qué hora
   es? **2.1**
**What's happening?** ¿Qué
   pasa? **LP**
**What's his/her/your** (formal)
   **name?** ¿Cómo se llama? **LP**
**What's your** (familiar)
   **name?** ¿Cómo te llamas? **LP**
**when** cuando **2.2**
   **When?** ¿Cuándo? **2.2**
**where** donde
   **Where?** ¿Dónde? **2.2**
   **(To) Where?** ¿Adónde? **2.2**
   **Where are you from?** ¿De
      dónde eres es usted
      (familiar)/(formal)? **LP**
   **Where are you going?** ¿Adónde
      vas? **2.2**
   **Where is he/she from?** ¿De
      dónde es? **LP**
**Which?** ¿Cuál(es)? **3.1**
**a while** un rato
   **once in a while** de vez en
      cuando **2.1**
**white** blanco(a) **4.1**
**Who?** ¿Quién(es)? **3.1**
   **Who is he/she/it?**
      ¿Quién es? **LP**
**Why?** ¿Por qué? **3.1**
**wind** el viento
   **It is windy.** Hace viento. **LP**
**window** la ventana **2.2**
   **ticket window** la ventanilla **4.2**
**winter** el invierno **4.1**
**to wish** desear
**woman** la mujer **1.2**
**to work** trabajar **1.1**
**world** el mundo
**worse** peor **3.2**
**to write** escribir **1.1**
   **to write e-mails** escribir correos
      electrónicos **1.1**
**writing** la escritura

**year** el año **3.2**
   **New Year** el Año Nuevo
   **to be... years old** tener...
      años **3.2**

**yellow** amarillo(a) **4.1**
**yes** sí **LP**
**yogurt** el yogur **3.1**
**you**
    **(sing., familiar)** tú **1.1**
    **(sing., formal)** usted **1.1**
    **(pl., familiar)** vosotros(as) **1.1**
    **(pl.)** ustedes **1.1**
**young** joven (*pl.* jóvenes) **1.2**
**younger** menor **3.2**
**your**
    **(sing., familiar)** tu **3.2**
    **(pl., familiar)** vuestro(a) **3.2**
    **(formal)** su **3.2**

**zero** cero **LP**

# ❋Índice

# Índice

# Créditos

## Acknowledgment

"Invierno tardío" by Antonio Colinas. Reprinted by permission of the author.

## Photography

**Cover** *center* Steve Dunwell/The Image Bank/Getty Images; *inset* Marc Bacon/LatinFocus.com; **i** *Title Page* Steve Dunwell/The Image Bank/Getty Images; *Half Title Page* Marc Bacon/LatinFocus.com; **iii** Marc Bacon/LatinFocus.com; **Back Cover** *top left* Steve Dunwell/The Image Bank/Getty Images; *top center* Rodriguez Joseph/Gallery Stock Limited; *top right* Panoramic Images/Getty Images; *bottom left* Doug Armand/Getty Images; *bottom center* David Noton Photography; *bottom right* P. Pet/zefa/Corbis; **iv** *top* Guy Jarvis/School Division/Houghton Mifflin Harcourt; *bottom left* Jaime Puebla/AP Images; *bottom right* Alberto Martin/Agencia EFE; **v** *bottom left* Gregory Bull/AP Images; *bottom right* Jennifer Szymaszek/AP Images; **vi** Ann Summa/Holt McDougal/Houghton Mifflin Harcourt; **vii** *left, right* Ann Summa/Holt McDougal/Houghton Mifflin Harcourt; **xxii** *top* Erich Lessing/Art Resource, New York; **xxiii** *top* Ann Summa/Holt McDougal/Houghton Mifflin Harcourt; *center, bottom* Ken Karp/Holt McDougal/Houghton Mifflin Harcourt; **xxv** *top* Jay Penni/Holt McDougal/Houghton Mifflin Harcourt; **xxvii** *left, right* Michael Goss/Holt McDougal/Houghton Mifflin Harcourt; **xxviii** *top left* Robert Galbraith/Reuters Pictures; *top right* Holt McDougal/Houghton Mifflin Harcourt; **xxix** *top left* Richard Wareham Fotografie/Alamy; *top right* Ann Summa Stock; *center* Edward Hernandez/Edward H. Photos; *bottom* Philip Coblentz/Brand X Pictures/Getty Images; **C2** *banner, left to right 1* Jesus Dominguez/Agencia EFE; *2-4* Rafael Diaz/Agencia EFE; *all others* Rafael Diaz/Agencia EFE; **C3** *top left, top right* Rafael Diaz/Agencia EFE; *bottom right* Jesus Dominguez/Agencia EFE; **C4** *banner, left to right* Juan Carlos Ulate/Reuters Pictures; The Brownsville Herald/Anthony Padilla/AP Images; Jose Luis Magana/AP Images; Agencia EFE; *bottom left* Hector Lopez/Agencia EFE; *bottom right* Marco Ugarte/AP Images; **C5** *top right* Kent Gilbert/AP Images; *top left* Daniel LeClair/Reuters Pictures; *bottom right* Juan Carlos Ulate/Reuters Pictures; **C6** *banner, left to right* Greg Smith/Corbis; Eduardo Verdugo/AP Images; Claudia Daut/Landov/Reuters Pictures; Les Stone/NewsCom/Zuma Press; *left* Laura Cano/NewsCom/Agence France Presse; *bottom right* Jacqueline Castellon/NewsCom/Notimex; **C7** *center left* Dennis Callahan/NewsCom/Notimex; *bottom right* Susana Vera/Reuters Pictures; *top right* Claudia Daut/Reuters/Landov LLC; **C8** *banner, left to right* Ann Summa; Robert Frerck/Odyssey Productions, Inc.; Denis Defibaugh; Rodrigo Abd/AP Images; *bottom left* Juan Barreto/Getty Images; *bottom left, inset* Ann Summa; *center left* Charles Bennett/AP Images; *top right* Marco Ugarte/AP Images; **C9** *top left* Glen Allison/Alamy; *top right* Eduardo Verdugo/AP Images; *bottom left* Jaime Puebla/AP Images; **C10** *banner, left to right* Marcelo Del Pozo/NewsCom/Reuters; Enrique Marcarian/Reuters Pictures; Juan Martin/Agencia EFE; Blake Sell/NewsCom/Reuters; *top left* Alberto Lowe/NewsCom/Reuters; *bottom left* Viesti Associates, Inc.; *bottom right* Leo La Valle/epa/Corbis; **C11** *top* Silvia Izquierdo/AP Images; *bottom* Desmond Boylan/NewsCom/Reuters; **C12** *banner, left to right* Dolores Ochoa R./AP Images; Marcou/Sipa Press; Denis Doyle/AP Images; Eric L. Weather/Lonely Planet Images; Luis Nereo Bueno Martinez/NewsCom/Reforma; *top left* Silvia Izquierdo/AP Images; *bottom right* Alberto Martin/Agencia EFE; *bottom center* Juanjo Martin/Agencia EFE; *bottom left* Olga Vasilkova/ShutterStock; **C13** *top right* Kryzsztof Dydynki/Lonely Planet Images; *left* Richard I'Anson/Lonely Planet Images; **C14** *banner, left to right* Miguel Vidal/Reuters/Corbis; Pablo Aneli/EPA/Sipa Press; Miguel Menendez V./EPA/Sipa Press; Andres Leighton/AP Images; *left* Elvira Urquijo A./EPA/Sipa Press; *bottom right* Martin Crespo/EPA/Sipa Press; **C15** *top left* Juan Barreto/Staff/Getty Images; *right* David Mercado/Reuters Pictures; *bottom left* Javier Galeano/AP Images; *bottom right* Guy Jarvis/Holt McDougal/Houghton Mifflin Harcourt; **C16** *banner, left to right 1* Kai Forsterling/Agencia EFE; *2* Hannah Levy/Lonely Planet Images; *3-5* Manuel Bruque/Agencia EFE; *bottom* Hannah Levy/Lonely Planet Images; *left* J.C. Cardenas/Agencia EFE; **C17** *right* Heino Kalis/Reuters/Corbis; *left* Kai Forsterling/Agencia EFE; **C18** *banner, left to right* Jack Kurtz/NewsCom/Zuma Press; Viesti Associates, Inc.; Viesti Associates, Inc.; Jack Kurtz/NewsCom/Zuma Press; *bottom right* Viesti Associates, Inc.; *left* Ann Summa; **C19** *top left* Pilar Olivares/Reuters Pictures; *bottom right* Viesti Associates, Inc.; *top right* Dolores Ochoa R./AP Images; **C20** *banner, left to right* Tyler Hicks/New York Times; Joe Raedle/Getty Images; Jorge Uzon/Getty Images; Damian Dovarganes/AP Images; *right, bottom left* Robert Galbraith/Reuters Pictures; **C21** *top right* Jose Luis Magana/AP Images; *center* Michael Springer/Zuma Press; **C22** *banner, left to right* © Keren Su/Corbis; Paolo Aguilar/Agencia EFE; *left* EPA/Corbis; *bottom right* Paolo Aguilar/Agencia EFE; **C23** *right* Guillermo Legaria/Agencia EFE; *left* Christian Lombardi/Agencia EFE; **C24** *banner, left to right* Dado Galdieri/AP Images; Tony Morrison/South American Pictures; Stuart Franklin/Magnum Photos; *left* Daniel Munoz/Reuters/Corbis; *bottom right* Jupiter Images/Comstock; **C25** *bottom* Pablo Corral V/Corbis; *top left* Stuart Franklin/Magnum Photos; *top right* "Símon Bolívar" (1830), José Gil de Castro. Oil on

Photograph by Ian Pearson/Mexicolore/Bridgeman Art Library; **94** *agenda* Jay Penni/Holt McDougal/Houghton Mifflin Harcourt; **95** *map inset* Royalty-Free/Corbis; **101** *bottom right* Jay Penni/Holt McDougal/Houghton Mifflin Harcourt; *6 map inset* Royalty-Free/Corbis; **103** *2, 3, 4, 5 left, 5 right* Ann Summa/Holt McDougal/Houghton Mifflin Harcourt; **109** "Alfabetización" ("Learning the ABCs") (1925), Diego Rivera. Mural, 2.06 m. x 1.33 m., Court of Fiestas, Level 3, West Wall, Secretaría de Educación Pública, Mexico City, DF, Mexico. © 2005 Banco de México Diego Rivera & Frida Kahlo Museums Trust, Av. Cinco de Mayo No. 2, Col. Centro, Del. Cuauhtémoc 06059, México D.F./ Photograph by Schalkwijk/Art Resource, New York; **113** Jay Penni/Holt McDougal/Houghton Mifflin Harcourt; **116** *center* Benson Latin American Collection/The University of Texas at Austin; *bottom* Danny Lehman/Corbis; **122** *paper* Jay Penni/Holt McDougal/Houghton Mifflin Harcourt; *pencil* PhotoDisc; *backpack* Guy Jarvis/School Division/Houghton Mifflin Harcourt; *clock rim* Willem Bosman/ShutterStock; *clock face* Andres Rodriguez/ShutterStock; **127** *modelo* Gabe Palmer/ Corbis; *1* Ira Block/IPNstock; *3 map inset* Royalty-Free/Corbis; **129** *3* HIRB/Index Stock Imagery; **135** Jay Penni/Holt McDougal/Houghton Mifflin Harcourt; **137** *left* "Autorretrato con collar" ("Self-portrait with Necklace") (1933), Frida Kahlo. Oil on metal, 35 cm x 29 cm. © 2005 Colección Jacques y Natasha Gelman, Cuernavaca, Mexico. © 2005 Banco de México Diego Rivera & Frida Kahlo Museums Trust, Av. Cinco de Mayo No. 2, Col. Centro, Del. Cuauhtémoc 06059, México D.F./ Photograph by Agencia EFE; *right* "Frida Kahlo" (1939), Nickolas Muray. Color photograph, assembly (Carbro) process, 40.1 cm x 29.9 cm. Gift of Mrs. Nickolas Muray. GEH NEG: 40130; 71:0050:0016. George Eastman House; **141** Jay Penni/Holt McDougal/Houghton Mifflin Harcourt; **142** *bottom left* Robert Fried/Alamy; *bottom right* Guy Jarvis/School Division/Houghton Mifflin Harcourt; **143** *right* Robert Frerck/Odyssey Productions, Inc.; *top left* Guy Jarvis/School Division/Houghton Mifflin Harcourt; **144** *bottom right* Lynne Guitar, Ph.D.; *bottom left* James Lyon/Lonely Planet Images; *top* Jay Penni/Holt McDougal/Houghton Mifflin Harcourt; **148–149** David Dudenhoefer/Odyssey Productions, Inc.; **149** *center* HIRB/Index Stock Imagery; *bottom* Dan Gair/index Stock Imagery; **150** Jay Penni/Holt McDougal/Houghton Mifflin Harcourt; **152** *pasteles* Martha Granger/EDGE Productions/Holt McDougal/Houghton Mifflin Harcourt; *flag* Image Club; **153** *bottom center inset* Kevin Schafer/Corbis; *center right* Angelo Cavalli/age fotostock; *bottom left* Robert Fried/DDB Stock Photography; **156** *eggs* Comstock; *yogurt* Jay Penni/Holt McDougal/Houghton Mifflin Harcourt; **157** *bottom right* John A. Rizzo/Getty Images; **158** *apple* Comstock; **159** *modelo right, 4 right* SuperStock; *modelo left* Royalty-Free/Corbis; *5 left* Comstock; *3 left* John A. Rizzo/Getty Images; *6 left* FoodPix/Getty Images; **161** *1* SuperStock; *3* John A. Rizzo/Getty Images; *8* FoodCollection/SuperStock; **163** Jay Penni/Holt McDougal/Houghton Mifflin Harcourt; **164** *bottom* Renee Comet Photography, Inc./StockFood; **170** © Rolf Richardson/Alamy; **174** *all* Comstock; **175** Jay Penni/Holt McDougal/Houghton Mifflin Harcourt; **176** *grapes* PhotoObjects/Jupiterimages Corp.; *the rest* Guy Jarvis/School Division/Houghton Mifflin Harcourt; **177** *whole pineapple* Jim Jurica/ShutterStock; *halved pineapple* Rudolf Georg/ShutterStock; *can label* Holt McDougal/Houghton Mifflin Harcourt; *the rest* Guy Jarvis/School Division/ Houghton Mifflin Harcourt; **178** *top* NOAA; *bottom* Tony Arruza/Corbis; **193** Kim Karpeles/Alamy; **199** *top*, "Lavandera" by Rafael Tufino, 1960, Oil on masonite, 48 x 28 inches (121.9 x 71.1 cm.), Collection El Museo del Barrio, NY, Gift of Edward Bejan, P92.125; Image Courtesy of El Museo del Barrio, NY; *bottom* "Smiling Country Girl" (2005), Fernando Sayán Polo. Oil on canvas, 15" x 21". Courtesy of the artist.; **202** Comstock; **203** Jay Penni/Holt McDougal/Houghton Mifflin Harcourt; **204** *left* Ed Kashi/Corbis; *right* HIRB/Index Stock Imagery; **205** *gift box* PhotoDisc; *all others* Edward Hernandez/Edward H. Photos; **206** *top* Jay Penni/Holt McDougal/Houghton Mifflin Harcourt; *bottom left* PhotoObjects/ Jupiterimages Corp.; *bottom right* David Stares/Alamy; **210–211** Jorgrn Schytte/Peter Arnold, Inc.; **211** *bottom* Terry Harris/Alamy; *center* J Marshall-Tribaleye Images/Alamy; **212** Jay Penni/Holt McDougal/Houghton Mifflin Harcourt; **213** David Sacks/Getty Images; **214** *bottom right* Martha Granger/EDGE Productions/Holt McDougal/Houghton Mifflin Harcourt; *center* Image Club; **215** *bottom left* Anthony Cassidy/Getty Images; *center right* "Don Quixote" (1955), Pablo Picasso. Gouache on paper. Private collection. © 2007 Estate of Pablo Picasso/Artists Rights Society (ARS), New York. Photograph by Bridgeman Art Library; *center* AP Images; *top left* Shizuo Kambayashi/AP Images; **218** *top right* Jon Ivern/ age fotostock; **219** *t-shirts* Jay Penni/Holt McDougal/Houghton Mifflin Harcourt; *shorts* Guy Jarvis/School Division/ Houghton Mifflin Harcourt; *Euros* Gary Conner/PhotoEdit; **220** *spring* Jonelle Weaver/Getty Images; *summer* José Pascual/age fotostock; *fall* M.A. Otsoa de Alda/age fotostock; *winter* Paco Ayala/age fotostock; **221** *3* Jay Penni/Holt McDougal/Houghton Mifflin Harcourt; *1, 6* Guy Jarvis/School Division/Houghton Mifflin Harcourt; *2, 4, 5, 7* C Squared Studios/Getty Images; *8* PhotoObjects/Jupiterimages Corp.; *modelo* Jessica Bethke/ShutterStock; **225** *shirt* PhotoObjects/Jupiterimages Corp.; *blouse* Jay Penni/Holt McDougal/Houghton Mifflin Harcourt; *socks* Burke/Triolo/ Getty Images; *hat* Stockbyte Royalty Free; *shoes* Michael Newman/PhotoEdit; *jeans* C Squared Studios/Getty Images; **226** Jay Penni/Holt McDougal/Houghton Mifflin Harcourt; **227** *1* Burke/Triolo/Getty Images; *2* Siede Preis/Getty Images; *3* Guy Jarvis/School Division/Houghton Mifflin Harcourt; *4, 8* Lara Barrett/ShutterStock; *5, 6* C Squared Studios/Getty Images; *7* Michael Newman/PhotoEdit; *hat* Stief & Schnare/SuperStock; **229** *bottom* The Persistence of Memory" (1931), Salvador Dalí. Oil on canvas, 9 1/2" x 13" (24.1 cm x 33 cm). Museum of Modern Art, New York (162.1934). Given anonymously. © 2007 Salvador Dalí, Gala-Salvador Dalí Foundation/Artists Rights Society (ARS), New York. Digital Image © The Museum of Modern Art/Licensed by SCALA/Art Resource, NY; **233** *right* Edward Parker/Alamy; *left*

Michelle Chaplow/Alamy; **236** *right* Getty Images; *left* PhotoSpin; **237** Jay Penni/Holt McDougal/Houghton Mifflin Harcourt; **238** *inset* Victor Lerena/Agencia EFE; *background* Guy Jarvis/School Division/Houghton Mifflin Harcourt; **239** *left* Yanik Chauvin/ShutterStock; *right* Guy Jarvis/School Division/Houghton Mifflin Harcourt; **240** *top left* Frank Vetere/Alamy; *top center* Royalty-Free/Corbis; *bottom right* F. Damm/Zefa/Corbis; *top right* Victor Kotler/age fotostock; **246** *steak, chicken, veggies* Jay Penni/Holt McDougal/Houghton Mifflin Harcourt; *fish* Rusty Hill/StockFood; **247** *bottom right* Mauricio-José Schwarz/Alamy; **248** *cake* Comstock; **251** *modelo* Christina Peters/Getty Images; *1* Jay Penni/Holt McDougal/Houghton Mifflin Harcourt; *2* Rita Maas/Getty Images; *3* Rusty Hill/StockFood; *5, 6, 7* Comstock; *8* J.G. Photography/Alamy; **253** *background* Stockbyte Royalty Free; **255** *top* Bruno Perousse/age fotostock; *bottom* Robert Frerck/Odyssey Productions, Inc.; **257** *modelo* Royalty-Free/Corbis; *1* Jon Ivern/age fotostock; *2* Guy Moberly/Lonely Planet Images; *6* Nigel Francis/Corbis; **259** *modelo* Christina Peters/Getty Images; *1* J.G. Photography/Alamy; *2* Jay Penni/Holt McDougal/Houghton Mifflin Harcourt; *3* Comstock; *5* Rita Maas/Getty Images; *6* James Carrier Photography/StockFood; *7, teen girl* Jay Penni/Holt McDougal/Houghton Mifflin Harcourt; *8* Rusty Hill/StockFood; **261** *right,* "Las Meninas" ("Infanta Margarita") (1957), Pablo Picasso. Oil on canvas, 194 cm x 260 cm. Gift of the artist, 1968, Museo Picasso, Barcelona (MPB 70.433)/© 2007 Estate of Pablo Picasso/Artists Rights Society (ARS), New York/Bridgeman Art Library; *left,* "Las Meninas" (1656), Diego Rodríguez Velázquez. Oil on canvas, 276 cm x 318 cm. Museo del Prado, Madrid, Spain. Photograph by Erich Lessing/Art Resource, New York; **265** Jay Penni/Holt McDougal/Houghton Mifflin Harcourt; *downtown Madrid* Nigel Francis/Corbis; **266** *bottom left* Ken Welsh/age fotostock; **267** *both* Yadid Levy/Alamy; **268** *top right,* "Landscape Near El Escorial" (1932), Ignacio Zuloaga y Zabaleta. Oil on canvas, 71 cm x 96 cm. Photograph by Erich Lessing/Art Resource, New York; *bottom right,* "Girl Under a Parasol" Lira, Pedro. © Whitford & Hughes, London, UK/The Bridgeman Art Library; *left* Jay Penni/Holt McDougal/Houghton Mifflin Harcourt; **272–273** David Dudenhoefer/Odyssey Productions, Inc.; **273** *center* Pierre Merimee/Corbis; *bottom* David Noton/Getty Images; **274** *teens* Jay Penni/Holt McDougal/Houghton Mifflin Harcourt; **278** *Ricardo* H&S Graphics, Inc.; *soup, soccer, hand with book, phone* Getty Images/PhotoDisc; *screen* Holt McDougal/Houghton Mifflin Harcourt; *skateboard, bike* Comstock; *guitar, charcoal drawing* Corbis; *Isabel* Holt McDougal; **281** *spiral notebooks* Victoria Smith/Holt McDougal/Houghton Mifflin Harcourt; *cafeteria, backpack, loose leaf paper* Don Couch/Holt McDougal/Houghton Mifflin Harcourt; *boy and girl talking in hall, pens, calculators* Holt McDougal/Houghton Mifflin Harcourt; **282** *bananas, grapes* Jupiter Images; *bread* Corbis; *bowl of soup, apple, sandwich, cup of coffee* Getty Images/PhotoDisc; *milk, yogurt, juice* Holt McDougal/Houghton Mifflin Harcourt; *burger* Brand X Pictures; **283** *grandfather, grandmother, father, mother, uncle, Pedro, sister* Don Couch/Holt McDougal/Houghton Mifflin Harcourt; *aunt, cousin* Corbis; **284** *jeans, shoes, red plaid shirt, blue sundress, women's sandals* Holt McDougal/Houghton Mifflin Harcourt; *green button-up shirt* H & S Graphics; *striped t-shirt* Don Couch/Holt McDougal/Houghton Mifflin Harcourt; *hunting cap, team jacket* Getty Images/PhotoDisc; *straw hat* Brand X Pictures; **285** *all* Holt McDougal/Houghton Mifflin Harcourt.

All other photography by Jorge Albán/Holt McDougal/Houghton Mifflin Harcourt.

**Illustration**

**4** *top* Anna Veltfort; **10** *all* Vilma Ortiz-Dillon; **12–15** *maps* Mapquest.com; **16** *keypad* Steve McEntee; **20** *map* Mapquest.com; **24** *all* Anna Veltfort; **26** *all* James Yamasaki; **28–29** *map* Mike Reagan; **39** *all* Vilma Ortiz-Dillon; **41** Beth Griffis Johnson; **45** *faces* Steve McEntee; **46** Pablo Torrecilla; **54** *map* Mapquest.com; **65** Steve McEntee; **68** Vilma Ortiz-Dillon; **71** *both* Anna Veltfort; **73** Anna Veltfort; **74** *both* Brie Spangler; **90–91** *map* Mike Reagan; **95** *clocks* Steve McEntee; **97** *digital clocks* Steve McEntee; **99** Steve McEntee; **108** *both* Brie Spangler; **114, 115** *logo* The American School Foundation of Guadalajara, A.C.; **116** *map* Mapquest.com; **124** *faces* Steve McEntee; **125** Steve McEntee; **130** *faces* Steve McEntee; **131** Anna Veltfort; **133** *faces* Steve McEntee; **136** Pablo Torrecilla; **151** Steve McEntee; **152–153** *map* Mike Reagan; **159** Vilma Ortiz-Dillon; **163** *faces* Steve McEntee; **165** Steve McEntee; **169** *all* Anna Veltfort; **171** Vincent Regimbald; **185** *calendar pages* Kenneth Batelman; **192** Steve McEntee; **197** *all* Anna Veltfort; **198** Pablo Torrecilla; **214-215** *map* Mike Reagan; **221** *top* Anna Veltfort; **232** Vincent Regimbald; **249** Vilma Ortiz-Dillon; **260** Tim Jones.

All other illustrations by Robin Storesund or Chris Wilson/Holt McDougal/Houghton Mifflin Harcourt.